Creating Identity
in the Victorian Fictional Autobiography

Creating Identity

in the

Victorian Fictional Autobiography

Heidi L. Pennington

UNIVERSITY OF MISSOURI PRESS
Columbia

Library of Congress Cataloging-in-Publication Data

Names: Pennington, Heidi L., author.
Title: Creating identity in the Victorian fictional autobiography / Heidi L.
    Pennington.
Description: Columbia : University of Missouri, 2018. |
Identifiers: LCCN 2017050788 (print) | LCCN 2017059015 (ebook) | ISBN
    9780826274069 (e-book) | ISBN 9780826221575 (hardback)
Subjects: LCSH: Autobiographical fiction, English--History and criticism. |
    English fiction--19th century--History and criticism. | Identity
    (Psychology) in literature. | Self in literature. | Narration (Rhetoric) |
    BISAC: LITERARY CRITICISM / General.
Classification: LCC PR830.A8 (ebook) | LCC PR830.A8 P46 2018 (print) | DDC
    823/.0820908--dc23
LC record available at https://lccn.loc.gov/2017050788

Typefaces: Bodoni and Caslon

In loving memory of Nana, Lance, and Laurel

Table of Contents

Acknowledgments

COLLABORATIVE, CREATIVE PROCESSES ARE AT the heart of this book in more ways than one. I am exceedingly grateful to all those whose support has enabled and enriched this project and made creative collaboration a lived reality for me.

I am deeply indebted to Emma Kafalenos for opening my eyes to the possibilities of narrative analysis. The impressive depth of her knowledge is equaled by her profound commitment to exceptional teaching and to the intellectual and professional development of her students. I am superbly lucky to have been one of those students: her teaching and wisdom continue to inspire me. Dr. Kafalenos's course Fictional Biographies and Autobiographies at Washington University in St. Louis in the spring of 2009 was particularly illuminating to me and significant for this project. Erin McGlothlin's course Truth or Fiction? Autobiographical Fiction and Fictional Autobiography similarly proved foundational to my thinking. I am grateful for her insights throughout the early stages of this project, as well as for her friendship. Sincere thanks to Guinn Batten, William McKelvy, and Wolfram Schmidgen for their time, their feedback, and their encouragement as I was completing the dissertation that inspired this project and beginning the process of writing this book.

Many thanks to James Madison University and to its College of Arts and Letters and its Office of Research and Scholarship, to The Graduate School of Arts and Sciences of Washington University, to the Department of English and the Program in Comparative Literature at Washington University, and to the Washington University Center for the Humanities for their generous support at various stages of this project's development. Parts of chapter 3 previously appeared in the *Victorians Institute Journal* as an article entitled "How Do You Solve a Problem Like Esther?: Reading *Bleak House* as Fictional Autobiography" (volume 41, 2013), and I thank the journal and its editors for graciously allowing their republication here.

I am particularly grateful to the faculty and staff of the James Madison University English Department for exemplifying collegial collaboration and for welcoming me into their community. Special thanks to Annette Federico for her kindness and her guidance, and to Dabney Bankert for her generous encouragement and advice, for her advocacy, and for all she does. To the many colleagues and friends who have read and reflected on my work at various stages, who have cheered and challenged me throughout the process, I give my sincerest thanks. Barbara Barrow, Jennifer Tate Becker, Philip Herrington, and Benjamin Trumbo: thank you for lending me your keen eyes and so much of your time. I appreciate the insights and feedback offered by the anonymous readers of my manuscript, which have strengthened this project. Without the dedication and thoughtfulness of Gary Kass, the care of the staff at the University of Missouri Press, and the engaged and sensitive copyediting of Gloria Thomas, this book would not have become a reality.

Miriam Bailin has been invaluable to me and to this project at every stage, in too many ways to name—though I will try. For her teaching and mentorship, her insightful and generous reading, her wisdom and humor so readily shared, her patience, and her frank perspective, I am profoundly grateful.

To my beloved parents, who model the beautiful flexibility of unconditional love each day, to my sister, and to my connected families—Smiths, Trumbos, LeLoups, Penningtons, Ashies—thank you for the unceasing support and the laughter: we do get silly. And, lastly, I acknowledge Ben and Felicity: if there is a core to any life, you are the happiness at the center of mine.

Creating Identity
in the Victorian Fictional Autobiography

Introduction

Fictional Self-Making in a Changing World

WHEN A READER FIRST ENTERS the world of Charlotte Brontë's novel *Jane Eyre: An Autobiography*, she might find herself disoriented. "There was no possibility of taking a walk that day," declares the famous first line, giving only a negation upon which to build an understanding of the diegesis. With no discernible speaker and referring to no human agents, this sentence tells the reader more about the gaps yet to be filled than it does about the facts of the fictional world. Who narrates? Who acts, or, in this case, who does *not* act? The discourse of *Jane Eyre* takes its time in definitively answering one of the fundamental questions that most readers automatically (if often unconsciously) ask when approaching a narrative: "Who?"

In the first five paragraphs the discourse progresses from having no determinable agents, to a plural first-person subject ("we"), to a distinctive singular first-person voice ("I was glad of it; I never liked long walks"), and, finally, to a clearly named narrating protagonist. But it is not Jane Eyre in her role as narrator who first introduces herself to the reader, as one might expect in a book subtitled "An Autobiography." Instead it is Mrs. Reed, her aunt, who names her even as she silences character-Jane within the narrated scene: "Jane, I don't like cavillers or questioners; . . . Be seated somewhere, and until you can speak pleasantly, remain silent."[1] What might seem to be a usurpation of Jane's right to speak, however, when considered in concert with the progressively particularizing pronouns of the opening paragraphs, becomes a logical starting point from which the narrating protagonist can construct her identity through how she tells her own story. Silence at the level of the story empowers her speech at the level of the discourse. By withholding her name for even a short space of discourse time, narrator-Jane piques the reader's interest in the primary concern of the novel—the nature of personal identity—and strategically prepares her audience to perceive her forward trajectory of development from powerless obscurity to self-determined individuality.

3

The foregoing interpretation of *Jane Eyre*'s opening passages is consistent with common thematic readings of the novel's protagonist, though it is unusual in its attention to Jane's strategic withholding. This episode of selective revelation in the novel's first paragraphs begins to construct the "Jane Eyre" who is often described as engaging in "rebellious self-affirmation," who becomes "independent, authoritative, and self-governing" through her narrative, and who is widely known for her "spiritedness and individuality."[2] Such descriptions demonstrate the extent to which readers integrate the choices of narrator-Jane with their impressions of Jane's identity overall. Often without comment, and sometimes without marked consciousness of the textual distinction between narrator and character in a text of autobiography (whether fictional or not), readers create their version of Jane Eyre's identity based on both what she tells about herself and how she chooses to tell it. In this book, I illustrate how such narration, as an instance of the subgenre of fictional autobiography, may transform readers' understanding of the nature of selfhood.

In the present example, the incremental filling in of the gap of Jane's literal identity at the novel's commencement initiates a pattern of audience inclusion in which readers are encouraged or provoked by the mode of narration to perceive the role they play in creating Jane's textual self. The act of telling from within the story world operates both as a mode of self-definition for the fictional autobiographer and as what Susan Sniader Lanser calls a "search for contact" with subjects outside the self of the teller.[3] As in all works of fictional autobiography, the process of narration becomes half the drama—if not of the plot, exactly, then at least of the reader's intellectual and emotional engagement with the being named Jane Eyre. The novel exhibits the fact that getting to know Jane Eyre involves the same cognitive activities as getting to know another person in the real world: filling in gaps, assigning motivations, and working both with and against the declarations of the autobiographer herself to generate a sense of her complex identity.[4] The fictional autobiography draws attention to this process of identity creation and to its structural parallels with understanding selves outside the text. The "blend of intimacy and autonomy"[5] that characterizes the narrative situation of the fictional autobiography has the potential to demonstrate to the analytical reader that the processes that make both intratextual and extratextual identities feel real are structurally identical across the perceived fiction/actuality divide.

In the coming chapters, I argue that the temporary gap of Jane's name in the opening pages of her narrative is just one illustration of how readers are invited to witness, to participate in, and to become aware of the practices of fictional self-making that make Jane Eyre, and her fictional autobiography

Jane Eyre, so very compelling and so very "real." Indeed, through the act of reading and thus creating Jane's real-feeling self, readers may come to see that Jane seems so real precisely because she is so explicitly fictional.

* * *

This book proposes that you and I, and everyone we know, are fictions. This fictiveness is not just in the sense that identity is artificial and contingent (though that idea is important, too). My claim is more specific: that the "selves" of people in the real world are fictional creations constructed using the same cognitive and affective processes with which readers animate fictional worlds, characters, and situations.[6] This book demonstrates how texts of fictional autobiography illuminate for the careful reader the sameness of self-making processes across the perceived ontological boundary between actual and textual selves. Much as the formal properties of *Jane Eyre* invite the reader to take part in the protagonist's self-making, so too do individuals participate in intensely social and narrative kinds of identity formation beyond the text, in real life. The sensation that people get of being who they are and of knowing who someone else is—both of these phenomena are the results of the processes of imaginative identity-narration in which they engage. This pervasive fictional self-construction can be undertaken consciously or unconsciously, by ourselves and in contrast to social narratives or collectively and reciprocally with others. But no matter how it happens, fictional self-making creates the identities we experience as real. The primary contentions of this book are that what is commonly called "personal identity" is the result of distinctly fictional processes and that the fictional autobiography in its Victorian moment is particularly suited to reveal as much to attentive readers. By constructing, adopting, telling, and revising creative stories of who we are, we become real to ourselves and to others.

A fictional autobiography is a first-person, retrospective account of the imaginary narrating protagonist's life story; this life story is self-consciously told through narrative conventions shared with the classical autobiography. Fictional autobiographies are always stories about identity. The interest of their tales lies in the elaboration and validation of the identity of the character-narrator. The fictional autobiography, particularly in the Victorian period, also promotes a rethinking of personal identity more broadly. Its unique phenomenology of reading engages readerly participation in the self-making processes of the main character in ways that simultaneously evoke readerly investment in the real-feeling identity of that main character. The fictional autobiography features the dual presence of conventions of fiction (an openly imaginary protagonist and story world) and conventions of reference (autobiographical content and style). These overlapping genre conventions lead to that unique phenomenology of reading that I claim for the fictional autobiography by creating in readers a doubled reading stance with respect to the text.[7] The experience of seeming to discover the genuine identity of the main character through the text coexists with the readerly awareness that this character's identity has no real-world referent to be discovered. In this way, the fictional autobiography reveals to the analytical reader the imaginative and collaborative narratives that underlie all real-feeling identities, whether fictive or not.

This book's central claim about personal identity emerges from key narratological and historical convergences in the Victorian fictional autobiography. I focus on the Victorian fictional autobiography not because this subgenre's textual traits belong only to that period's literature, but rather because the illuminating reading stance that I argue is its most engaging feature (and a result of its structural and generic characteristics) first became possible and widespread in the Victorian period with the growing public familiarity with the "conceptual category of fiction," as Catherine Gallagher calls it.[8] (More on the development of fictional and nonfictional discourses follows, in chapter 1.) As demonstrated by *Jane Eyre*'s opening passages, the carefully rendered omission of Jane's name invites the reader to become an active—if not always a conscious—partner in her narrative self-making. In this and a variety of other ways, which are more fully explored in chapter 2, the fictional autobiography encodes the reader as the necessary link between text and world; fictional potential becomes experiential reality only through readerly intervention.

The following pages repeatedly pose and variously answer the question, How might Victorian readers—and those readers shaped by a Victorian understanding of literary fictionality—have experienced the conceptual implications of these individual texts? And though I am most interested in the potential interpretations open to Victorian readers, expectations of the novel and traditional autobiography have changed little in the past century and a half, or at least the assumptions about reality and identity that undergird them. Thus, the claims I make about potential interpretations by Victorian readers often double as claims about potential readings available to present-day readers; this connection is developed in the coda.

The methodology of this book is therefore a doubled one, attentive to the interpretive potential of literary form for readers in specific historical moments. My approach takes a cue from the literature itself and traverses the disciplinary line between formal and historical modes of inquiry. I have laid out the theoretical foundations of my argument in two successive (though mutually referential) sections of the book. This introduction focuses primarily on the narratological elements of the fictional autobiography, with some attention paid to the philosophical and cultural backgrounds that give these formal traits their interpretive potency. Chapter 1 builds on these narratological and conceptual foundations by exploring the historical specifics of genre development, while paying close attention to the emergence of a cultural consciousness of fictionality and how that consciousness influences the interpretive potential of the fictional autobiography for readers in the Victorian period.

The fictional autobiography, by operating across the boundary between the actual and the fictional, discloses a latent Victorian awareness that the structures of realist fiction are analogous to the imaginative narratives that shape real-world experiences of personal identity. Indeed, this subgenre suggests that the Victorians were exploring fictional processes of self-invention long before postmodern thinkers could claim the deconstruction of the stable, inward self as their own intellectual breakthrough. In tracing the history of ideas about the self, the Victorian experiment with constructivist identities can boast not just an earlier moment in time than the postmodern writers but also a greater potential to reach the public directly. The Victorian fictional autobiography and its latter-day forms, unlike the writings of postmodern philosophers, were and continue to be essentially democratic texts: they had and continue to have widespread appeal and large reading audiences. Popular and elite literatures were severed in the late nineteenth and early twentieth centuries—a split that, despite postmodernism's work to counteract it, for most practical purposes remains intact today—and how many general readers now are familiar with, let alone emotionally invested in, the philosophies of Derrida or de Man? Compare that number to the legions of dedicated *Jane Eyre* fans or Dickens devotees. The continued popularity of the fictional autobiography is part of what makes it both interesting and significant.

Although the Victorians anticipated their twentieth-century counterparts in examining the constructivist dynamics of self, their approaches were both more implicit and more exploratory, coming as they did at a historical moment of massive social, technological, and scientific change. The rapid proliferation of new technologies of production, communication, and mobility affected every aspect of nineteenth-century life and transformed the last vestiges of older social structures into recognizably modern ones. As Thomas Hardy's narrator puts it in chapter 3 of *Tess of the D'Urbervilles*, the gulf that existed between people of two consecutive generations in the mid-nineteenth century had the same practical and affective impact of "a gap of two hundred years as ordinarily understood."[9] This persistent state of external change inspired a profound cultural investment in the concept of personal identity as an essential inward property, borrowing its dynamics of permanence from the Christian concept of the soul. Even as developments in fields such as psychology and physiology actively challenged the possibility of viewing the individual as a "unified agent," Sally Shuttleworth notes, "a new interiorized notion of selfhood arose" in the Victorian period.[10] The era's upheaval of values and experience made the ideal of an immutable core self all the more enticing for the stability it seemed to offer.

Enlightenment Inheritance, Postmodern Articulation: Narrative, Imagined, and Social Selfhood

When I claim that identity is a fundamentally fictional phenomenon, I am claiming three main things about selfhood: it is narrative, it is imagined, and it is social. While my ability to perceive and articulate these traits owes much to more recent theoretical developments, these integral dynamics of personal identity received careful exploration long before the twentieth century in the philosophies of John Locke, David Hume, and Adam Smith. Even before the volatility of the Victorian age, such philosophers were thinking about the imaginative boundaries of the self. This tradition influenced the Victorian engagement with identity, if often in covert ways.

As early as 1689, Locke introduced a vision of personal identity as narratively based in *An Essay concerning Human Understanding*. Although Locke's work in political economy and materialist philosophy is widely recognized to have had a profound influence on nineteenth-century thinkers, many overlook the latent presence of his radical notions about identity in Victorian literature and culture.[11] Locke insists that consciousness of the self *as* the self at diverse points in time and space is what makes "personal identity" a knowable and distinguishable category. He defines a "person" as "a thinking intelligent being, that has reason and reflection, and can consider itself as itself, the same thinking thing, in different times and places."[12] In other words, only by linking distinct events (including actions and thoughts) in some kind of chronology can one claim a continuous identity beyond the present moment of being. If self, then, is the result of connecting events in time, its structure is nearly identical to the basic structure of a "narrative," defined by H. Porter Abbott as *"the representation of an event or a series of events."*[13] While Locke does not specify "representation" as essential to forming an idea of selfhood, when he insists that a person must be able to "consider itself as itself, . . .

in different times and places," he is describing self-consideration as a basic mental re-presentation of past actions (impressions, thoughts, etc.). Locke's conception of personal identity thus is formed upon a fundamentally narrative construction of self.

In the eighteenth century, David Hume brought the role of imagination to bear upon the experience of personal identity in *A Treatise of Human Nature*. Hume rejects the idea of a "constant and invariable" self, a thing of "perfect identity and simplicity," labeling the ideal of such a permanent and continuous identity a "fiction." Instead, he proposes, the "perpetual flux and movement" of mental impressions produces the effect of constant internal sameness because people tend to confuse fixed sameness (absolute identity) with those things that succeed each other in time and are "connected together by a close relation." Personal identity, he suggests, is constructed from experiences of the latter kind. Nonetheless, humans attempt to justify the impression of (and perhaps desire for) an essential self by inventing "some new and unintelligible principle" to "disguise the variation" of identity over time; it is in this way that conventional thinking "run[s] into the notion of a soul, and self, and substance."[14]

Adam Smith's *Theory of Moral Sentiments* further theorizes the significance of invention in the human ability to understand the sensation of selfhood and reality, specifically through an individual's attempt to understand (i.e., sympathize with) another person.[15] As Rae Greiner describes it, Smith proposes that "when we 'put ourselves in [another's] case,' we can conjure feelings 'from the imagination' that do not derive from the sufferer's 'reality.' . . . The burden of proof falls away." Smith's version of sympathetic imagination locates value in the creative, narrative attempt to understand someone else while recognizing the impossibility of ever directly experiencing the self of another, Greiner argues. Smith's imaginative procedures of sympathy insist on the social dimension behind the impression of the reality of individual selves: "[Smith] sees great value in this uncertainty [about others]. The insistence that sympathy deals in representations alone turns private emotion into public currency. The result is a conception of feeling as profoundly social, and a flexible sympathy in which thinking of others thinking of us, and the reverse, is the psychological mechanism enabling the sense of self." "Thinking of others thinking of us," indeed, even "comes to serve as the basis for reality itself."[16] Our selves, this suggests, depend upon an intricate and often unconscious *mise en abyme* of imaginative creation with (and of) other human beings. Greiner's expansion upon Smith's theory confirms how explicitly social acts of imagination, and consensus or conflict through fiction, underlie not just our sense of self but our entire notion of what is real.

Locke, Hume, and Smith thus laid the conceptual foundations for the narrative, imaginative, and social dynamics of fictional selves lying latent in the Victorian fictional autobiography. But the deep historical roots of constructivist ideas about identity in British culture are only half of the critical inheritance upon which the present project builds. My claim that fictional processes generate the illusion of inner self-permanence resonates with the work of many more-recent theorists, from Émile Benveniste to Judith Butler and others.[17] Benveniste in "Subjectivity in Language" (1971) and Butler in *Gender Trouble: Feminism and the Subversion of Identity* (1999) each note a foundational confusion of effect with cause when considering the implications for identity of English grammar, which places the subject ("I") before the predicate.[18] The order of the grammatical elements erroneously suggests that consolidated identity precedes rather than results from action and utterance. The fictional autobiography illuminates the mistaken equation of effect with cause. This subgenre makes visible how the processes of fiction, as they are enacted both within and beyond the literary text, shape the chaos of lived experience into a sensation of self-permanence that regularly is assumed to be its own original cause rather than the effect of distinctly creative processes.

To put my argument into Wolfgang Iser's terms, in his anthropological study of fiction *The Fictive and the Imaginary: Charting Literary Anthropology*, personal identity is an undefined imaginary possibility until it is shaped by the creative narrativization that he calls "fictionalizing acts." Iser describes the imaginary as "a featureless and inactive potential" that can be defined into specific forms by the process of fictionalizing. According to Iser, realist fictions—texts that turn determined realities of the world into multivalent signs within the literary work—in fact transform and make flexible the same realities they fictionalize. Conversely, the imaginary becomes more fixed when given a determined form through the linguistic and narrative particulars that make up a text. In both cases, "the act of fictionalizing is a crossing of boundaries"; it is a transformative process that challenges categorical borders, whether it is disrupting or defining what is assumed to be real. For this reason, Iser holds, most literary fictions are self-conscious and draw attention to the act of fictionalizing through "self-disclosure." Literary fiction thus stands in contrast to "institutions, societies, world pictures," and other "nonliterary fictions" that "mask their fictional nature."[19] The perception of personal identity as an essential property, I argue, is just such a "nonliterary fiction," indeed amounting to a persistent cultural institution.

The following chapters demonstrate how the fictional autobiography "unmasks" the fictionality of lived selfhood and discloses that the processes that construct literary fictions and real-world selves are structurally indistinguish-able acts. The fictional autobiography beginning in the Victorian period is uniquely positioned to disclose more than just its own fictionality, a function that most (if not all) literary fictions perform, as Iser and others have claimed. Through those acts of self-disclosure, the fictional autobiography unmasks the fictionality of lived, extratextual identities more perceptibly than do other types of novels, as I show later in this introduction (in the sections "Reading for Fictional Selves" and "The Fictional Autobiography vs. the 'Omniscient' Realist Novel"). This subgenre's doubled existence as an overtly fictional form that explicitly makes meaning through autobiographical genre conventions reveals how readers' impressions of recognizably imaginary selves can come to feel as authentic as the readers' own sensations of self.

* * *

Even considering the benefits of retrospection and a nuanced critical vocab-ulary, and even taking into account Victorians' inheritance of radical En-lightenment philosophies of the self, to position Victorian texts of fictional autobiography as constructivist may yet seem counterintuitive. After all, Vic-torian writing often explicitly values essentialist ideals of personal identity; the rhetoric of essential inwardness remains present throughout most fiction-al autobiographies. And yet, upon closer inspection, the nineteenth-century literary practices of identity—especially in texts of fictional autobiography—show themselves to be much more constructivist in nature, and self-consciously so. Consider, for instance, the overtly metatextual opening utterances of the narrating protagonists in fictional autobiographies such as Mary Brunton's *Discipline: A Novel* (1815) and Amelia Ann Blanford Edwards's *Barbara's History: A Novel* (1864). Brunton's Ellen Percy opens her first chapter by med-itating on the act of "writ[ing one's] own history" and guessing the reader's impression of her "merits as a narrator."[20] Edwards's Barbara Churchill begins her preface with the statement "I am about to tell the story of my life—that is, the story of my childhood and my youth."[21] These initiating statements demonstrate a fictional self-awareness that both embraces and challenges the novels' invocations of personal authenticity. Each text works this doubled effect by highlighting the generic conventions of autobiography in openly fictional bildungsromane. Eliza Lynn Linton's *Autobiography of Christopher Kirkland* (1885) even more forcefully demonstrates the constructivist self-awareness characteristic of the fictional autobiography, acknowledging in the opening preface, signed by "Christopher Kirkland," "It is impossible to write an absolutely candid autobiography" because no text can ever show "the whole process of construction."[22]

The following chapters illuminate how the fictional autobiography makes legible the processes of fictional self-making that often were, for the Victorians themselves, as tacit and nuanced as Jane Eyre's delayed revelation of her identity. This engagement with the idea of fictional selves represents a significant facet of Victorian literature that could have repercussions for a twenty-first-century understanding of the cultural past and for our experiences of lived identity. After all, we inhabit a historical moment in which the widespread advancement of digital technologies and the corresponding public debates about the individual's proper role in the social collective mirror in their degree of extremity the Victorian experience of rapid modernization and destabilizing change. This book proposes to situate us—and our senses of self—not on more stable ontological ground but rather in good (Victorian) company, which models identity as something narrative, imagined, and inherently social.

Definitions, Doubleness, and Contextualized Analysis

At present, there is no widely recognized definition for the term *fictional autobiography*, although several scholars who have employed the label use it as I do. In *The Implied Reader: Patterns of Communication in Prose Fiction from Bunyan to Beckett* (1978), Iser uses the terms *fictional autobiography* and *autobiographical fiction* interchangeably.[23] Lanser, in her 1992 monograph *Fictions of Authority: Women Writers and Narrative Voice*, uses the term to describe *Jane Eyre* in an exploration of the narrational category of "personal voice."[24] Hsiao-Hung Lee (1996), James Phelan (2003, 2005), Rachel Ablow (2012), and Anna Gibson (2017) have also written about texts of "fictional autobiography," meaning works featuring the first-person, retrospective telling of the fictional narrator's life story.[25] Nonetheless, *fictional autobiography* is not a term whose definition or referents are at all agreed upon, even among literary scholars. And, complicating matters further, Victorian reviewers tended to discuss these texts in diverse ways, usually opting for something along the lines of the "autobiographical novel."

Somewhat paradoxically, given the lack of sustained critical attention it has received, the fictional autobiography was and today remains a fairly recognizable form to most readers. The first-person, retrospective account of the narrator's life parallels what one expects to find in classic autobiography, and the intimate accounting of the narrating protagonist's inner self corresponds to the primary concerns of nearly all nineteenth-century realist novels: the nature of the individual and her place in a social world. In fact, I conjecture that the formal and thematic traits of the fictional autobiography have become so familiar in the life stories of memoirists and in the narrated interior monologues of novels' protagonists that most readers and scholars have overlooked the significance of their mutual appearance in the fictional autobiography. For this reason, very few critics have recognized this form as a distinct subgenre with a history and phenomenology of its own.

The fictional autobiography produces in readers a doubled stance with respect to the text. Expanding upon the work of narratologist Dorrit Cohn, I propose that the doubled reading stance solicited by the text is a result of the combined presence of literary conventions based in extratextual experience (autobiography) and those based in imagination (fiction). More specifically, the form invites the reader's desire for genuine knowledge of the protagonist's inner self while simultaneously alerting the reader to the protagonist's essential fictionality. In this way, the fictional autobiography asks readers to recognize the extent to which their own imaginative involvement with the narrative generates the emotional reality of the main character's identity.

Cohn is one of only a few scholars who have not only recognized fictional autobiography as a distinct form of the novel but also analyzed its phenomenology of reading. Cohn writes from a rigorous narratological perspective and expands on the autobiographical theory of Philippe Lejeune. Lejeune proposes that autobiography and fiction are not defined by textual features, but rather by the reader's impression of the author's ontological relation to those features. In the case of an "autobiographical pact," the author, narrator, and protagonist are all assumed by the reader to be one and the same being, often because they are referred to by the same proper name in both the text and the paratext.[26] Fictional autobiographies often flag their fictional status through the use of proper names in their paratexts: seeing that the "autobiography" of Alton Locke is authored by Charles Kingsley, for instance, immediately signals both its autobiographical commitments and its overt fictionality.

Cohn claims that there is a "*double* pact" in place when readers approach fictional autobiography, in which an "autobiographical pact" is "impacted within a fictional" one. In highlighting this "telescoped" experience of the autobiographical within the fictional, Cohn proposes that readers seek to "establish the distance between authors and narrators." While I too emphasize the "doubled" reading experience evoked by these texts, Cohn conceives of this doubleness differently. For Cohn, the "literally equivocal origin of the discourse"—its pretense of having an imaginary author in addition to its flesh-and-blood creator—marks out the hierarchy of investment for readers. According to Cohn's theory, readers are most interested in delineating the differences between the identities of the fictional and the real-world authors. Judging by Cohn's examples, which focus solely on cases of narratorial unreliability in twentieth-century texts, the "double pact" of the fictional autobiography operates through a strict pecking order of readerly curiosity. The reader's primary concern is not in engaging with the fictional world or the fictional teller, but in learning about the real-world author through the fiction. Cohn posits that we are most interested in "the authorially intended meaning [that] passes from author to reader—behind the narrator's back."[27]

In contrast to this model that downplays readers' investment in the identities of the fictional tellers, the present study elaborates another possibility. The most captivating doubleness of the Victorian fictional autobiography, I argue, can be understood as a reworking of the emphasis in Cohn's hypothesis: what proves at least equally compelling in this subgenre is the act of reading the narrating protagonist as if she were her own author, all the while knowing her to be a fictional creation. The popularity of both the fictional novel and the nonfiction autobiography in the Victorian era made their respective conventions very familiar to nineteenth-century readers, thus enabling them to consider the narrating protagonist of a fictional autobiography on two levels simultaneously: as her own teller and agent and as having no real-world existence. Here I wish to accentuate the fictional autobiography's potential to stimulate a marked and simultaneous awareness of fiction and actuality, rather than Cohn's "impacted" and hierarchical (though no less doubled) reading approach. In other words, what makes the fictional autobiography such a compelling form is how it invites readers to grant agency to fictional characters who feel real, while also inviting readers to witness the narrative processes through which they come to make these characters into the emotionally real beings they seem. Indeed, fictional autobiographers feel like real people to many of us precisely because we construct them in the same way that we construct ourselves and the selves of others.

Cohn is not the only scholar to resist taking fictional autobiographers seriously as their own fictional writers. Alison Case has similarly argued that the interpretive strategy of granting agency to the fictional teller of a story proves less than productive in cases of "'paradoxical' paralipsis." Case describes this phenomenon, adapting it from the work of James Phelan, as the "omission or misrepresentation of information on the part of a retrospective homodiegetic narrator that appears to be inconsistent with the knowledge and perspective otherwise assigned to that narrator."[28] In other words, paradoxical paralipsis occurs when a first-person narrator omits something that she should know or feel in the present moment of narration but that her character-self (the written, past self) would not have known or felt at that point in the story. Case takes Esther Summerson's autobiographical narration in *Bleak House* as her prime example. She points out seeming inconsistencies in Esther's evaluations, most especially in the continually generous manner in which she narrates her own poor treatment by her godmother (whom narrating Esther now knows to be her biological aunt). For Case, if Esther is read as an autobiographer within her fictional world, the generous narratorial treatment of her aunt becomes a canny deception about her own naïveté that invites readers to distrust Esther's narration.[29] Case instead reads Esther's inconsistencies as evidence of Dickens's gendered assumptions. However, there is another way to read Esther's "paradoxical" narration here. Consistent with her character-self, Esther's narrator-self works to enlist her imagined readers in her affective community by interesting them in her life, and trying to "win some love" for herself.[30] Indeed, as does Jane Eyre with her delayed revelation of her "I," Esther proves her skill at controlling the order and style of her self-revelations to produce a compelling life story. Taking Esther as her own teller within the story world, her narration demonstrates not deception but rather what I call narrative competence.[31] I argue this point in detail in chapter 3, but for now it is crucial to recall that Esther's chapters explicitly evoke the conventions of autobiography that were widely recognizable to and popular with Victorian readers in the 1850s. To ignore that the novel promotes a recognition of Esther as her own teller with at least some level of agency means ignoring how the novel encouraged Victorian readers (whether successfully or not) to use their genre expectations of nonfictional autobiography to help them understand *Bleak House* and Esther Summerson.

As my argument for the validity of recognizing Esther's narrative competence suggests, the phenomenology of the fictional autobiography cannot be fully understood without also considering its history. Any theory about its phenomenological distinctiveness must take into account its existence as a historically situated form, to which particular and contextualized readerly expectations are attached. Nonetheless, in the rare scholarly conversations about the fictional autobiography, it is usually considered a form without its own past. Cohn and other writers describing its development tend to conceive of it as a derivative genre. In the *Routledge Encyclopedia of Narrative Theory*, for instance, there is no entry for *fictional autobiography*, but it gets a brief mention in the entry for *autobiography* as a copy of that form: "There has also been, in addition to autobiography, a prominent tradition of fictional narratives *imitating* its form."[32] Cohn, too, declares that these works are "deliberate, artificial simulations of this referential genre [of autobiography]."[33] But the history of this form does not support that assertion. Rather than fake invocations of autobiographical conventions, they are instead fictional engagements with the same thematic and formal concerns that occupy most referential autobiographies.

The textual traits common to both the referential and the fictional autobiography—which are elaborated below in more detail—include a preoccupation with the accuracy of the writer's account, moments of conscious self-reflection, and the realization of the protagonist's "true" self and his place in the social world. The primary shared formal characteristic is the first-person, retrospective telling. These conventions, I propose, are less borrowed from the autobiography than simply shared by the fictional and nonfictional forms of the genre. After all, first-person accounts of imagined life stories were around long before anyone could "deliberately simulate" the genre of autobiography. This is primarily because autobiography did not surface as its own genre (let alone as a term to consolidate and signal this genre to readers) distinct from religious-conversion narratives, memoirs, and confessions until the last decade of the eighteenth century.[34] Long before then, however, Daniel Defoe was delighting and intriguing readers with novels that featured distinctive first-person tellers of their own life stories, and Laurence Sterne was humorously exploring in *The Life and Opinions of Tristram Shandy, Gentleman* the impossibility of telling an entire life without the shaping narratorial act of selection. I explore in chapter 1 why novels such as *Moll Flanders* and *Tristram Shandy* are more protofictional autobiography than fictional autobiography proper; however, their very existence suggests not a derivative history for the fictional autobiography, but a synergy between three popular forms that concern themselves with the biographies of individuals: the novel, the autobiography, and the fictional autobiography. Chapter 1 demonstrates that the fictional autobiography is a genre that develops in conjunction with the novel and the autobiography throughout the seventeenth, eighteenth, and into the nineteenth century. In my analysis, the history of the fictional autobiography helps elucidate the interpretive valences it possessed for Victorian readers and for readers today whose expectations of fiction and autobiography are remarkably similar to their Victorian counterparts'.

Reading for Fictional Selves

Before proceeding, I will draw a conceptual road map to trace how the fictional autobiography brings attention to the narrative, imagined, and social aspects of personal identity. While I will continue to fill in the details and the detours of this map throughout the following chapters, I will lay out here the concise version of the subgenre's interpretive phenomenology. Readers of fictional autobiography are engaged by the author in the self-making procedures of the main character through certain narrative strategies; namely, their participation is solicited through narrative gaps and the rhetoric of reader inclusion.[35] Through interpretive and sometimes affective interaction with these narrative strategies, readers become invested in the main character's emotional reality. That is, the fictional autobiographer's selfhood begins to feel real to invested readers. But the blatantly fictional self-making in which the audience takes part remains disguised from the overt awareness of many readers by the text's rhetorical similarities to nonfictional autobiography; the shared rhetoric of inwardness, self-discovery, and development often continues to "mask," as Iser might phrase it, the reader's active fictional creation of the narrating protagonist's real-feeling identity. The passages that most involve the reader in the collaborative animation of the main character's identity resemble the passages in nonfictional autobiographies that seem to promise revelations (rather than construction) of the writer's inmost self. The presence of autobiographical conventions thus effects a rhetorical and emotional sleight of hand. The genre expectations that Victorian readers brought to autobiographical content led them to seek out signs of authentic interiority, textual indications of the writer's essential self. And so even as readers are enlisted in the act of fictional self-making for the protagonist, they may overlook their creative role and mistake the sensation of intimacy they receive from their reading as proof of some ineffable, extratextual "true self" emerging through the text.[36]

But the fictional autobiography thwarts such essentialist assumptions about identity if only one reads it closely enough. After all, the reader remains persistently aware of the protagonist's fictionality. Thinking too intently about Jane Eyre's "real" self, for instance, will only lead the savvy reader to conclude, per Catherine Gallagher's use of the term in *Nobody's Story*, that Jane is literally "nobody" beyond the text.[37] Without the reader's cognitive and emotional participation, Jane's self can be reduced to the flat page and the printed word. Indeed, it is precisely Jane's fictional nobodyness that permits the reader's sense of "who Jane really is" to guide the text's self-making so actively. In the absence of a fixed and preexistent identity—an absence signaled by the text's fictionality—the reader in concert with the narrator must supply the attributes that make a given character feel as real as a living person.

So how do these texts engage readers in this challenging reconsideration of identity? There are two primary structural features that involve the reader in the intimate processes of identity creation around which the tales revolve. First, there are gaps in the narrative (whether temporary or permanent) that invite readerly imagination to fill them in active, conscious ways. The readerly recognition of gaps highlights what is told, what is withheld, and when things are told by the narrating protagonist, simultaneously indicating the narrative spaces to be filled by readers' imagined interventions. Second, there are instances of reader inclusion, which include direct address (explicit invitations to participate, or warnings to desist from it), rhetorical provocation (tonal and stylistic features that pointedly invite readerly response), and thematic invocation of the reader through depictions of interpretive acts. Reader inclusion functions by calling the reader's attention to the discourse's features and the discourse's agent, the "how" of narration and the "who" of the fictional teller whose choices, in the world of the fiction, determine the style and content of the discourse. Not all fictional autobiographers employ the same combination of reader-inclusion strategies, but all seek to shape the reader's response in some or all of these ways and all call attention to the fact that they are doing so.

Fictional autobiographies promote a rethinking of personal identity by eliciting certain readerly emotions and inciting particular imaginative responses in the reader through these two methods (gaps and reader inclusion). For example, when Lucy Snowe of Charlotte Brontë's *Villette* elaborately refuses to tell her tragic family history, readers are invited not only to imagine what her past life might have been like but also to surmise that her feelings about this past are deep and profound—so deep that her desire for self-preservation and control over her own self-image prevents her from taking us into her confidence. Edwards's narrating protagonist in *Barbara's History*, perhaps following the lead of her fictional predecessor Lucy Snowe in the method of concluding her tale, explicitly provokes readers to recognize their own interpretive acts. She references the futility of her filling in the final fates of her characters, for, she writes, such is the audience's own power of creation: "What are all these but pictures which each reader will long ago have conceived for himself, and which no colouring of mine can bring before him more vividly?"[38] Though the type, presentation, and frequency of gaps and other reader inclusions differ from text to text, and from teller to teller, these fictional autobiographies all engage in similar narrative strategies that reveal to readers the absence of an essential selfhood at the core of their emotionally potent protagonists. Careful readers discover through their self-consciously imaginative acts that absences underlie even the most real-feeling identities—perhaps, in a version of transitive equivalence, even their own.

Literary Siblings

The fictional autobiography shares features with both novels and autobiographies, thus evoking similar reading expectations in its audience. But because of the fictional autobiography's unusual positioning astride the ontological divide between fiction and reference, the meaning of such shared textual features gains new and different imaginative life when read in the context of this subgenre. Below I elaborate the convergences and divergences of the themes and structures among these related forms. I conclude that while the similarities show how Victorian readers could bring parallel expectations to fictional and nonfictional autobiographies, and to novels with and without an autobiographical first-person narrator, the differences between these forms enabled the fictional autobiography to undercut nineteenth-century readers' security in their essential notions of self in more pointed ways than its sibling genres did.

The Fictional Autobiography vs. the Nonfictional Autobiography

The fictional and nonfictional versions of the traditional autobiography share thematic concerns (as they do, too, with the nineteenth-century bildungs-roman, discussed below in the section "The Fictional Autobiography vs. the 'Omniscient' Realist Novel"). It is this overlap that in part primes readers to desire, and to seek, knowledge about the "authentic" or "real" self of the narrating protagonist in a fictional autobiography. Sidonie Smith and Julia Watson, describing the traits of Jean-Jacques Rousseau's *Confessions*, help to frame the general thematic and plot concerns that characterize traditional autobiography as it was understood in the nineteenth century: "For some [interpreters], Rousseau inaugurates modern autobiography, with his focus on childhood, his retrospective chronology, his radical individualism, and his antagonistic relationship to both his readers and posterity."[39] Versions of these thematic traits structure each of the Victorian fictional autobiographies with which I am concerned, though the precise combination of factors alters—appropriately for realist texts—according to the individual circumstances of each narrating protagonist. Let me rework, and thus in part qualify, these categories. Autobiographies of the nineteenth century demonstrate (1) an investment in the narrator's origins and development, particularly in his childhood and education; (2) a desire to represent an individual self, with the attendant if often implied stipulation that it be an expression of an essential self; and (3) a desire for—sometimes becoming a rhetorical insistence upon—social recognition of that self's worth and authenticity. I refer to these three thematic focuses as origins, self-representation, and social recognition of the self.

In addition to these three thematic traits, the autobiographical act is a self-conscious one, inextricably linked to the consolidation and naming of the genre "autobiography" at the end of the eighteenth century. As James

Treadwell notes, there is a "particular self-consciousness" associated with publishing a text of life-writing to be consumed and evaluated by the public, and this self-consciousness becomes a recognizable convention of the genre as it emerges into its modern incarnation.[40] Autobiographical discourse reflects this personal and textual awareness through overt references to the narrating situation: both writers of autobiography and—even more particularly—fictional autobiographers make it a feature of their works to write about the act of writing. The three foregoing thematic preoccupations, along with this discursive self-consciousness of the writing act, signaled to Victorian readers that, like their nonfictional counterparts, fictional autobiographies were deeply interested in validating the narrating protagonist's personal identity within a specific social context.

Of course, such questions of existential truth and authenticity foreground the fact that autobiographies of both persuasions can only make meaning through specific epistemological commitments. As both types of text are told in retrospect, questions of accurate knowing and telling feature prominently in each, though often to different extents and effects. After all, unlike the fictional autobiography, which creates its own story world, the nonfictional autobiography stands in a "competitive relation with other texts" that attempt to refer to the real world, according to Marie-Laure Ryan.[41] Cohn clarifies that, while "a work of fiction itself creates the world to which it refers by referring to it," referential texts can only offer what they implicitly claim to be an accurate representation of the reference world they share with their readers.[42] Although many theorists of autobiography, including Paul de Man, James Olney, and Paul John Eakin, have substantially complicated the unsophisticated connection of autobiographical truth to empirical factuality, prominent theorists of nonfictional autobiography (including Lejeune and Eakin himself) continue to recognize some notion of reference—some direct connection between the world and its textual representation—as essential to how readers approach the genre. This is important for two reasons: (1) we can separate the kinds of truth claims that fictional versus nonfictional autobiographies make while (2) we keep in mind that both types of autobiography maintain a crucial investment in epistemology—in what the autobiographers know and how they know it.

As highly personal texts of memory, both fictional and nonfictional autobiographies must convince their readers that the narrators' proffered versions of events are accurate versions, or at least sincere attempts at accuracy. As Martin Löschnigg notes, "subtle authentication strategies" characterize the "mimesis of autobiographical memory" in Charles Dickens's *David Copperfield* as well as in referential autobiographies.[43] Telling not only what one knows but also how one manages to know and to remember the information forms a key part of appealing to the judgment and emotions of the reader of autobiographical texts. Victorian audiences in particular brought certain epistemological expectations to texts operating through autobiographical conventions. Namely, a Victorian approach to these texts combines an empirical sensibility with a profound commitment to the validity of subjective truths.[44]

The similarities between fictional and referential autobiography lead Löschnigg to declare that only "extra-textual parameters" can distinguish the two types of narrative from one another.[45] Cohn (building on the work of Käte Hamburger) also finds that first-person fictions and first-person nonfictions are impossible to differentiate based solely on their formal traits. Cohn observes that "there is nothing distinctively fictional about the discourse of an imaginary 'I.' The only mark of its fictionality is the nonreferential identity tag affixed to the person, the mind, the voice of its speaker."[46] She later describes the fictional autobiography as "mim[ing] the language of a real speaker telling his past experiences."[47] The claim of formal indistinguishability seems to hold true in terms of grammatical person, tense, and mood, but there are nonetheless differences in what fictional versus nonfictional autobiographers tend to include in their respective texts.

In nineteenth-century fictional and nonfictional autobiographies, there are features of both form and content that allow a reader, with substantial accuracy, to distinguish one from the other. Further, these same distinguishing features make the fictional autobiography particularly compelling by encouraging readers to recognize the fictionality of some of the most poignant passages about personal identity. Fictional autobiography in part signals its essential fictionality by including enriching details only representationally possible in fiction. Löschnigg makes the point that fictional autobiographies often feature more focalization of the past character-self than do referential autobiographies.[48] Precise recounting of long-past conversations as dialogue; extended, in-depth scenes of action, including accounts of even the smallest gestures; confessions of dreams and secret hopes in the exact language in which the teller first experienced them: these features properly belong in the novel, in which reality is created and not just remembered and represented. In a novel, these tropes overtly construct the reader's sense of the main character's identity. But in the case of the fictional autobiography, these same textual features coexist with the structural and thematic traits of the nonfictional autobiography, including its persistent appeal to real-world epistemology.

Rachel Ablow also notes a difference in content between fictional and nonfictional autobiographies in the nineteenth century, claiming that fictional autobiographers were more likely to write about their emotional lives than were real-world Victorian autobiographers. Emphasizing the private-sphere concerns to which this subgenre appealed, Ablow maintains, "This focus on the emotions in fictional autobiographies contrasts strikingly with non-fictional autobiographies of the period, where the emphasis is most commonly placed on the professional lives of their authors," citing Charles Darwin, Anthony Trollope, John Stuart Mill, and others as examples.[49] Ablow's distinction between fictional and nonfictional autobiography, however, also aligns with the different focuses of works within the field of nonfictional autobiography itself. There were two prominent modes of autobiography in the Victorian period. The res gestae memoir tradition (about one's public life, accounting for the "things done") contrasts with the introspective self-interpretation that had carried over into the nineteenth century from the spiritual life-writing texts of earlier generations. Indeed, the latter form of referential autobiography is what Linda Peterson identifies as the main precursor to the secularized, but still introspective, Victorian autobiographical tradition.[50] Thus Victorian readers could associate the intimate self-reflection characteristic of works such as *David Copperfield* or George Eliot's *The Lifted Veil* with both fictional and nonfictional autobiographies, thanks to their inheritance from the practices of spiritual autobiography of earlier centuries (though this particular genre name only came into use after the term *autobiography* emerged in 1797, as is discussed in chapter 1).

And yet, while both fictional and nonfictional autobiographies may contain passages of self-reflection, it is the level of specificity in those self-reflections and the frequency of formal features such as quoted dialogue that distinguish the fictional autobiography from its referential sibling in the Victorian period. While explicitly interested in accuracy, fictional autobiographies have the freedom to follow the epistemological standards expected of autobiography in a much looser fashion. For instance, readers who are constantly (even if not actively) aware of the text's fictionality will not question Esther Summerson's detailed recounting of a fever-dream she had eight years prior to the telling in *Bleak House*. However, if Anthony Trollope attempted the same in his posthumously published *Autobiography*, or if he claimed to recount word for word a conversation of long ago, accuracy-seeking readers would become suspicious. In this way, the different truth claims that fictional and nonfictional autobiographies make contribute not only to how they are told but also to what they can legitimately tell while still retaining readerly investment in the teller's authenticity.

This increased freedom of the fictional autobiography to stretch real-world standards of epistemology functions, broadly speaking, in two ways. First, it allows the reader more access to the innermost thoughts and feelings of the protagonist than would a nonfictional autobiography; the fictional auto-biography seems to "reveal" more of the narrating protagonist's interiority. Second, it promotes in the reader an enriched sense of the fictional protagonist's place in her social world by allowing the reader more direct access to that social world through extended representations of direct discourse and dramatic scenes than does the nonfictional autobiography. The fictional autobiography cultivates contact between teller and reader through recounting detailed interpersonal interactions that are long past in the chronology of the story world. Such scenes' status as memory would make them epistemologically troublesome in nonfictional autobiography, but not in the fictional autobiography, in which a consciousness of fictionality persistently guides interpretation. By this richness of intimate detail and the frequency of featured dialogue and scenes among characters, the fictional autobiography signals its fictive status through content and form. These same traits also stake out a place for the fictional autobiography as a subgenre of the realist novel, invested in the textures and specifics of the world surrounding the narrating protagonist (discussed further in the section "The Fictional Autobiography vs. the 'Omniscient' Realist Novel," below).

To sum up the claims made in this comparison of fictional and nonfictional autobiographies, they are both highly self-conscious narrative forms, and they share the three general content concerns that I call origins, self-representation, and social recognition of the self. Thanks to these thematic preoccupations and their rhetorical self-awareness as public texts about personal identity, the two forms also share an investment in real-world epistemology. How the narrating protagonist can know and validate not just the reported narrative information but also the very self that this narrative information collectively reveals (or rather, constructs) is constantly at issue. This attachment to real-world epistemology is signaled throughout even the fictional discourse by the narratorial acknowledgment of what is known or unknown, and how that knowledge came to be achieved. However, there is a distinction between the specific types and the extent of narrative information that readers will tolerate from nonfictional and fictional autobiographies. Anything highly detailed or subjective—thoughts from long ago, the minutiae of dreams, extended recounting of direct discourse and dialogue—usually appears only in fictional autobiographies, in which readerly awareness of fictionality encourages readers to relax their often-strict empirical standards of knowing. Further discussion of these elements, their interpretive effects, and the parallel histories of the genres takes place in chapter 1.

The Fictional Autobiography vs. the
Non-autobiographical First-Person Novel

Not all first-person fictions are fictional autobiographies; this must be distinctly understood, or nothing wonderful can come of the theory I am trying to relate (to paraphrase Dickens). According to Gérard Genette, there are two main types of first-person narration: homodiegetic and autodiegetic.[51] I propose that "fictional autobiography" serves as a productive further subdivision of the "autodiegetic" category of narration. To explain the distinctions among these types of first-person narration, the reading experience differs significantly between first-person fictions with a broader content focus (homodiegetic narration) and first-person fictions with a focus on the life experiences of the teller (autodiegetic narration). Most significantly, homodiegetic texts lack a primary investment in the three thematic preoccupations of autobiography when it comes to the life of the telling agent himself; the narrator's origins, self-representation, and social recognition of the self are not the novel's main points of interest.

But these three autobiographical-content categories are not necessarily the main interest of all autodiegetic narrators, either, even if personal events from the teller's life are the focus of the tale. As Genette notes, the autodiegetic narrator is simply "the hero of his narrative."[52] The category of autodiegetic narration, while including fictional autobiography, is not necessarily synonymous with nor limited to autobiographical self-reflection. Understanding and validating the self of the narrator is at most a secondary concern in homodiegetic fiction, and even in some autodiegetic fiction. The complex identities of the tellers are not the reader's focus when reading the narration of David Balfour in Robert Louis Stevenson's *Kidnapped* (autodiegetic), Nick Carraway in F. Scott Fitzgerald's *Great Gatsby* (homodiegetic), or Ishmael in Herman Melville's *Moby Dick* (arguably both, at different moments of the discourse). Genette describes Ishmael as a narrator who "plays only a secondary role, which almost always turns out to be a role as observer and witness";[53] yet the opening chapters of *Moby Dick* are also what one might call autodiegetic if not autobiographical. But because of his primary focus on the madness of Captain Ahab, and the effect of Ahab's obsession on an isolated group of culturally diverse men, as a narrator Ishmael proves ultimately uninterested in the detailed epistemological accountability characteristic of both fictional and nonfictional autobiography. Indeed, breaking the presumed rules of knowledge that guide nonfictional autobiography and most realist fictional narratives, Ishmael recounts everything from his own firsthand experiences to Ahab's private and fevered thoughts.

Not only does his narration openly transgress the bounds of epistemological possibility in the real world, but his telling also has almost no bearing on the reader's relationship to Ishmael himself as an individual about whom he wishes to know more. First-person fictions that are more invested in particular events and/or in people who are not the teller thus raise epistemological questions that to some extent discourage readerly investment in the accuracy of the teller's identity. Further, because biographical identity is not the centerpiece of the novel's content, the reader's desire to know the narrating fictional self of the text diminishes, or disappears, beneath the themes and stories that are more relevant to the world of that particular novel—as occurs when one is reading *Kidnapped* or *Moby Dick*. In other words, Ishmael's identity is just less relevant to *Moby Dick* as a work of art than, for instance, Lucy Snowe's is to *Villette*.

Even a narrating protagonist like Stevenson's autodiegetic Balfour, who relates his own adventures as a young man, is uninterested in specifically autobiographical material (that is, in exploring the three main content concerns of autobiography). And unlike in a fictional autobiography, Balfour as a narrator avoids writing about his writing; he is not a remarkably self-conscious autobiographer. Metanarrative moments, which are essential to attracting the reader's attention to the interpretive implications of the fictional autobiography, are sparse in such non-autobiographical autodiegetic fictions. Balfour shows little interest in his narratees' or his readers' opinions of him in general; there is almost no reader inclusion, even in its more implicit forms, and his choices as a narrator are rarely recognized and discussed as such. In these ways, the actual reader is less frequently reminded of his position as a reader, and is thus permitted to remain a much more passive recipient of the discourse (if the reader wishes) than is the case with the figured and provoked readers of texts of fictional autobiography.

Reviewing Case's hesitance to interpret first-person tellers as their own narrative agents helps to solidify the foregoing points about non-autobiographical first-person narrators, both homodiegetic and autodiegetic. Case cites Emily Brontë's *Wuthering Heights* as an example in which seeking to explain the narration by means of granting Lockwood, the narrator, agency proves rather unproductive. Although "readers are clearly invited to form judgments about the character of Lockwood . . . the fact that Lockwood is apparently recording in his journal day by day every word Nelly Dean tells him . . . is obviously *not* intended to contribute to the novel's portrait of Lockwood." Instead, "Lockwood's labors in recording Nelly's narrative are a fictional necessity for getting this story told, but as regards his character, they are simply irrelevant." To put it another way: *how* Lockwood tells matters little precisely because *what* he tells is not about himself. Indeed, Case says, only over-reading Lockwood as having "superhuman" powers of memory and transcription, or "obsessive-compulsive disorder" at the very least, could make him fit a "mimetic" model of narration. For the most part, this assessment seems right: such a reading of Lockwood could prove ridiculous, and it might take attention away from the primary focus of the novel, "the lengthy story of the Earnshaw family."[54] But in using *Wuthering Heights* as an example, Case's argument underscores my point: *Wuthering Heights* is not a fictional autobiography. It is a multi-narrator, framed fiction whose concern lies with Cathy, Heathcliff, and the rest of the troubled Earnshaws. In *Bleak House*, however, Esther's identity and value as a Victorian woman are primary focuses of the novel. Lockwood, unlike Esther, does not tell his own life story, and readers have very little interest in discerning his identity or engaging with his inward self. On the contrary, he is primarily a narrative device—the figure of the naïve outsider—that allows access to the other selves and story events, in which the audience is more interested. In other words, readers have utterly different concerns when reading Lockwood or Balfour or Ishmael than when reading Esther and other fictional autobiographers. Only in encounters with the latter category of narrators is the identity of the teller herself of great— even primary—importance to the audience, and only then does how she tells matter as much as what she tells.

The Fictional Autobiography vs. the "Omniscient" Realist Novel

In this section, the "how" of narration will be the central point of distinction between two closely related forms of the Victorian novel. Like the fictional autobiography, many nineteenth-century novels narrated anonymously in the third person are bildungsromane concerned with the individual interiority and personal development of their protagonists. The Victorian realist novel is indeed known for its focus on the biography of the singular individual in a so- cial world. But despite the overlapping thematic concerns and plot structure, it is the type of narrator, how she narrates, and the relationship to the reader this constructs that creates extensive interpretive differences between novels such as Jane Austen's *Pride and Prejudice* and George Eliot's *Mill on the Floss* and a fictional autobiography such as Charlotte Brontë's *Jane Eyre*.

The fictional autobiography occupies a special place within the literary category of realism. I use *realism* to designate a mode of fictional narrative in which the details of the diegetic world, invented in themselves, illustrate something true about the nature of reality. This definition, if somewhat broad, is consonant with predominant critical understandings of realism, most of which identify the complex connections among invention, representation, and actuality as the central focus of realist texts.[55] While the Victorian realist novel proposes to examine—through fictional means—certain truths about the world beyond the text, the fictional autobiography is distinctive in its sharper focus: it proposes to illuminate certain truths about the nature of selfhood and of identity's foundations in fictional processes.

The fictional autobiography achieves this enhanced focus by calling attention to the particularly autobiographical dynamics of the relationship between the reader and the narrator-protagonist in the two separate narrative roles she occupies. The impression the fictional autobiography cultivates of direct contact between the narrator-protagonist and the reader—with no narrative middleman, as it were—doubles the interpretive impact of all its narrative elements. The fictional autobiographer's style of telling, including tone, diction, syntax, discourse order, even perhaps typography, contains just as much information about her identity as does the content of her story. Unlike in *Pride and Prejudice*, in which a so-called omniscient narrator selects what to reveal and how and when to reveal things about the protagonist, Lizzy Bennett, and other characters, in a fictional autobiography the reader is asked to attribute those choices within the fictional world directly to the narrating protagonist herself and to imagine her identity based upon the act of selection implied by that narrative information. In other words, the reader of the fictional autobiography is not merely actively enlisted in shaping the protagonist through reading and interpreting the story (a process that characterizes most realist novels). Most significantly for understanding the distinctive nature of this subgenre, the reader is asked to notice the creative modes of self-making through which the narrating protagonist, with the guided input of the reader, makes her *self* feel real. The fictional autobiography's doubling of genre—novel and autobiography—and its doubling of its central character—narrator and protagonist—allows it to operate in an enhanced mode of novelistic realism that hones the reader's focus on the processes through which individuals construct and socially legitimize their personal identities.

A comparative analysis of two thematically similar passages from Charlotte Brontë's *Jane Eyre* and George Eliot's *Mill on the Floss* demonstrates how the dynamics of the narrator-protagonist-reader relationship in the fictional autobiography illuminate the fictional structures of personal identity more pointedly than do the dynamics of the omnisciently narrated realist novel. Formally speaking, Eliot's extradiegetic-heterodiegetic narrator, often referred to as an omniscient narrator, in *The Mill on the Floss* is removed from the story events and external to the fictional world.[56] Brontë's narrating protagonist in *Jane Eyre* is autobiographically autodiegetic, or preoccupied with her origins, self-representation, and the social recognition of her identity; she "belong[s] to the diegetic universe of [her] narrative" and is "the hero of [her] narrative."[57] For brevity and ease of reading, however, I refer to these two narrator types as an anonymous third-person narrator and a fictional autobiographer, respectively. Beyond an interest in the lives of the main characters, in this case Eliot's Maggie Tulliver and Brontë's Jane Eyre, the following examples also indicate a more profound commitment to examining the gendered struggle for forward motion that these bibliophilic, rebellious, affectionate protagonists experience in their self-consciously female bildungsromane. Indeed, these two novels work well as formal foils to one another precisely because their content concerns are remarkably similar.

Brontë's 1847 novel, *Jane Eyre: An Autobiography*, tells the story of an orphaned girl who is rejected by her wealthy relatives and sent away to a grim charity school. At eighteen, she seeks "a new servitude" and becomes the governess at Thornfield Hall for the ward of the mysterious, and initially absent, Mr. Rochester. In the first twelve chapters, we learn that Jane is a bibliophile who reshapes her often hostile world through the narratives she reads. Her rebellious and affection-starved nature is both soothed and stimulated by her expansive imagination of the wider world beyond her isolating occupation. She paces the grounds of the great estate and the upper floors of the house, imagining "more vivid kinds of goodness" and listening to "a tale my imagination created, and narrated continuously; quickened with all of incident, life, fire, feeling, that I desired and had not in my actual existence."[58] Similarly, in Eliot's 1860 novel, *The Mill on the Floss*, the protagonist Maggie Tulliver finds herself "too [a]'cute" for a miller's daughter in the provincial English town of St. Ogg's. Maggie finds not just interest but solace in her reading. Each of the texts Maggie reads serves as the basis for the imaginative and ethical exercise of her large-minded sympathies. Even her beloved brother Tom fails to respond to Maggie's defining "hunger of the heart," leaving Maggie's narrative imagination both to exacerbate and to attempt to fulfill her longings for mutual understanding when her family falls on hard times.[59] Consider the thematic parallels contained in the two following passages, the first from Brontë's *Jane Eyre*:

> Anybody may blame me who likes, when I add further, that, now and then, when I took a walk by myself in the grounds; . . . or when . . . I climbed the three staircases, raised the trap-door of the attic, and having reached the leads, looked out afar over sequestered field and hill,

and along dim sky-line—that then I longed for a power of vision which might overpass that limit; which might reach the busy world, towns, regions full of life I had heard of but never seen; that then I desired more of practical experience than I possessed; more of intercourse with my kind, of acquaintance with variety of character, than was here within my reach. I valued what was good in Mrs. Fairfax, and what was good in Adèle; but I believed in the existence of other and more vivid kinds of goodness, and what I believed in I wished to behold.

Who blames me? Many, no doubt; and I shall be called discontented. I could not help it; the restlessness was in my nature; it agitated me to pain sometimes. Then my sole relief was to walk along the corridor of the third story, backwards and forwards, safe in the silence and solitude of the spot, and allow my mind's eye to dwell on whatever bright visions rose before it—and, certainly, they were many and glowing; to let my heart be heaved by exultant movement, which, while it swelled it in trouble, expanded it with life; and, best of all, to open my inward ear to a tale that was never ended—a tale my imagination created, and narrated continuously; quickened with all of incident, life, fire, feeling, that I desired and had not in my actual existence.[60]

and the second from Eliot's *Mill on the Floss*:

It is in the slow, changed life that follows [the first shocks of trouble]—in the time when sorrow has become stale and has no longer an emotive intensity that counteracts its pain, in the time when day follows day in dull unexpectant sameness and trial is a dreary routine—it is then that despair threatens: it is then that the peremptory hunger of the soul is felt, and eye and ear are strained after some unlearned secret of our existence which shall give to endurance the nature of satisfaction.

This time of utmost need was come to Maggie, with her short span of thirteen years. To the usual precocity of the girl, she added that early experience of struggle, of conflict between the inward impulse and outward fact which is the lot of every imaginative and passionate nature; and the years since she hammered her nails into her wooden fetish among the worm-eaten shelves of the attic, had been filled with so eager a life in the triple world of reality, books and waking dreams, that Maggie was strangely old for her years in everything except in her entire want of prudence and self-command that made Tom manly in the midst of his intellectual boyishness. And now her lot was beginning to have a still, sad monotony, which threw her more than ever on her inward self.[61]

Despite their similarities, reading a novel like *The Mill on the Floss*, narrated by an anonymous third-person entity, feels notably dissimilar to reading a fictional autobiography like *Jane Eyre*, narrated by the protagonist herself. Jane's role as narrator allows her to become an immediate, distinctive, even a combative, narrative presence to her readers. This affective difference leads readers down diverging interpretive paths. The differing fictional origins of the narration (highlighted by Cohn, as described above) subtly but substantially affect how readers understand the identities of the novels' main characters.

In the above passage, Brontë's heroine seems to write herself into being as she openly provokes and persuades the reader to animate her character in certain ways. The sheer number of first-person pronouns she uses—twenty-four in the two full paragraphs from which the above excerpt is taken—reiterate her agency as teller as well as her subjective experience as the most significant object of her discourse. Jane chooses to share her inner life with the reader, explicitly validating her past feelings as she recounts them. Maggie, in stark contrast, plays no active role in what is said about her by the narrator. In the third-person anonymous mode of narration the reader distinctly lacks Maggie's expression of what her "inward self"—although explicitly evoked by the narrator—might hold for her. While the narrator later reveals in indirect discourse some of Maggie's longings at this point in the story, by the very nature of the discourse we are not privy to Maggie's own account of herself. When put into conversation with *Jane Eyre*, this moment raises the question of how conscious Maggie is of her own double-mindedness, her own dissatisfaction and its causes. What does Maggie know and think about herself, about her circumstantially hemmed-in identity? And what would she choose to tell her readers, if she could express herself through the narration? While both Jane and Maggie may feel "real" to the invested reader, only Jane's self-making and self-conscious narration simultaneously expose the distinctly fictional processes that construct her identity's emotional reality.

The narration in *Jane Eyre*, since it is a fictional autobiography, comes from Jane herself within the fictional world, and Jane shows that she is a highly self-aware autobiographer. She explicitly calls the reader's attention to her role as a singular kind of narrator by declaring in chapter 10 that "this is not to be a regular autobiography."[62] The passage excerpted above marks another moment of self-conscious narration, in which Jane represents both her past sensations and her present evaluation of those circumstances and feelings. The case she narrates is specific to herself even to the extent that her narration anticipates and attempts to circumvent the kind of personal judgments that readers might level at her based on her self-revelations. Indeed, this passage contains two examples of reader inclusion in the form of provocations when Jane declares that "anybody may blame me [for my restlessness] who likes" and when she, further, affirms that no doubt "many" will do so.[63] The reader and her potential opinions are rhetorically figured and explicitly resisted by narrator-Jane. The two indefinite pronouns *anybody* and *many* gesture to the readerly act of interpretation, challenging the agents outside her text either to accept Jane's own interpretation of her past self or, this rhetoric implies, to fail to understand who she really is. Jane's discursive choices give the impression that she desires to be rightly understood by her audience, and the language she uses to marshal the reader's response itself affects the construction of her identity. Jane does not beg for a particular interpretation of her identity; rather, she rhetorically resists unjust readings—as she tells Helen Burns she intends to do with all injustice in chapter 6—and she thus emerges in the discourse as defiant, independent, and (paradoxically) autonomous of her readers.

Moments like this show how Jane's self comes to feel like and to operate in ways parallel to the actual selves a reader engages with beyond the text. The similarity of sensation between Jane's identity and extratextual identities is achieved in two ways. First, Jane seems more directly knowable since she is her own teller, deciding what to reveal or conceal, and how; her telling is itself an act of characterization. Second, she not only overtly insists that she is personally different from the reader but also claims that she is independent of any external imagining of who she is. This second feature—her blatant insistence on her own unique autonomy—implicitly appeals to the cultural assumption that personal identity in the real world is founded upon a permanent and inward essence. This passage, and others like it throughout *Jane Eyre*, rely on the fictional autobiography's realist mode to promote the idea that Jane is an individual distinct from her readers through the (fictional) details she relates about herself. Yet in this apparent individuality she is also more profoundly "like" her real-world audience by seeming to possess an essential inner self. The realism of "Jane Eyre" seems to be, at first glance, that her distinctive, invented details model the real-world truth of essential identity. Notice her rebuff to the disapproving "many" her narration tries to control: "I could not help" having those longings, she explains; "the restlessness was in my nature." She legitimizes her personal traits by claiming them as innate and so not affected by the reader's disapproval or (implicitly) by the reader's imaginative acts.

In contrast to Jane's personal narration and the autonomy it projects, Eliot's anonymous third-person narrator claims to relate the circumstances not only of Maggie but also implicitly of anyone who has experienced the wearisome burden of "unexpectant sameness and trial" without the support of kindred spirits. In fact, the description of Maggie's life proves nearly equally descriptive of Jane's situation and sensations: both women mentally stagger under the weight of a "slow, changed life" that lacks—as Jane herself puts it—"incident, life, fire, feeling," or, at the very least, "more of intercourse with my kind." To say it another way, the narration of *The Mill on the Floss* captures the isolation of these two young women in terms that extend beyond Maggie's individual strife. This narrator asks readers to understand Maggie's despair through their own modern experiences of the "conflict" between "inward impulse and outward fact," claiming that everyone with an "imaginative and passionate nature" like Maggie's desires to find "some unlearned secret of our existence" in times of trouble. The pronoun *our* is plural and inclusive. It explicitly expands the target of the narrator's words, making the details of the reader's own sense of identity the key to understanding Maggie's life and self. This inclusive narration, which emphasizes a very specific kind of sameness between the reader and the protagonist, encourages an entirely different self-understanding than does the narration of Jane Eyre.

The incomplete separation of Maggie from the reader, paradoxically, is what lends Jane the advantage in producing the sensation of an actual, extratextual individual. Readers are invited to learn things about Maggie and the world beyond the text through reference to their own experiences. Readers can even know things about Maggie that Maggie might not know about herself; as suggested earlier, this passage raises the question of how self-conscious Maggie is about her own double-mindedness in the midst of her troubles. In being asked to relate to Maggie through reference to themselves, readers need not grant Maggie individual agency—indeed, this mode of telling discourages it. Maggie is an affecting fictional presence, but her character operates as a metonym for any isolated individual in a shifting social world. In this way, Maggie is both a single character and a symbolic way to comprehend an entire network of extratextual realities (such as gender, family, a changing social system, and more). Maggie's figurative function avoids interrogating directly the nature of individual identity by failing to embody the cultural ideal of an autonomous, singular identity in her structural as well as in her thematic characteristics. Maggie lacks agency, both within her fictional world and in the discourse that creates her. Her textual presence is not structurally aligned with how "real" selves are assumed to operate in the extratextual world.

Jane's resistant narration and evocations of autobiography, by contrast, insist upon her difference from the reader. She uses rhetoric that places us at a distance from her, and in doing so she seems to embody the kind of authentic, essential identity that readers are likely to believe characterizes lived personhood. Jane promotes herself as distinctly other from the reader in a way that invokes a fellowship of essential individuality among individuals—whether fictive or embodied. While the fictional details of "who Jane really is" and how she experiences life differ from the actual details of her readers' lives, it is this very difference that makes Jane feel most like her audience members.

And yet, this same moment of resistant narration represents just one of many reader inclusions in which Jane's discourse simultaneously gestures at the reader's animating function within the text. *Jane Eyre* is an explicitly fictional novel whose fictiveness is signaled even before one opens the book by the discrepancy between the proper name in the title and that in the authorial byline—*Jane Eyre: An Autobiography*, by Currer Bell/Charlotte Brontë. This overt fictionality means that even as Jane speaks for herself her utterances invite the reader's imagination to fulfill her narrative self-making. Her self-conscious narration registers its own existence—and Jane's identity—as text in need of the reciprocal imaginings of the reader in order to come to life through a seeming resistance to the reader's mental construction of "Jane Eyre." Brontë's Jane, by resisting the hypothetical reading she supplies to her audience and insisting on her independent existence, simultaneously engages the reader in the process of creating her self.

In refusing the reader's judgment of her, Jane accomplishes two things: (1) she invokes the cultural ideal of essential identity by appealing to the reader's desire to know the essential "Jane" signaled by the autobiographical conventions of narration, and (2) her words simultaneously compel the reader to create in his imagination that very essence of her identity that he so wishes to discover. Jane's insistence that she is distinct from her reader and that we read her wrongly activates the reader's own sense of personal integrity and simultaneously feeds the desire to know more about Jane's true self. Her refusal of hypothetical judgments suggests that there *is* a right way to read her identity. Of course, as most readers when questioned would concede, the essence of Jane is a fictional construct. Her selfhood is a construct that we, as the readers, are in part responsible for animating into an emotionally potent and intellectually compelling phenomenon—that is, for making it feel real. This is one of the ways that the fictional autobiography stands out from other realist texts: the presence of antagonistic reader inclusion to insist on a likeness-through-difference between narrator and reader subverts the ideal of identity that it initially trades in. Readers are in fact "like" Jane in that their sense of an inward personal reality derives from fictional processes, processes that this same textual moment itself initiates in the reader's mind.

In a subgenre that superficially privileges transcendent individualism, it is especially significant that the desire to discover the protagonist's inviolate inner essence brings the reader to the interpretive cruxes that, when analyzed carefully, demystify such an essentialist conception of identity. Seeking the essential self of the narrating protagonist exposes the collaborative and constructivist mechanisms that create the feeling of reality that attaches to selfhood. In other words, while the fictional autobiography seems to be about consolidating autonomous self-permanence through narrative, it simultaneously undercuts the notion that such a form of self exists. The fictional autobiography demonstrates to the careful reader how socially contingent imaginings give us the impression of a selfhood that exists beyond the stories we tell.

While many types of fictional encounter can provoke a rethinking of what Iser calls the reader's "natural attitudes,"[64] the fictional autobiography encourages a total reevaluation of the role fictional processes play in creating the reality of selfhood. This does not mean that other types of realist novels have nothing to say about the connections between fiction and the world: the foregoing close reading outlines how *The Mill on the Floss* makes its own significant claim about the nature of the intersections of imagination and reality. Through Maggie-as-metonym, Eliot's novel has the capacity to demonstrate that fiction functions as a useful hermeneutic device for understanding the complexities of the real world, potentially including the specific conditions of an individual reader's own life. Theorists as diverse as Catherine Gallagher, Wolfgang Iser, Blakey Vermeule, and Lisa Zunshine have argued along these same lines that fiction and the reading processes it requires serve as an ideal instrument for thinking analogically about the world beyond the text.[65]

While this hermeneutic view of fiction (which is discussed further in chapter 1) is productive in many ways and informs the argument of the present study, as the foregoing example illustrates, the fictional autobiography asks readers to see fictional processes as constituents of reality itself. Fictional processes, this subgenre contends, construct the feeling of essence behind the most intimate reality most of us know: our selves. The fictional autobiography—more pointedly than its nonfictional (autobiography) and its fictional third-person ("omniscient," Austenian) siblings—makes visible not only those truths universally acknowledged but also this disquieting truth almost universally ignored.

The Victorian Need for Fiction: Adaptable, Flexible, Implicit

The possibility that identity was not an essential property but a narratively constructed experience was a challenging one for Victorian writers and audiences to accept. The ideal of a fixed and internal core self certainly received widespread expression throughout Victorian literature. This notion of self was valued (and indeed, often fetishized) for offering the individual some kind of ontological security in the unstable social, political, and economic world of nineteenth-century Britain, whose imperial claims to global dominance were being challenged by the volatility at home. From national to personal identity, few categories of existence went unquestioned during this period. As Anna Gibson notes, "a broader ideological shift" was happening, "away from theories of the person as stable, . . . and toward an understanding of the person" as a being whose existence was physiologically and psychologically "processual."[66] Indeed, the marked emphasis on an essentialist ideal of identity in Victorian literature mainly verifies its absence from lived realities. For these reasons, the adaptability inherent in understanding the self as a collective fictional process also appealed to nineteenth-century audiences. If stability was not to be achieved, then flexibility could become a productive (and perhaps was the only) alternative.

And how could any Briton of the time feel truly secure when, as Jerome Buckley puts it, "the Victorian, looking outwards, could see his whole age in perpetual motion"?[67] The new abundance of periodicals; the rise in mass literacy; the growing reach and efficiency of the postal service; the invention of the telegraph, the typewriter, the telephone, and the phonograph; and the expansion of the railroads: these technologies of knowledge and innovations in communication were often lauded as signs of progress. But "progress" could be a destructive—or at least disturbing—phenomenon, too.[68] The increased geographic and economic mobility of the Victorian era indeed led to the simultaneous deracination of a predominantly rural society; the period witnessed vast numbers of citizens being forced to migrate to overcrowded urban and industrial centers for subsistence. This ambiguously valued mobility, Buckley notes, was indeed perceptible in every aspect of life. Though class and status had never been wholly fixed concepts—let alone practices—the changes of the Victorian era blatantly demonstrated the potential for precipitous upward *and* downward movement of the individual in society, which made this period feel especially uncertain to many who lived it. After all, Robin Gilmour points out, the Victorians transformed "a 'feudal' society into a 'modern' state," emphasizing with these terms the radical nature of the change. Gilmour notes of the resulting widespread uncertainty, "The Victorians confronted their unique historical exposure without the security of a confident world-view. . . . The acceleration of everyday life, and the accumulation of knowledge about a new society which left individuals conscious of crisis but impotent to act, bred a new kind of *angst*—pervasive but unfocused."[69] And so, while "progress" pushed on, it provoked new anxieties about epistemological uncertainty and, thus, ontological instability. The key, if often implicit, question became one of assured values. What mattered if everything was variable, malleable, subject to alteration?

The Victorians attempted to deal with this ontological uncertainty in two main ways, broadly conceived. They explicitly clung to notions of essence and eternal permanence, which stemmed from Judeo-Christian religious belief. As the focus of a human's value began to shift from the "soul" to the individ- ualist "self,"[70] this led to an idealization of a fixed, inward, and autonomous personal identity based on older notions of the "divine spark." This is the Victorian ideal of selfhood. However, the concurrent and opposite approach to the experience of instability was a growing interest in and practice of imag- inative adaptability (in all its timely significance) when it came to establish- ing the value of individual humans. In this way, Victorians questioned their own need for permanence by an increasing interest in cultivating collective, creative identities that could adapt to the ever-changing world around them. This is the appeal of fictional selves and imaginative, social self-making. It can never suffer the suffocating stasis of a fixed essence, or the alienation of that which is utterly autonomous.[71] Throughout the following chapters I trace how the practices of Victorian identity in these texts of fictional self-making coexist with while challenging an explicit attachment to the ideal of an es- sential, inward self. These categories—ideals and practices—are neither mu- tually exclusive nor comprehensive when it comes to Victorian conversations about identity. However, they do help to explain how the Victorian fictional autobiography could suggest the seemingly radical idea that personal identity is a fictional creation yet remain widely popular despite its subversion of such a treasured cultural ideal.

* * *

The following chapters focus most closely on popular works by Charles Dick- ens and Charlotte Brontë. Chapter 1 examines the cultural conditions and genre histories that make the experience of reading the fictional autobiog- raphy in the Victorian period distinctive, closing with a comparison of the different effects of truth-telling conventions in a fictional autobiography, *Jane Eyre*, and a referential one, Anthony Trollope's *Autobiography*. *David Copperfield* and its evocation of the author as a cultural placeholder for as- sumptions about personal identity occupy chapter 2. The second chapter also examines Jane Eyre as a self-conscious author of autobiography who—unlike David Copperfield—cautiously embraces the social dynamics of such a posi- tion. Chapter 3 examines *Bleak House* and Esther Summerson as a domestic autobiographer, an identity category that—similarly to the figure of the Victorian author—illuminates the textual structures of selfhood in the period. Chapter 4 examines the Victorian ambivalence about the social dynamics of fictional identity creation through representations of domestic difficulties in *Copperfield* and Brontë's *Villette*. Lucy Snowe ultimately rejects traditional conceptions of home, replacing limiting domestic relationships with contentious yet collaborative modes of cross-ontological self-making.

I have chosen these example texts for several reasons, not the least of which is the substantial readerly devotion they have inspired over the years, including in myself and my students. Not only were these works popular at the time of their publication, but they continue to inspire ardent reader responses even today. This is a substantial benefit for a study that hypothesizes their phenomenology of reading: after all, there must be something about these texts that gives readers pleasure, or that frustrates them, or that sparks their curiosity. The consistent readerly attention these works have attracted makes them culturally significant in themselves, and, pragmatically speaking, will allow as many readers as possible to follow and assess the claims I make about the subgenre of fictional autobiography through close readings of their narrative elements. Further, each text provides representative examples of the key features that distinguish the subgenre from its literary siblings.

For this reason, the limited number of my example texts is not necessarily a reflection of the state of the subgenre in the Victorian period itself. The absence of definitive terminology and a set definition for the form makes it impossible to trace exactly how many fictional autobiographies were written and published throughout the nineteenth century. Nonetheless, "autobiographical novels" (as they were sometimes, if inconsistently, called) had a distinctive presence. These works include *Discipline*, by Mary Brunton (1815), and *Caroline Mordaunt*, by Mary Martha Sherwood (1835), both of which, as fictional autobiographies and "governess novels," have been identified by Susan Sniader Lanser as possible precursors to *Jane Eyre*.[72] Victorian examples of fictional autobiography include *The Luck of Barry Lyndon*,[73] by William Makepeace Thackeray (1844); *Agnes Grey*, by Anne Brontë (1847); *Alton Locke, Tailor and Poet: An Autobiography*, by Charles Kingsley (1850); *Aurora Leigh*, by Elizabeth Barrett Browning (1856, a "verse novel" as well as a fictional autobiography); *The Professor*, by Charlotte Brontë (published posthumously, 1857); *The Lifted Veil*, by George Eliot (1859); *Great Expectations*, by Charles Dickens (1860);[74] *The Morgesons*, by Elizabeth Stoddard (an American example, 1862); *Barbara's History*, by Amelia Ann Blanford Edwards (1864); *Cometh Up as a Flower: An Autobiography*, by Rhoda Broughton (1867); and *The Autobiography of Christopher Kirkland*, by Eliza Lynn Linton (1885). These are just some of the fictional autobiographies that were read by Victorian audiences whose texts are still available today. The foregoing list is not exhaustive, and the present study has no pretensions to provide a complete taxonomy of the fictional autobiography in the nineteenth century. Instead, the above list indicates the decided presence of this literary subgenre in the public marketplace throughout the nineteenth century, despite the numerical predominance of novels narrated in the omniscient perspective.

Yet even the comparative rarity of the fictional autobiography speaks to its subversive interpretive potential. Victorian reviewers identified fictional autobiographies as difficult productions to write well, and as the subsequent chapters demonstrate, the way this subgenre troubles concepts of essential identity might further account for its limited numbers. The "I" of the narrating protagonist is precariously poised between stability and transformation, and the extratextual sensation of self becomes, by implication, an uncomfortably contested reality in an already changing world.

The fictional autobiography is above all a form that wavers on and wonders about self: how does one reconcile the fictional dynamics of identity with the lived sensation of inward self-permanence? The following chapters explore the varied and ambivalent solutions to that conundrum as proposed by some of the most popular texts of Victorian fictional autobiography. In the process, I hope to reflect some light on this question that urgently persists in our own lived experiences of a rapidly changing, digital world.

CHAPTER ONE

The Victorian Fictional Autobiography in Context
Fiction, Reference, and Reader Expectations

Fictional autobiographers frequently prompt their narratees—and, by imaginative extension, their readers—to read their texts and their textual identities in particular ways. Such self-conscious narration treats the act of narrating as itself a significant part of characterization and is one of the most important distinguishing features of the fictional autobiography. Whether it is Barry Lyndon's arrogantly "presum[ing] that there is no gentleman in Europe that has not heard of the house of Barry of Barryogue"[1] or Jane Eyre's resisting the "many" who may "blame" her for her restlessness at the start of chapter 12, the more the narrating protagonist coaches her audience to have or to avoid certain responses, the more readers are encouraged actively to perceive and not just unconsciously to experience the reciprocal cross-ontological identity construction this subgenre enables. By implicit suggestion, explicit provocation, or one of the more familiar forms of direct address, among other possible methods, the central writing characters of fictional autobiography offer readers abundant counsel on how best to understand their identities and the stakes of their stories.

Given the amount of attention the form pays to its own internal processes of interpretation, it is curious to note how infrequently the fictional autobiography is studied as a form unto itself. This absence of sustained attention signals the critical uncertainty about whether the fictional autobiography represents an interpretively distinct subgenre or a mere imitation of other forms of literature. Indeed, without even opening a text of fictional autobiography, one can see that the subgenre's very name indicates how a handful of theorists over the last few decades have expected readers to respond to these texts; namely, they treat them as hybrid works that fictionally reproduce the traits of referential life-writing. Dorrit Cohn, consolidating the opinions of several scholars of first-person writing, denominates fictional autobiography a "deliberate, artificial simulation" of autobiography.[2] But thinking of the fictional autobiography as a derivative hybrid form—presumably cobbled together from the already established conventions of the two broader genres suggested by its name—assumes a belatedness of the subgenre, obscuring how texts of this kind took shape alongside the nascent novel and autobiography genres throughout the seventeenth and eighteenth centuries. Indeed, the historical "consanguinity" among the three forms (which Cohn and others deny)[3] in part determines how nineteenth-century readers understood the distinctive interplay of overt fictionality and referential tropes in the fictional autobiography. To ignore the history of invented first-person life stories is to overlook some of the key factors that determine how this subgenre could be interpreted and understood in and beyond the Victorian period.

Victorian readers were avid consumers of fictional autobiographies, novels, and autobiographies, and they understood the ontological difference between the truth claims made by the two latter forms in the same way as contemporary readers do: that is, as metaphoric and referential claims, respectively. The now-familiar conceptual separation of the three sibling genres occurred at the same moment as—and in part because of—the growing tendency in the eighteenth century to conceive of fictional and referential discourses as two distinct modes of narrative truth-telling that claimed different connections to the actualities of the world. According to Nicholas Paige, realist fiction as a mode of communication makes a "soft" (or metaphoric) truth claim, as opposed to nonfiction's "hard (i.e., literal)" assertions of accuracy.[4] By the early nineteenth century, these distinctions were fully operational for the majority of readers, to the point of being nearly invisible. Broadly speaking, most readers would not have had to think consciously about the genre of a text to conceive in what relation it stood to the facts of the world. Early Victorians were one of the first generations implicitly to understand fiction and reference as distinct ontological modes of veracity in literature, and thus they were arguably the first historical audience for whom texts of fictional autobiography encouraged its characteristic doubled reading stance.

In contrast to more recent accounts of this subgenre, Victorian reviewers of fictional autobiography did not rhetorically marginalize this literary form by associating it with imitations of autobiography. Further, their engagement with these texts often demonstrates the form's doubled reading stance in action. Works such as *Cometh Up as a Flower: An Autobiography*, by Rhoda Broughton, seem most often to have drawn some version of the label "autobiographical novel" and to have been treated as a fictional novel that engaged its readers through the familiar structural and thematic tropes that it shared with the autobiography. The difference is slight but essential. To Victorians, these were not novels faking the form of the autobiography and asking readers to detect the potential duplicity of their character-narrators,[5] nor were they primarily assumed to be lightly fictionalized versions of the flesh-and-blood writer's own autobiography; instead, they were explicitly fictional texts that explored the identities of imaginary characters through narrative techniques also characteristic of a literary genre best known for personal referentiality. One Victorian reviewer of *Washington Grange: An Autobiography*, by William Pickersgill, comments in the *Literary Gazette* that "among the most pleasant" forms a "man of genius" can select for his canvas of invention is the "autobiographical form of novel-writing."[6] This casual if clunky phrase suggests that this nineteenth-century writer understood the thematic and formal traits affiliated with autobiography to be enhancements of the overtly imaginative experiences of novel-writing and novel-reading. The declared fictionality of the fictional autobiography was an essential aspect of the form's pleasure-giving potential for this writer, rather than a sign that it was copying or attempting to simulate the referential genre with which it shares certain features.

Victorian critics also remark on this subgenre's special charm for readers: namely, they find that the intimacy the form constructs between fictive teller and actual reader increases both the excitement of the reading experience and the reader's sense of the narrative's authenticity.[7] In an 1867 review of Broughton's novel *Cometh Up as a Flower*, an anonymous reviewer in the *Times* (London) describes it as the "autobiographical form of narrative, or, as children more simply style it, 'An I story.'" The reviewer argues, "The disadvantages attending the autobiographical novel are pretty obvious. The I of the book ought to be especially interesting. He (or she) is almost necessarily the most prominent character, for he must be present at every incident, and take the lead in every conversation." He notes that this necessity for the narrator to be simultaneously the protagonist places certain narrative rigors and constraints on the flesh-and-blood author of such productions. The reader, on the other hand, is drawn to the "autobiographical novel" precisely because of the excitement such autodiegetic "I" narration promises.[8] This reviewer makes the case for the compelling nature of the fictional autobiography thus: "It is more startling to say, 'I thrust my dagger into the caitin's [*sic*][9] breast' than to say that X, Y, or Z performed that thrilling feat. In the first case the reader is permitted to hold actual converse with the assassin; in the latter case the assassin is separated from us by a third person who professes such an intimate acquaintance with all his characters that we are inclined to doubt his veracity."[10] Coming from a position opposite that of later critics, this writer seems to find extradiegetic-heterodiegetic—more commonly called omni-scient narrators—*less* credible than their first-person, autobiographical coun-terparts. After all, fictional autobiographers are frequently accounting for the sources of their knowledge and making clear gestures to maintain standards of real-world epistemology; not so with the more numerous all-knowing (if not all-telling) narrators of most Victorian fiction.

The *Times* reviewer identifies the potential for readerly intimacy with the fictional autobiographer as part of the subgenre's increased appeal over other novelistic productions. Because "the reader is permitted to hold actual con-verse" with the fictional being who both acts in the story and narrates those actions in the discourse, the emotional response is enhanced. (In his sensa-tional example, readers are "startled," though presumably the effect functions across diverse modes of feeling as well.) He even goes so far as to denomi-nate the narrating protagonist of *Cometh Up* as "the authoress" of the work, remarking on her personal characteristics both at the level of the story and as they are reflected in her style of narration. He specifically quarrels with the predominance of "slang" in parts of the discourse, and instead prefers when "the authoress" is behaving in a more discreet and domestic manner (a significant preference in itself, and one of the reasons I refer to this reviewer as male): "For ourselves, we prefer the authoress in her calmer and more se-rious moods—when she is sitting by her poor old father, weighed down with debt and disappointment; or when she is striving to solve some of the many puzzles of our existence."[11] Elsewhere in the review when he refers to the "au-thoress," however, he clearly means the unnamed Broughton, the actual writ-er of the novel, talking of her potential for future literary productions. In the well-known review of *Jane Eyre* in the *Quarterly Review* of December 1848 by Elizabeth Rigby, the writer's phrasing suggests a similar slippage between real-world author and fictional autobiographer. Rigby attributes to Brontë (as "Bell") insufficient knowledge and incorrect portraiture of her main character in several passages. She asserts that Jane is "not as artless" as her writer would have readers believe, but that if the "high-souled" woman of chapter 27 who resists Rochester's threats and temptations "be Jane Eyre," then the author and not the skeptical critic has done Jane a disservice. Yet Rigby also credits Jane herself with the composition of certain scenes. Rigby criticizes Jane as both narrator and writer when she complains that "when Jane Eyre sets [Mr. Rochester's guests] conversing, she falls into mistakes which display . . . a vulgarity of mind inherent in herself."[12]

In both reviews, the identification of the overtly fictional character-narrator as the author of her text, all while explicitly treating her as distinct from the actual living writer of it, attests to the fact that these two historical readers experienced the fictional autobiography's doubled reading stance. Both the *Times* reviewer and Rigby grant at least some agency to the narrating protagonists as their own tellers, and, as a result, these critics seem to feel they possess personal knowledge of the narrating protagonists' identities based on how these main characters narrate their life stories. This persistent doubling of authority between real-world author and fictive narrator, and the potent impressions thus made on readers by the narrator's identity—despite the readers' consciousness of its fictionality—demonstrates this subgenre's remarkable phenomenology of reading. These reviews illustrate that the fictional autobiography can and did operate for Victorian readers as more than a mere "facsimile" imitating autobiography and that its interpretive possibilities are distinct from non-autobiographical realist novels narrated in the third person.

The fictional autobiography occupies the intersection of two modes of truth-telling by sharing conventions with both novels and autobiographies; the above-cited reviews demonstrate just some of the potential interpretive effects of these shared features and commitments. Even as the interpretive effects of the fictional autobiography show it to function in more nuanced ways than as a simple copy of its sibling forms, the genre expectations of novels and autobiographies nonetheless play an essential role in understanding how the fictional autobiography as a related subgenre shapes reader interpretation. After all, as Justin Sider argues, "many readers, particularly of conspicuously 'genred' works, attach their sentiments less to the particular text in question than to the fulfillment of the generic contract."[13] The fact that individual texts of fictional autobiography openly invoke the genre expectations of both novels and autobiographies, in other words, can play a significant role in how readers interpret these texts and in how they invest their imaginative energies in the identities of the narrating protagonists. When reading the nonfictional autobiography, readers seek to find the writer's authentic identity in and through the scrupulously accurate telling of his life. In the novel, readers seek intersubjective intimacy with fictional characters, achieved through a level of epistemological certainty (absolute assurances of created truth) that would be impossible to achieve in first-person accounts of the real world. In the fictional autobiography, readers seem to find it all.

What may be gained in satisfaction from reading the fictional autobiography, however, comes with the attendant cost that traditional notions of personal identity—modern selfhood being the central concern of all three genres—lose some of their apparent stability. The fictional autobiography invites readers consciously to cross the line between the actual and the imaginary. Far from breaking down the line between the fictional and the referential, however, the fictional autobiography relies on the boundary's relative stability in literary matters: only if Victorians were convinced of the essential difference between fictional creation and referential representation could the fictional autobiography trouble the nature of self by landing that "self" squarely on the side of the fictional. This, however, means that the literary transgression of the actual/imaginary boundary is displaced outside of literary experience into the realm of lived experience. In its most extreme effect, reading a fictional autobiography fundamentally detaches the notion of personal identity from anything eternal or objective while simultaneously reinforcing the reader's investment in "self" as the most significant category of human existence. "I" becomes not just a contingent grammatical category, pitching us into an abyss of nonexistent referents. What is so disruptive in the fictional autobiography's challenge to everyday assumptions about identity is that this genre never allows the attentive reader to forget that the experience of being a self—even if that self is indeed a flexible fiction—remains an intimately personal lived reality for each human being.

Historical Consanguinity: The Autobiography, the Novel, the Fictional Autobiography

The novel and the autobiography—as discrete genres whose conventions are established and signaled to readers by their genre names—developed concurrently. If we can talk about "the rise of the novel," then we can also talk about "the rise of the autobiography" over the course of the eighteenth century. Although the terminology for the fictional autobiography remains persistently unfixed even today, it nonetheless shares common literary ancestors and thematic concerns with the novel and the autobiography, making it demonstrably historically consanguineous with its sibling forms. From the work of Michael McKeon to the writing of Roy Pascal, the emergence of the novel and the autobiography, respectively, are often traced to texts that feature the life story of an invented first-person teller—that is, to protofictional autobiographies. For McKeon, the first English novel is Samuel Richardson's epistolary novel *Pamela*.[14] For Pascal, Daniel Defoe's *Moll Flanders* is superior to many early texts of referential life-writing in its autobiographical presentation of a developing personality.[15] These common progenitors for all three literary forms demonstrate their shared cultural roots and preoccupations: specifically, all three are distinctly modern forms concerned with validating the identity of the singular individual in a social world.

By the end of the eighteenth century, a newly capitalist social and economic order had emerged that fed upon the Enlightenment premise that the autonomous individual human is the center of knowable experience and thus the locus of ultimate value in the world. As Ian Watt puts it, "individual experience" of the world became "the ultimate arbiter of reality."[16] Watt and McKeon each locate the novel's success and its cultural relevance in its focus on the individual life; they also show that its genesis throughout the eighteenth century freely traversed the as-yet-nonexistent line between fictional and referential modes of discourse. It was only in the late eighteenth century, when most readers began actively to conceive of fictional works as separate both from tales with reference to the real world and from deception and lying, that the genre of the novel could truly be said to exist as such, according to Catherine Gallagher.[17] Watt and McKeon each frame the rise of the novel as both participating in and reflective of a change in consciousness, an emerging sense of modernity.[18] The rise to prominence of this modern consciousness and the modern individual's "unique" identity accounts not only for the novel's cultural success but also for the popularity of life-writing genres.

Watt's emphasis on personal originality as the key to relevance in the modern world[19] is also particularly applicable to the modern genre of autobiography. In autobiography, acts of introspective self-interpretation, according to Linda Peterson, are not just the central objective but the primary points of interest in the narrative.[20] Michael Mascuch and Martin Danahay also align the rise of an individualist ideology with the consolidation of the autobiographical genre as it came to operate in the early nineteenth century, following its somewhat reluctant naming in 1797 by William Taylor in a review of Isaac D'Israeli's *Miscellanies, or Literary Recreations*, which contained the essay "Some Observations on Diaries, Self-biography, and Self-character."[21] So by the turn of the nineteenth century, Taylor's *autobiography* had emerged as the primary term to refer to texts of life-writing featuring retrospective first-person narration in which the thematic focus is the teller's origins, self-representation, and social recognition of self. Although related types of life-writing had been around for centuries, the autobiography's individualist focus diverges significantly from some of its precursors, even from the similarly introspective spiritual autobiography of earlier periods. As Martin Löschnigg highlights, in the spiritual autobiography descriptions of the state of the soul, its sins, and its ultimate redemption have a didactic, universalizing purpose, presenting the main character as a model for readers to emulate;[22] not so with the modern autobiography and its approach to personal identity. According to James Treadwell, by the beginning of the Victorian period autobiography was an "apparently distinct and recognizable genre [that] had naturalized it-self in the eyes of readers." Treadwell connects this newly consolidated genre with modern perceptions of selfhood, claiming that "the presentation (or publication) of a singular identity" comes to seem like "an end in itself" for texts of autobiography.[23]

The classical autobiography's commitment to validating the writer's singu-lar inward individuality means that, even for its earliest audiences, the genre "raise[d] questions about motivations, purposes, and, inevitably, about au-thenticity," particularly regarding the identities it purported to represent.[24] To complicate the genre's implications for personal identity even further, unlike memoirs of well-known figures in the res gestae tradition, religious confessions that model a path to salvation for others to follow, or other first-person works with "autobiographical content," a classical autobiography, Pas-cal contends, is not the portrait of a "static personality," nor is its central purpose to explore events external to and persons other than the writer. In-stead, autobiography is "historical in its method, and at the same time [is] the representation of the [writing] self in and through its relations with the outer world."[25] In this way, the subject of classical autobiography shares a central dynamic with Georg Lukács's "problematic individual," or the seeker figure at the center of the novel genre.[26] Both the classical autobiographer and the problematic individual of the novel struggle to manifest their inward origi-nality externally, in the arbitrary structures of the social world that surrounds them.

In *The Theory of the Novel*, Lukács posits a shift in consciousness that rup-tures the "epic" mind-set of the past and leaves us alienated, displaced, self-conscious—in a word, modern. "Totality," in the days of ancient epic, was only a matter of finding one's "*locus*" in the universal system, "for knowledge is only the raising of a veil, creation only the copying of visible and eternal essences, virtue a perfect knowledge of the paths." The modern subject and its literature, by contrast, are born of "the rift between 'inside' and 'outside,' . . . the essential difference between the self and the world." As a result of this loss of faith in unity and knowable universal principles, modern subjects have become "other" to themselves. Because the interior experience of self is the only certainty of modern living, according to Lukács, "the outward form of the novel is essentially biographical." The problematic individual seeks the totality of a real—organic, objective—and thus stable identity. But the subjective narrative that creates the illusion of authenticity for this identity, and that is supposed to stem from a point outside that same narration (from something "organic"), brings the immediacy of the loss of totality, and the yearning for it, to the fore of the novel's concerns. Although totality is un-reachable, Lukács writes that the novel is "the epic of an age in which the extensive totality of life is no longer directly given, in which the immanence of meaning in life has become a problem, yet which still thinks in terms of totality."[27]

This desire for and attempt to construct a now-displaced totality, and the yearning to perceive, attain, and prove the efficacy of universals, governs more than just the nineteenth-century novel. Theorists of autobiography have long associated this loss of and longing for totality (though in other words) with that genre as well—a genre whose referential mode of representation in itself complicates the quest for unity at which the novel's fictionality excels. In describing the classical autobiography of the nineteenth century, Pascal's theory dovetails with Lukács's work on the dynamics of internal and external in the modern individual's life. Pascal writes that "perhaps one might say that [autobiography] involves the philosophical assumption that the self comes into being only through the interplay with the outer world."[28] The problem-atic individual in classical autobiography, like the problematic individual of the nineteenth-century novel, can only be expressed—perhaps only comes to exist—through engagement with what is supposedly external and alien to it. Both the novel and the autobiography, as vehicles for negotiating the modern experience of individuality in a social world, imply that the self is socially constituted, or at least that it is only confirmed through a collective act of interpretation.

This is the core "problem" in the problematic nature of the individuality at the center of all three of these genres: if the modern self is most valued for its inward permanence as the one stable point in a chaotic world, then its reliance on social discourses for expression and on the reader for interpre-tive confirmation of its existence undercuts its supposed ontological stability. Mascuch notes this paradox in the autobiography's goals and phenomenology of reading: one of autobiography's defining generic tropes is to establish the autonomous authority of its writer-protagonist, yet an autobiography can only establish the authority of its author's self through a public, published repre-sentation of his identity as a socially determined construct.[29] As in the novel, the newly consolidated form of the autobiography in the early nineteenth century seems to be striving "both for the immediate unity of life and for a completely rounded architecture of the system"[30] in the narratives of identity the works create.

The fact that novels, autobiographies, and fictional autobiographies all ad-dress and negotiate modern subjectivity through their biographical focus is significant because such a focus in all three genres indicates the thematic trajectory of readerly attention in these texts. In these sibling genres, readers are primed to invest in questions of identity and sociability, personal autonomy and intimacy with others, though to different interpretive ends in each genre. These "different interpretive ends" are a result of the genres' distinct ontological relationships with (and thus have implications for how readers understand) the identities they construct. Where the novel is acknowledged to create its own reality—achieving a limited sort of unity through its self-conscious artifice—the autobiography remains more directly tethered to the outside world in its readers' minds. For this reason, the key distinction of communicative mode resurfaces: the phenomenological difference between reading a referential text and reading a fictional text proves to be vast. The novel constructs imagined worlds and selves that are entire in themselves precisely because they are invented creations.[31] The autobiography and the selves it undertakes to represent and validate, on the other hand, are assumed to be tied to real-world actuality, which is by its nature disputable (as discussed in the section "The Fictional Autobiography vs. the Nonfictional Autobiography" in the introduction). The fictional autobiography takes the central ontological assumption of autobiography—that the essence of the individual is her inner self but that it can be understood (paradoxically) only in relation to the outer world—and works through it in an overtly fictional mode wherein questions of being and knowing seem to operate in the hazy middle distance, one step removed from the real world.

The understanding that fictionality and referentiality are two different modes of truth-telling is a historical and cultural phenomenon of the late eighteenth century. While protofictional autobiography was around as a nascent form in and before the eighteenth century, the doubled reading stance that fictional autobiography encourages could not come into effect until the communicative categories of fictional and referential discourse were clearly delineated and understood by most readers, as signaled by the establishment of the genre categories "novel" and "autobiography." For example, at the time of their writing and first reading, Daniel Defoe's *Robinson Crusoe*, *Moll Flanders*, and *Roxana* were considered neither fictional *nor* referential. They were what Nicholas Paige, using Barbara Foley's term, calls "pseudofactual" texts that function on assumptions fundamentally different from those that now inform our reading of the rhetorical categories of fictional and nonfictional discourse. The pseudofactual "narrative posture" operates on the principle that "the more you take the spectacle for reality, the greater its effect on you." Consonant with eighteenth-century aesthetic theories, Paige explains, art and literature were taken to be "rather a substitute for reality, a simulation that is, unfortunately but necessarily, always a bit off." The less a work makes us think about its inventedness, according to eighteenth-century assumptions, the more powerful will be its effect. This belief explains Defoe's insistence on maintaining the found-manuscript trope in *Robinson Crusoe*, despite at least some public recognition of the protagonist's invented status, and Samuel Richardson's similar frustration at being named the "author" (and not the editor) of *Clarissa* by one of the novel's preface-writers.[32] The assumption that a readerly awareness of invention diminishes a work's aesthetic and ethical impact is also in marked contrast to more modern notions of "high" literary fictionality, in which texts often self-reflexively register their inventedness and in which metafictional and metatextual moments are often paramount to how these works communicate their messages.

Paige is among the scholars of genre history (including Catherine Gallagher) who claim that "fictionality" as we have known it since the nineteenth century is a distinct mode of literary creation and communication. As Paige phrases it, a fictional text proclaims, "I am about to tell you how the world really is, as opposed to something that really happened."[33] Fiction as such did not exist in a widespread way as a popular writing and reading posture until the late eighteenth century, and it reached its modern zenith in the mid-Victorian period. To reframe this history in terms important for the current study, throughout much of the eighteenth century readers generally did not interpret literary truth claims in the same ways and through the same categories as readers have since the early nineteenth century. Whereas for most of the eighteenth century popular audiences were generally encouraged to avoid consciousness of a text's invented status when seeking to experience its full aesthetic effect, by the nineteenth century many readers could not help but become immersed in the active conversations that covered the pages of popular periodicals about the creative, metaphorical (rather than factual) connections between explicit fictions as works of art and the world beyond the text. The Victorian audience's historically new capacity to appreciate fiction's truth-telling potential is what enabled the fictional autobiography to produce in readers its distinctive doubled reading stance, and thus to challenge the ideals of identity that govern modern subjectivity.

Although the doubled reading stance of the fictional autobiography was not a distinct interpretive possibility until the early nineteenth century, life stories of imaginary first-person tellers appealed to readers from at least the early modern period on—long before "the novel" or "the autobiography" existed as intelligible sets of conventions to shape readers' expectations of those works.[34] Defoe, though popular, was hardly the first author to publish such tales. Charles Haskell Hinnant indicates several first-person texts upon which Defoe might have modeled his own invented first-person accounts. One "pseudo-memoir" (or protofictional autobiography) that preceded and likely informed Defoe's texts was *Mémoires de la vie de Henriette-Sylvie de Molière*, by Marie-Catherine Hortense Desjardins, who wrote under the name Madame de Villedieu.[35] Published in six parts from 1672 to 1674,[36] this epistolary memoir of an imaginary protagonist was popular in both France and England, and it inspired other "pseudo-memoirs" and pseudonymous memoirs—personal romans á clef, one might say.[37] Despite the basic structural similarities to fictional autobiography (an imaginary protagonist telling her life story in first-person, retrospective narration) the primary concern of the fictive Sylvie is markedly different from those of later Victorian character-narrators in the fictional autobiography. External events and public scandal provide the main interest of the *Mémoires de la vie de Henriette-Sylvie*. Further, the separation between character-narrator and real-world writer was often tantalizingly incomplete, which was one of the main appeals of the text: contemporary readers in the know recognized many similarities between the details of the life of Desjardins and the details of the life of Sylvie, according to Donna Kuizenga.[38] And though Sylvie as a narrator is explicitly invested in staking claims to her individual worth in a social world, inwardness as a sign of individuality is not an essential part of her story or purpose. In other words, she is not yet a "problematic individual" in the ontologically complex, Lukácsian sense. The minimal interest the text takes in the interiority of Sylvie is also characteristic of *Robinson Crusoe* and Defoe's other invented autodiegetic narratives,[39] making their main characters feel less modern than the narrating protagonists of the Victorian fictional autobiography.

But Desjardins's and Defoe's works demonstrate that, even before the line between artistically whole and legitimate fictions and accurate yet artistically sophisticated nonfictions became firm; even before a secular self, whose inviolate inwardness was both a mark of permanence and a social problem, became the dominant way of thinking about identity; even before our contemporary mind-set took nascent shape in the Victorian period, readers wished to engage with the first-person tale of an imaginary individual's life. Perhaps this is because such tales present the mechanisms through which so many humans intuitively, if unconsciously, experience existence as narratively unified social beings. The following section explores how the crucial generic and narratological distinction between fiction and nonfiction discourses might have operated for Victorian readers as they contemplated the nature of individual identity in (and as) creative narrative. The fictional autobiography, by illuminating the tensions inherent in truth claims that cross the fiction/reference divide, makes the fictional mechanisms of identity both more visible to readers and easier to accept, even as the subgenre challenges the modern subject's attachment to the illusion of self-permanence that fictional processes create.

Fiction and/as Reality

This section traces recent theories of fictionality, and their resonance with Victorian beliefs about fiction and the world, to demonstrate how fictional processes structure readers' sense of personal reality. As signaled in the introduction and as the following chapters illustrate, fictional autobiographies fulfill the audience's desire for intimacy with and knowledge of the narrator-protagonists through reader-inclusion strategies that require the audience to take part in the creation of the identities with whom they seek communion. Through such active reader engagement—whether undertaken consciously or not by any given reader—imaginary characters engender vivid intellectual and emotional experiences for audiences. Recent work in cognitive literary theory by scholars such as Lisa Zunshine and Blakey Vermeule underscores the experiential reality of fictional characters to real-world readers. Vermeule proposes that encounters with fictional characters provide readers "with the most intense cognitive stimulation imaginable" by making readers feel they are privy to "social information" and "the deep truth about people's intentions"[40] and, by extension, their identities.

Enabling the cognitive and affective potency of a character's selfhood—the impression of knowing the "deep truth" of another subjectivity—is the reader's tacit understanding of what Catherine Gallagher calls the "conceptual category of fiction."[41] Before readers feel comfortable filling in these animating gaps of a narrating protagonist's identity, they must have a sturdy if implicit grasp of the fiction/reference divide. Indeed, as has been the case beginning with certain audiences and novelists in the eighteenth century, far from confusing "textual with actual people," Gallagher argues, "readers attach themselves to characters because of, not despite, their fictionality."[42] As Gallagher's theory of fictional "nobodies" in several of her works illustrates, to take an active and creative role in a fictional "nobody's story" is appealing precisely because "nobodies and their stories" do not "belong to anyone in the real world."[43] Readers can be "acquisitive without impertinence" when they imaginatively construct these overtly fictional selves, argues Gallagher, adapting a phrase from Edmund Burke, because these fictional nobodies do not refer to any actual, embodied selves beyond the text.[44] Gallagher's twist on Burke's phrase—highlighting the readerly desire to possess the truth of another self without imposing upon what is presumed to be an independently existing identity—begins to reveal the existential anxieties that accompany such social acts of creative self-making, even in a consciously fictional encounter. If one can construct an authentic-seeming self for another distinctive being through fictional processes, the implications of that creation are potentially worse than mere impertinence. Knowingly participating in the creation of a real-feeling selfhood becomes a direct challenge to the belief that identity is the permanent inward property of each living individual.

This is where "the conceptual category of fiction" works its magic in the experience of reading the fictional autobiography. Both contemporary theorists and numerous Victorian readers and writers have understood fiction to be at once separate from and intimately connected to the world of the reader.[45] Fictional works' metaphoric connection to actuality seems, at least at first blush, to free the reader from the destabilizing implications of actively constructing fictional selves that nonetheless feel—cognitively and affectively—like the embodied selves one can encounter in the world. Gallagher suggests that fictions provide a secure mental space in which to engage in suppositional play, allowing readers to test out scenarios akin to those experienced in the real world without risking themselves.[46] The recognizable fictionality of the fictional autobiography at once shields readers from the immediate implications of collaborative self-making and draws attention to the imaginative, social, and narrative processes that make the resulting selves of the narrating protagonists feel so real.

The fictional autobiography comes to operate for readers on two planes. As an explicit fiction that creates its own story world, the fictional autobiography seems to give readers access to the kinds of truth humans cannot fully possess in and about the real world.[47] And, as a text that employs conventions of reference and intimacy shared with the genre of classical autobiography,[48] the fictional autobiography seems to promise definitive knowledge of another's genuine self. But those same conventions of autobiography complicate readers' engagement with the fictional self in the text; their affiliation with real-world reference makes the parallel between knowing another in the real world and knowing another in the fictional world all the more apparent. The narrative manner through which a reader comes to feel she knows the truth of the narrating protagonist's identity, the fictional autobiography reminds the attentive reader, is identical to the processes by which she generates her own sensation of selfhood and her impression of knowing real-life others. The reader's "knowledge" of *any* identity is at least in part attributable to her collaborative creation of that identity. The detailed, invented points of difference that make the narrating protagonist seem personally distinct from the reader only reinforce the structural and affective likeness of these equally fictional selves.

The tension, then, between referential and fictional modes of truth-telling, whose conventions intermingle in the fictional autobiography, could also be considered a dialectical collaboration between two types of knowing and two types of existence that, in their mutual presence, give rise to a related third possibility. Adapting Gallagher's vocabulary to my argument, the fictional autobiography tells nobody's story through genre conventions that usually characterize the tale of an actual somebody; this subgenre thus exposes that nobodies often feel like somebodies precisely because they emerge from the same foundational processes in which selves come to exist through imaginative, socially informed narratives. The fictional autobiography, after all, does not ask its readers to distinguish between narration that constructs real selves and narration that constructs false or simulated selves. Indeed, as a form it tends to demonstrate the fact that, as Richard Walsh points out, "all narrative, fictional and nonfictional, is artifice. Narratives are constructs, and their meanings are internal to the system of narrative."[49] By activating reader expectations in this dialectical manner, the fictional autobiography achieves its interpretive specialty: to make visible identity's narrative artifice and to make this artifice appear productive rather than threatening to the self of the reader.

In *The Distinction of Fiction*, Dorrit Cohn articulates some of the crucial differences between reader expectations associated with the fictional and with the nonfictional autobiography that illuminate how the dialectical effect of the fictional autobiography functions. Cohn's work implicitly draws attention to the different ontologies of identity that each type of text relies upon and makes possible. Citing the work of Philippe Lejeune, Elizabeth Bruss, and Michál Glowiński on autobiography, she suggests that its nonfictional form is referential not only in the factuality or precise accuracy of its content (or in readers' expectations of accuracy) but in the ontological status of its author and narrator. Cohn quotes Bruss, "Whether or not what is reported [in an autobiography] can be discredited, . . . the autobiographer *purports* to believe in what he asserts."[50] That is, as long as the author seems to believe in the accuracy of his representation of the world and himself, then the factuality of the content becomes secondary in determining whether or not a text is referentially autobiographical. From this complication Cohn concludes that

> the truth claim of autobiography in no sense implies the *actual* truth of an autobiographer's statement. . . . It now becomes clear that the referential nature of autobiography can only be theoretically secure by a shift

of emphasis from its content to its speaker. For if the genre is defined by way of the reality of its speaking subject, then it remains no less real when the subject lies or fantasizes about his past than when he utters verifiable truths.[51]

In other words, Cohn's analysis proposes that the distinction between reading autobiographical first-person fiction and reading autobiographical first-person nonfiction—the difference in the phenomenology of processing those claims—lies in how the reader perceives the ontological status of the text's narrator-protagonist, whether her name refers to an extratextual being or an exclusively textual and imaginary one. In Cohn's theory, as in the work of Philippe Lejeune and others, the essence of the referential genre is in how readers approach it, which is determined, in turn, by how they understand the existence of its narrator-protagonist.

One of the central differences in effect between fictional and nonfictional autobiography, then, relies upon the reader's genre-specific assumptions about the ontological status of the main character. The reader's understanding of the narrating protagonist's existence, furthermore, influences how he understands the other truth claims made by the text: are they the metaphoric claims of fiction or the empirical, literal claims of nonfiction? In autobiographies both fictional and nonfictional, readers continue to look for some kind of accuracy, even if each type of reading approach elicits specific kinds of accuracy seeking (which will be discussed later in this chapter). The reader's attentiveness to accuracy in all autobiographical genres is an extension of the persistent modern desire for access to definitive knowledge of the world, of the self, and of the other. After all, as Lukács claims, modern subjects still think in terms of totality, which means they seek a coherent truth—or at least the fictional representation of it—in the "created totalities" of literature.[52] Readers wish to establish a connection between the seemingly more knowable worlds of narrative fiction and the truths of their own existence, especially when the genre is one whose appeal is built upon conventions of intimacy, and—significantly—even when the protagonist is acknowledged to be ontologically "other" from the world of the reader.

Despite a common and often implicit understanding of fiction as constituting a kind of ontological otherness, Richard Walsh theorizes how fiction nonetheless enables meaningful real experiences for readers. His claims both reinforce the Victorian understanding of fiction's value and mark an important entry in recent critical accounts of fiction's significance today. In his monograph *The Rhetoric of Fictionality*, Walsh defines fiction as "the serious use of a language's representational capacity for fictive—imaginary, not literally assertive—purposes," resisting the tendency to perceive fiction as a type of verbal play, something secondary to "serious" language. He insists that readers take satisfaction in their construction of fictional worlds when they can "bring them into relation with the larger context of their own experience and understanding."[53] But taking fiction seriously in this way, I propose, does not mean overlooking the fact that most readers associate fictionality with some type of ontological difference from embodied realities. In marking the connections that exist between their lived experiences and the fictional world, readers remain cognizant (even passively so) of the ontological separation between fictive realities and their own. Fictional encounters, nonetheless, far from becoming unimportant because of their fictionality, instead possess a distinct kind of relevance for readers.[54] This special relevance in turn explains the ability to invest oneself in narratives of the nonactual: as Gallagher and others have claimed, fiction serves as a particular—metaphoric, flexible, and less risky—way to experience reality.

Walsh further argues for the significance of fiction, noting that "the production and consumption of fictions is both an application of the capacity for narrative understanding we already possess and an opportunity to enhance it."[55] Linking this rationale of fictional communication to the poles of particularity and generality associated with realist representation, Walsh identifies "the mimetic process" as the cognitive capacity that makes fiction beneficial:

> So, with fiction, the relation of particular to general is the dialectical relation of imaginary data to narrative understanding, the former largely for the sake of the latter. It is the particulars that are fictional, not the mimetic process, which does not reside in these particulars themselves, but in their narrative articulation. The reciprocity between these two, the general faculty and the imaginary particulars, secures the real-world benefits of engaging with the unreal.[56]

He concludes that "what we understand, feel, and value may be ultimately grounded in the abstract and the general, but it is not in general terms that we experience understanding, feeling, or valuing it. Fiction enables us to go through that process, for the sake of the experience."[57] The fictional particulars of a text catalyze the mental narrative processes that characterize cognition both in and beyond fictional encounters. Walsh's argument that readers enjoy invented stories not only because they rehearse us in processing real-world sensations through narrative but also because they allow us to experience directly those same real-world sensations resonates with and expands upon Gallagher's theory on the function of fiction in the world. His argument also implicitly supports Victorian beliefs about fiction's capacity to teach feeling and understanding for real-world application. Like the Victorians before them, many recent scholars argue for various versions of what I call the hermeneutic view of fiction: it is a tool, a simulation of the world, that indirectly enriches one's understanding of extratextual existence. As already mentioned in the introduction, Gallagher, Iser, Vermeule, and others promote a version of the hermeneutic view of fiction and its real-world significance.[58]

What none of these theorists go so far as to suggest, and what I am drawing attention to here and throughout this project, is that fictional processes are the foundation for, and not merely the practice versions of, two of the most central aspects of modern living: namely, the experience of being a self and of knowing other selves. As Walsh implies and as recent research into cognition is revealing, the intellectual and emotional experiences activated when reading literary fictions can be very real indeed, even becoming empirically measurable to a limited extent.[59] The potentially literal nature of engaging with a fictional being, moreover, depends upon the readers' recognition of the text as fiction in order fully to fulfill that interpretive potential. The fact that an implicit awareness of a work's fictionality enhances the reader's cognitive and affective experience of its reality suggests that the processes of understanding fiction—of creating its reality—are identical to the processes that make the extratextual world feel real; this is especially the case with realities (such as personal identity) that are considered transcendent, ineffable. The fictional autobiography, going further than other types of novels, promotes an explicit recognition of identity's fictionality by inspiring in careful readers its special brand of cognitive dissonance. The subgenre illuminates that fictional selves are more than creative allegories for real-world identities by both acceding to and undermining the ideal of essential identity that underwrites the conventions of the realist novel and the classical autobiography that coexist in its pages. The openly fictional selves that emerge from this subgenre are explicitly invented, necessarily collaborative, and also—as a result of these two preceding conditions—very real cognitive experiences.

Being Real and Structuring Selves in Victorian Literature

Because literary fiction was widely believed to have an ethical impact on the world of its readers, Victorian reviewers spent considerable time and ink discussing the merits of good character construction by authors. Their arguments over what makes a character believable as a human-like entity (and thus valuable for what it can tell readers about the general truths of being human) also expose underlying assumptions about the nature of human identity, ideals that the fictional autobiography challenges. The critical reviews of William Makepeace Thackeray's historical fictional autobiography *The History of Henry Esmond* reflect the intricacies of defining fictional authenticity in the Victorian period. Thackeray's novel is a borderline case of fictional autobiography set during Queen Anne's reign. Henry Esmond, the narrator-protagonist, rarely uses the first person, referring to his character-self almost exclusively in the third person. It is easy to forget the linked identities of the character and the narrator, a fact that emphasizes the historical interest of the novel above the (fictionally) autobiographical. For some reviewers, this lack of intimacy between narrator and character, and between narrator and reader, does not mean a lack of authenticity. In his review of the novel in an 1852 issue of the *Spectator*, George Brimley suggests that the novel's "unity" derives from how external events, both personal and historical, "bring out" and "ripen" the "qualities" of the main characters in a way that productively imitates what "happens in life." Brimley insists that the working of the plot upon the characters makes this piece of fiction authentic; he comments that "the book has the great charm of reality."[60]

John Forster's review of *Henry Esmond*, which came out a week later in the *Examiner*, however, finds fault with the novel precisely for its lack of lifelike characters, and Forster gives as his justification the same reason that Brimley found it so charmingly real. For Forster, the characters lack the agency to be authentic, and their lack of an inner life is precisely what prevents their becoming real enough to be recognized in living men and women as types. Forster declaims that he read the novel from start to finish "without receiving . . . a distinct impression of vitality." He complains, "We cannot persuade ourselves that there is a single character described at any length in this history which could belong to any being made of flesh and blood" because Thackeray "hangs over the fictitious people on his paper too much as their creator and their judge. He does not think his own way among them, and talk of them as a man should talk of men. If they be men and women, he must be the God who judges them."[61] In other words, readers must be able to believe in the potential of these fictional beings to be as real as themselves and to have credible agency of their own within their fictional world—fictional agency that operates somehow in concert with that of their real-world creator. For Forster, fictional characters must impress the reader with outward manifestations of a unique inward essence—as the defining human characteristic—at the same time that they are knowably fictive.

Perhaps the closest that one may come to a Victorian consensus on character is that the best-drawn, most instructive, and most literary characters are those that, as Anthony Trollope expresses it in his *Autobiography*, maintain a "consistency" from the beginning of the story to the end and (in his case) from one novel to the next. He adds that it is equally necessary that characters exhibit, at the same time, "those changes which time always produces." To untangle the implications of Trollope's stipulations, it seems that truly human-like characters must exhibit both sameness and difference—an original inner self that can be developed into showing outward signs of that originality—rather than a "hard exactitude, [which] would have been untrue to nature."[62] Trollope's implied vision of human identity parallels John Stuart Mill's perspective in chapter 3 of *On Liberty*, "Of Individuality as One of the Elements of Well-Being." Mill presents productive individualism as a mode of being that leads to a socially informed (though not socially dependent) development of that which is already innate and "natural" (his word) in the individual. In Mill's vision of Victorian identity, the ideal of a permanent core self becomes partially reconciled, through the need for adaptability, with the practice of conscious self-making.[63] The self's original potential is predetermined, even though it must be realized through self-cultivation of those original urges. Mill's conception of individuality thus predicts and explains the dynamics of the Lukácsian problematic individual, the figure of selfhood at the center of the novel, the autobiography, and the fictional autobiography: an immutable inner essence precedes and structures the social possibilities of a self, even as that essence remains unrealized until brought into contact with the otherness of the outer world, and particularly with other selves.

Illustrating (even as it anticipates) both Trollope's and Mill's conceptions of individuality in and through literature, Brimley wrote in a review of *Bleak House* in 1853 that the plot was faulty because it insufficiently affects the identities and behaviors of the protagonists. He complains that "Mr Richard Carstone is not made reckless and unsteady by his interest in the great suit [of Jarndyce and Jarndyce], but simply expends his recklessness and unsteadiness on it, as he would on something else if it were non-existent." In the same vein, he later adds that the plot "is so unskillfully managed that the daughter [Esther] is in no way influenced either in character or destiny by her mother's history."[64] The irony here seems to be that Brimley, in his rejection of Dickens's ability to craft a convincing story, suggests through his own critical approach that, at the very least, Dickens has produced some very convincing characters, despite—or perhaps because of—their obstinate consistency with themselves over time.[65] After all, Brimley addresses Richard's personal failings as if they somehow preexisted the "mere plot" of the story, as if Richard, somehow, could have acted similarly in any other (fictional) situation. He likewise seems to overlook the characters' special brand of "non-existence" (to repurpose his word) when he critiques the fictional autobiographer Esther. He writes that her "unconscious goodness" is evident in her writing, as if the center of her identity somehow were extratextual, existing beyond the words that "unconsciously" depict the goodness that is her primary trait. And while the latter observation—of her unwitting self-revelation—can be a functional one if we think of Dickens, not Esther, as the actual author of herself and her story, Brimley nonetheless takes the novel at its word (in a critical exaggeration of real-world reading practices), talking about Esther as an unlikely "autobiographer" who may be better off "superintending the jam-pots" of Bleak House.[66] So while the events of *Bleak House* seem to the reviewer to be insufficiently motivated and motivating in reference to the characters, the characters themselves, because of their persistent permanence of personality, are treated to some extent by Brimley (and other reviewers) as if they were living beings, with identities wholly separate from the text in which readers encounter them.

These selections from the Victorian debates on character authenticity and the nature of selfhood suggest that, even if it is a complicated equivalency, readers generally process realist fictional characters as human-like beings, with all the attendant tendencies, potentialities, and shortcomings of humanity in general. Shlomith Rimmon-Kenan calls this kind of reading of character "mimetic."[67] A mimetic interpretation of character is implicitly invited by the realist mechanisms of the Victorian fictional autobiography; readers are encouraged to assume "minimal departure"[68] (or as little difference as possible) between real-world human nature and the nature of the fictional protagonists, specifically in the sense of a structural likeness. The details of each individual character mark them as invented and separate from the reader's self, even while the character's authenticity is assumed to emanate from a permanent inward essence, consonant with Victorian readers' ideal of identity.

However, the feeling of authenticity that readers sense in their interpretation of fictional beings is not the result of preexisting character entities, but rather grows out of readers' own imaginative composition of characters. Walsh invokes the case of Dickens's character Little Nell in *The Old Curiosity Shop* and the shifting critical evaluation of her (from angelic and properly affecting to overbearingly maudlin, and back) over the course of the last century and a half to illustrate the impact of historically situated readers' attitudes on the understanding of the identities of fictional characters. He argues that these ever-changing opinions prove that "emotional involvement is the recognition of values inherent in the discursive information given by a narrative, rather than in the actuality of the characters this information generates."[69] In other words, the relevance of fictional narratives and the real-feeling identities they present is not inherent in its characters as beings. After all, "Fictional being does not precede, but follows from, the evaluative, emotional dynamics of fictional narrative."[70]

As persuasive (or even as self-evident) as the foregoing statement by Walsh might seem, the experience of investing intellectual and emotional energy in the identity of a fictional character often obscures the processes through which that identity comes to exist as a felt reality. Responding to a character mimetically, after all, is encouraged by most realist fictions, though (as demonstrated in the introduction) not all realist fictions focus on the fictionality of selfhood. In a fictional autobiography, however, encouraging readers to experience the sensation of a likeness-through-difference with the fictional autobiographer is just the first step in unmasking the fictionality of extratextual identity. To that ultimate end, this subgenre invokes readers' essentialist assumptions about human nature through its rhetoric of authenticity and truth-telling.

Making Selves with Less and More: Gaps and Details in Fiction and Autobiography

The ideals of identity that emerge in Victorian debates about character construction are simultaneously accommodated and questioned by the narrative strategies of fictional autobiography. Just as readers expect accuracy as a measure of personal authenticity in the life stories of nonfictional autobiographers, so too do readers attempt to assess the genuineness of their fictional tellers through the choices those tellers make. When a reader is seeking the sensation of contact with the fictional identity of a narrator-protagonist, both omissions and unexpected knowledge can become epistemologically problematic, even as these elements prove affectively and cognitively stimulating for the reader of fiction. The fictional autobiographer's strategies for constructing the authority to tell fictional truths—particularly those linked to the "deep truths" of selfhood—are almost identical to those used by authors of referential autobiography to communicate to readers their sincere efforts to "reveal" their genuine selves. The fictional text's truth-telling techniques may be different in degree, but generally not in kind, from those of the referential text. Attending to Lubomír Dolezel's strategies for fictional authentication highlights the moments in fictional autobiography that signal the character-narrator's attempts to establish authority in her fictional authorship, and in turn draws attention to the text's dynamics of fictional self-making and to readers' assumptions about personal identity.

In his article "Truth and Authenticity in Narrative," Dolezel enumerates certain conventions in first-person fiction that seek to establish the narrator's authority to tell the truth from within and about the fiction. Writing from the perspective of speech-act and possible worlds theories, Dolezel suggests that for a first-person narrator to establish authority to tell the story, "devices limiting the scope of the narrator's knowledge" and "devices identifying the sources of his knowledge" must be appealed to in order to "earn [the narrator's] authentication authority."[71] In the following example from *Jane Eyre*, by certifying the accuracy of the stated information, Jane-as-narrator also testifies implicitly to her own inner genuineness. The opening chapter of the novel is known for the glimpses it offers of Jane's ardent, determined personality. What makes this more interesting is that Jane's narration suggests this image of herself precisely by highlighting her limited knowledge, her structural likeness to the reader in epistemological potential and liabilities, and her inner depths. Through these strategies, she bolsters the fictional authenticity of her discourse, her authority to tell it, and—ideally—the reader's impression of the authenticity of her inner self. Having been discovered reading in her hiding place by John Reed, the bullying eldest son of her aunt and uncle Reed—the latter of whom has died and committed orphaned Jane to his widow's contemptuous care—Jane withstands the boy's blows, both verbal and physical. Demonstrating her particularly embodied and limited knowledge of the world around her, she writes that John commands her,

> "Go and stand by the door, out of the way of the mirror and the windows."
> I did so, not at first aware what was his intention; but when I saw him lift and poise the book and stand in act to hurl it, I instinctively started aside with a cry of alarm: not soon enough, however; the volume was flung, it hit me, and I fell, striking my head against the door and cutting it. The cut bled, the pain was sharp: my terror had passed its climax; other feelings succeeded.
> "Wicked and cruel boy!" I said. "You are like a murderer—you are like a slave-driver—you are like the Roman emperors!"
> I had read Goldsmith's "History of Rome," and had formed my opinion of Nero, Caligula, etc. Also I had drawn parallels in silence, which I never thought thus to have declared aloud.[72]

Not only does Jane reinforce her first-person subject position through her younger self's pointed inability to see into John Reed's devious mind as he prepares to throw the book at her, but her explanation of the precocious, if just, epithets she in turn hurls at her tormentor also signals a literal and literary accounting for the "sources of her information." It is well remarked in the criticism on *Jane Eyre* that Jane, as a bibliophile and an iconoclast, tends to use intertextuality as a means for distinguishing her individual perspective on the world through texts and ideas that were widely recognizable to the novel's historical audience.[73] In this case, the reference to Goldsmith establishes for her the intellectual authority to justify the very act of her telling.[74] While John Reed may, as he says, own the books, Jane is clearly the one who interprets them more effectively, qualifying her as the best teller of her own life. After all, she models the ideal reading practice, even if the application is, in this case, overblown. She makes use of what she reads by drawing critical analogies between her texts and her own real world, while all John Reed can do is assert physical possession of the books and apply them as material objects of domination. While young Jane can have no notion of what passes through the boy's malicious mind, being herself no more than a fictionally embodied mortal, and thus narrator-Jane voluntarily limits what she tells us, this narration simultaneously asserts an originality of mind for herself that the brute, John Reed, clearly cannot equal. This originality is the basis for her identity's genuine worth, as well as for her authority to tell the truth of her life and her self.

Further tempting the reader to imagine Jane's inner depths into existence in this scene is the curious claim by narrator-Jane that this outburst against John Reed not only takes her antagonist by surprise but also shocks her written self. When narrator-Jane remarks that her younger self had "drawn parallels in silence, which I never thought thus to have declared aloud," she is not only proving her capacity to see metaphoric connections between past and present, text and life, but she is also asserting the peculiar ability to astonish herself. Her reaction to John's new torture is so visceral, her feelings so profound, this statement suggests, that their revelation in the moment of crisis comes as a surprise even to her. Just a few chapters later, Jane again shocks herself when she challenges Mrs. Reed to imagine the counterfactual scenario in which Mr. Reed could judge his wife's treatment of the orphan child (more on this moment in chapter 2). When Dolezel writes about "authentication authority," the authenticity he refers to is not identical to the type of inwardness that Jane's narration works to construct. Nonetheless, it seems appropriate that in the same opening scene in which Jane conscientiously limits the scope of her own report and reports the source behind her odd if fitting analogy, thereby securing the reader's trust in her as a teller of fictional facts, the very depths of her self are also "revealed," as it were, because they surface even against her will. Jane's inner life is so genuine, this rhetorical move proposes, that it cannot be concealed. This kind of depth, the suggested and yet unspeakable profundity of a character's inner life, represents a distinctly Victorian ideal of essential selfhood.

These self-conscious reporting strategies are not isolated to fictional autobiography. Referential autobiographers also strive to communicate their authority to tell the truest version of their life stories. Indeed, many gestures of factual accuracy and fidelity to life in referential autobiography read quite similarly to strategies for establishing authenticity in fictional autobiography. Comparing the foregoing example from *Jane Eyre* with the use of authenticating gaps by a referential autobiographer illustrates how the fictional autobiography both evokes and expands upon the rhetoric of genuineness that became predominantly recognizable to Victorian readers through the many popular texts of nonfictional autobiography available at that time.

Trollope, in his *Autobiography*, is careful to distinguish, as does Jane, between what his younger, written self knows in the moment he depicts and what his writing self now knows in retrospect. Neither reveals their "future" knowledge until it also dawns upon their younger selves. This strategic ordering of the discourse both limits what their character-selves can know and preserves for us, as readers, the chronological experience of their past reality. Writing of the last of his father's many financial failures, Trollope describes being summoned to drive his father to London despite the older man's illness:

> It was not till we had started that he told me that I was to put him on board the Ostend boat. This I did, driving him through the city to the docks. It was not within his nature to be communicative, and to the last he never told me why he was going to Ostend. Something of a general flitting abroad I had heard before, but why he should have flown first, and flown so suddenly, I did not in the least know till I returned. When I got back with the gig, the house and furniture were all in the charge of the sheriff's officers.[75]

As this episode of fleeing from his debtors exemplifies, Trollope's father, at least in the *Autobiography*, serves only as a negative example for his son; he is financially and literarily a failure. The image that this passage calls up of the young, alienated boy unknowingly assisting his father's flight allows Trollope to portray himself as what Sarah Gilead calls the "literary orphan,"[76] a stance from which he can most effectively throw into relief his later self-made success. As in the example from *Jane Eyre*, the order and manner of telling determines the interpretive outcome of the teller's identity. Further, the careful demarcations of the limits of the character-narrators' knowledge not only help to establish the fidelity of the tellers to epistemological standards that readers recognize as credible and, therefore, as authoritative. This limitation of knowledge also permits the narrators to re-create in the experience of the readers the same order of events and, ideally, the same emotions—for instance, surprise and dismay—as the written selves of the protagonists also must have felt in the recounted circumstances. Such effects further encourage readers to imagine the subjective inner lives of the narrating protagonists, whether they belong to nonfictional or fictional tellers.

But despite these striking similarities between texts of fictional and nonfictional autobiography, as discussed in the introduction (in the section "The Fictional Autobiography vs. the Nonfictional Autobiography"), there remain two important differences in what these texts include that affect their phenomenology of reading. The creative freedom of the fictional autobiography permits these texts to indulge in extensive focalization of the protagonist's written self and to include extended passages of quoted dialogue, neither of which are common, especially at any length, in referential autobiographies of the period. Martin Löschnigg posits that the increased presence of focalization—or narration that takes on the perspective—of the character-self in fictional autobiographies renders more "narrativity" to these tales, appealing to Monika Fludernik's definition of narrativity as experience centered on individuals and individual perceptions, rather than on external events.[77] In texts of referential autobiography, extensive focalization of the written self would no doubt trigger reader incredulity: how could the author possibly remember in such detail his former thoughts and feelings?

Similar questions would arise should a referential autobiographer attempt to record dialogue as if it were a word-for-word transcription. Often the referential autobiography will summarize conversations, or merely describe their outcomes; rarely are they dramatized at all. Extended, detailed passages of direct dialogue are common enough in fictional autobiography, however: consider the long accounts of the visiting gentry at Thornfield in *Jane Eyre* or the fraught and extensive dialogue between Jane and Rochester as she plans her escape in chapter 27. If a referential autobiography took on the task of reporting long-past conversations word for word, the pages of quoted discourse would immediately evoke an incredulity response: how does she possibly remember all that was said exactly, and if she remembers incorrectly, how does that change her story? As a result, the substance of the conversation would become a secondary, and perhaps a suspect, element in readers' interpretations. Not so in fictional autobiographies, however. The reader's tolerance for unlikely feats of memory is much higher (though not infinite) in fiction, in part because there is no living person and no existing document that could offer an alternative version of events. Readers only know what they are told, even if how it is told often allows them to evaluate its fictional-truth status.

There is a difference in degree, then, in the level of accuracy readers demand when it comes to fictional versus nonfictional autobiography. For the nonfiction narrator of his life story, readers maintain a higher degree of vigilance and a lower tolerance for unlikelihood when it comes to reporting things of the past, especially subjective, personal things that are unverifiable and easily altered, such as dreams, conversations, or feelings. David Copperfield may protest, repeatedly in fact, his memory's accuracy; but this gesture, while echoing a characteristic of autobiographical convention, does not cause most readers to doubt (at least, not in itself) the fidelity of the detailed childhood home scenes he then narrates as if they were present before his eyes.[78] The repeated focalizations of his younger self and the intensity of minute description that fill the first several chapters of *David Copperfield* would be suspect to many readers of a referential autobiography. But in David's life story, as readers know it to be fictional, they can recognize the gestures of autobiographicality in his promises of fidelity without expecting the same rigid limits to apply to David-as-self-narrator as to (for instance) Anthony Trollope-as-self-narrator. The autobiographical commitments implied by his statements instead turn readerly attention to evaluating the genuineness of his identity more broadly, rather than to wondering whether the housekeeper, Peggotty, said just this or just that to him when he was five years old.

With the increased feasibility, and affective efficacy, of representing the fictional self and the fictional world through focalization and dramatized dialogue, the fictional autobiography offers a form that is much more artistically open than its nonfictional counterpart, at least for Victorian writers (life-writing today, of course, is a different story). Furthermore, when readers are allowed more direct access to subjective features of the narrator-protagonist's life experience, the effect of reading a fictional autobiography often seems more intimately personal than the experience of reading a classical referential autobiography. This is so because readers are largely relieved of the task of policing factuality. And, since the gestures of fictional authenticity operate mainly in service to the more relevant issue of constructing the teller's self-hood, fictional autobiography enables a more focused study of the processes of fictionality and identity creation than does referential autobiography. The fine balance the form constructs between expectations for fictional and for referential modes of knowing means that readers may even feel that they know the fictional protagonist on a deeper level than they could know a being from their own world.

But while readers may hope to and feel that they do know intimately the character-narrators in fictional autobiographies, the idea of "knowing" them at all is exposed by the example texts I have selected as a somewhat misleading notion. In fact, as the following chapters demonstrate, it is the constantly renewed illusion of depth, of interiority, of an authentic self that the narrator-protagonists reveal and challenge through their labors to create that very essence. It is never the idealized essential self that can be assembled from the narratives of identity in these texts. Rather, what we find is the disassembling of the notion of a stable, extratextual self in service to an adaptable identity generated through fictional practices. Each of these texts, neither celebrating nor declaiming the breakdown of older ideas of self, posits the possibilities and risks of fictional selves. From David Copperfield's attempts at authorial singularity to Jane Eyre's (literally and literarily) "social heart," chapter 2 examines how the cultural touchstone figure of the author gives apparent stability to and thus opens a space for the formation of the narrative, imagined, and social selves of two of Victorian literature's most famous fictional autobiographers.

CHAPTER TWO

The Author and the Reader

The Individual and/as Narrative Community

In the preface to the 1850 edition of *David Copperfield*, Charles Dickens confesses that "no one can ever believe this Narrative, in the reading, more than I did in the writing."[1] In what, though, does the Inimitable purport to believe? Certainly Dickens's belief pertains to his conviction in the precepts enacted through David's life story. For instance, Dickens no doubt could be said to believe that hard work and compassion for others form the foundation of personal success. Likely, Dickens's belief adheres to the other—less appealing—implicit morals of the story as well, for instance, that "fallen women" may be forgiven, if usually from a great distance. But his profession of belief also applies to the "many companions" from whom he is now separated. Quite simply, he is saying that he will miss David, and Peggotty, and Aunt Betsey. Like other authors', Dickens's sentimental attachment to his characters is unsurprising: he is their creator, after all. They are his imaginative progeny and his intellectual property.[2]

But in this confession of credence Dickens does not confuse any of "the creatures of his brain" with actual human beings.[3] He ardently attests to his belief in them, in the "Narrative" that gives them life, precisely because they are nonactual. His belief derives from his own (temporary) omnipotence over these creations. And despite Dickens's specifically privileged relationship to *Copperfield*, all dedicated readers of fiction have experienced—on slightly altered terms—this same kind of belief in narrative, thanks to the emotional reality of the companionate connections they form with texts and the characters therein signaled. But why and how does this happen? Is a reader's sense of conviction a product of some mediated connection to Dickens himself through the text? Perhaps: there is certainly a strong appeal for some readers in the idea of textually communing with the author himself (for reasons I will explore later in this chapter). In contrast, however, I argue that this sensation of credence in fiction derives not from some metaphysical or archaeological link to the flesh-and-blood author. Rather, the attachment to fictional characters and their narratives grows out of the same act as that which connects Dickens himself to "the shadowy world" constructed by his text.[4] As this chapter will make clear, the act of creation is inseparable from the experience of emotional and cognitive investment. Our belief in fictional characters reciprocally derives from and informs our collaboratively authorial role in their animation. We believe in them, we feel with them (or against them), all because, in conjunction with Dickens's words and structures, we create them. In the following pages I examine how creative authorship begets affective investment, which in turn fosters belief in the real-feeling identities communally conceived. Indeed, these acts of authorship by readers are paralleled and influenced by the figure of the author embedded in Dickens's fictional autobiography—David himself. Understanding how the idea of authorship functioned in Victorian culture becomes essential to tracing how *David Copperfield* and, later in this chapter, *Jane Eyre*—both coming-of-age stories about realizing an authorial identity—make the case for the affective reality of fictional selves.

* * *

The Victorian obsession with the figure of the individual author enacted the desire for a lost totality that Georg Lukács identifies as the central motivating factor of the modern world and its literature. Modern subjects still "[think] in terms of totality";[5] they yearn for contact with individual truths because of their perceived synecdochal connection to the universal. In this way it is unsurprising that creative authorship became a cultural touchstone for the Victorians. After all, it seems to reconcile inner potential with outer communication, unique individualism with universal truths.[6] The figure of the author seems to suture personal experience into a kind of totality by converting subjective individuality into the necessary access point to something objective, true, authentic. The experience of autonomous individuality (often named as the founding problem of modern living), when authentically expressed through text, seems to become the key to escaping the limits of the subjective. In this way, the figure of the Victorian author serves as an ideal representative of the paradoxical nature of modern selfhood.

To the Victorians, acts of authorship were laden with complex assumptions about identity and existence. The figure of the author was valued for its ability seemingly to negotiate the urgently troubling binaries of inner/outer, self/other, subjective/objective that characterized modern experience. In *Past and*

Present, first published in 1843, Thomas Carlyle exemplifies this as he anatomizes genius, privileging innate, spiritual truths as both the proof and the goal of the existence of genius in society:

> Genius is "the inspired gift of God;" it is the clearer presence of God Most High in a man. Dim, potential in all men; in this man it has become clear, actual. So says John Milton, who ought to be a judge; so answer him the Voices of all Ages and all Worlds. Wouldst thou commune with such a one? *Be* his real peer then: Does that lie in thee? Know thyself and thy real and apparent place, and know his and his real and his apparent place, and act in some noble conformity with all that.[7]

In this passage, and throughout Carlyle's work, the figure of the genius—and specifically the literary genius—becomes an exemplar for the "potential in all men." But although his reference to Milton, and his challenge to his reader in the command *"Be* his real peer," situates "genius" in the realm of creative literary works, his concomitant admonition "Know thyself and thy real and apparent place" suggests that, for Carlyle at least, "being" one's truest self is not just an issue of self-cultivation through applied creative practice. It is the realization of something already existent inwardly. His injunction rehearses the familiar modern desire to reconcile the outer world's conditions with the inner sensations of self. Carlyle invokes "God Most High" as an element of spiritual universality rather than as a specifically Christian religious reference. The presence of divinity in Carlyle's work marks a belief in an absolute truth, one that is accessible through original individual experience but that somehow remains untainted by the contingency of the human subjectivity through which this truth is realized.

There is a similar yearning for contact with the universal through the authenticity of the individual[8] in Carlyle's earlier definition of the "Hero as Man of Letters" in his fifth lecture in *On Heroes, Hero-Worship, and the Heroic in History* (1840):

> There are genuine Men of Letters, and not genuine; as in every kind there is a genuine and a spurious. If *Hero* be taken to mean genuine, then I say the Hero as Man of Letters will be found discharging a function for us which is ever honourable, ever the highest; and was once well known to be the highest. He is uttering forth, in such a way as he has, the inspired soul of him; all that a man, in any case, can do. I say *inspired*; for what we call "originality," "sincerity," "genius," the heroic

quality we have no good name for, signifies that. The Hero is he who lives in the inward sphere of things, in the True, Divine and Eternal, which exists always, unseen to most, under the Temporary, Trivial: his being is in that; he declares that abroad, by act or speech as it may be, in declaring himself abroad. His life, as we said before, is a piece of the everlasting heart of Nature herself: all men's life is,—but the weak many know it not, in most times; the strong few are strong, heroic, perennial, because it cannot be hidden from them. The Man of Letters, like every Hero, is there to proclaim this in such sort as he can.[9]

For Carlyle, the genuine author is a man whose identity is determined by both his "True, Divine and Eternal" inner essence, "which exists always, unseen to most," and his ability to express outwardly the truth of that essential inwardness in and as literature. The Victorian figure of the author is born between the poles of a fixed interior self—whose very fixity and ineffability makes it a type for both the individual and the universal—and the obligation to communicate to others the double reality of this innate core self.[10] But Carlyle's prose registers the founding contradiction of this ideal of authorship. The inward essence that defines the author's identity has value as something permanent and "true" only insofar as the Man of Letters is capable of "declaring himself" to others "by act or speech."[11]

Even in Carlyle's most impassioned calls for social progress through self-knowledge there are hints that knowing the genius within and recognizing the genius without depend uncomfortably on validating an innate, ineffable worth through outward signs (linguistic or otherwise). While he despises the "Temporary, Trivial," he cannot escape the formal dynamics of communication that rely on the "function" of the Man-of-Letters Hero in the world to prove he is inwardly what he claims to be outwardly by "uttering forth . . . the inspired soul of him." Communication is essential. The function by which others recognize the true Hero of whom Carlyle speaks is not only through making his inner connection to the universal legible to "the weak many [who] know it not" but also through revealing this pervading truth to his fellow humans as a potential that they, too, possess—if in proportionally lesser forms. Precisely because the life of a great man is "a piece of the everlasting heart of Nature," he must extrude this inner truth through representation so it may be verified by and communicated to the outer world.

This is where the tensions in Carlyle's ideal of true genius become evident: representing any inner truth through language necessarily engages the same narrative processes as literary creation. The mode of making one's personal essence knowable to others obscures its extralinguistic existence; how can self-expression be distinguished from self-making if the processes are identical? The confusion between essential expression and identity creation leads to certain inconsistencies in Carlyle's rhetoric. These moments in which Carlyle's writing vacillates in its representation of self and text as either transparent to the right kind of reading or hidden and requiring more explicit expression (a dynamic that easily blurs revelation with activities of outright construction) introduces the unstable binaries that riddled Victorian ideals and practices of identity. The fundamental contradiction troubling the essentialist ideal of identity is that in order for the true self of the author to be shared beyond its defining inward sphere, that self has to be constructed through language and published for its readers to consume and validate. The necessary practice of externalizing the inward in order to verify its genuineness undercuts its ability to typify anything stable or eternal. Tracing the logic of this kind of authorial identity-making in texts of fictional autobiography illustrates that this idealized inner self is a blank space for creation rather than something made knowable through transparent representation. It is through the often-overlooked interactive processes of narrative construction that the persistent sense of an inner self is generated and legitimized.

The required "alienation" of one's identity as a practice that confirms its genuineness is not only a theoretical issue for understanding selfhood through textual dynamics but also a description of the literal relationship of the flesh-and-blood author to her literary creation, an act that becomes particularly fraught when that creation is autobiographical. As Clinton Machann argues, implicitly paralleling Carlyle's uncomfortable contradictions that arise in defining the heroic Man of Letters, a work of literature can only really belong to its author through the marketplace processes of publication. Machann captures one of the defining paradoxes of Victorian authorial identity when he asserts that "it is ironic that writers must give up their ideas and creations, must alienate them from themselves through publication before they can be said to own them, for ownership can only be validated in public, social terms through printing and the publication process. In terms of autobiography, this can be said about the very selfhood the author 'creates.'"[12]

Machann's description of Victorian authorship helps to contextualize two features of the fictional autobiography. First, his specification of what publication can mean for autobiographers—that it entails a giving away of the created self and, I would add, an exposure of the conditions of its creation—illuminates the implications of the rhetorical choices of David Copperfield, Jane Eyre, and other fictional autobiographers. The tellers, in attempting to embody the Victorian ideal of the authorial autobiographer, must also attempt to direct readerly perceptions of them as such. The implicitly acknowledged power of the reader to participate in the protagonist's self-creation, and thus to determine the relative success or failure of these characters as (fictional) authors, becomes a primary concern in these works. For this reason, the readers figured by these novels, much like the selves of the fictional autobiographers, are often treated ambivalently. And yet, even as the fictional autobiographers grapple rhetorically with the potential to be misconstrued by their readers, the readers' interpretive acts (solicited by these rhetorical choices) lead them to form attachments of varying emotional valence with the fictional beings they have the power collaboratively to create. Second, and building upon the affective potential of the collaborative self-making foregrounded in this subgenre, Machann's attention to the implicit risks of writing a nonfictional autobiography for Victorian men and women of letters makes the real-world appeal of the fictional autobiography clearer. Without compromising artistic freedoms, and without relinquishing the visceral immediacy and intimacy of a first-person exploration of identity's shaping moments, the actual writers of these fictional autobiographies distanced their own sense of self from their narrators' identities, all while solidifying their public, published claims to the identity of "author." Achieving and communicating one's right to self-author—even as it simultaneously necessitates the input of an audience—remains one of the main concerns of these fictional autobiographers, just as it was for so many flesh-and-blood Victorian writers.

In this and the subsequent chapters, the figure of the author and, later, the specifically female domestic autobiographer (a creator of both text and family), will serve as nodes for cultural contradictions that both contain and challenge their own constitutive paradoxes. These figures are anchors of culture in which conflicting values can have active play, precisely because these contradictions take place within recognizable categories of identity in recognizably fictional settings. The author, the homemaker, the autobiographer: these figures are founded upon the coexistence of the seemingly paradoxical traits of a specific innate vocation for creative labor and an intense work ethic to improve upon and realize the advances (artistic, scientific, familial, or social) that these beings are supposedly naturally enabled to achieve. In the parables of self-making posed by the protagonists of these texts,[13] the conflicting desires to be both autonomous and intimately connected with others, inherently original and yet progressing, will also shed light on the function of fictionality in the struggles of selfhood that surface throughout the nineteenth century. By appearing to conform to recognized cultural types, fictional

ing

autobiographers such as David Copperfield and Esther Summerson (in the following chapter)—and their creators—are able to deviate from the script in ways that prove disturbing, thought-provoking, and, possibly, productive for engaging in the processes of collaborative, imaginative self-making.

Dickens, *David Copperfield,* and the Author-Reader Relationship

David Copperfield is one of the most straightforward examples of how the desire to self-identify as an author, and the attendant anxieties about authority and identity, determines a narrator-protagonist's mode of self-creation. David's superficially linear story becomes a circular attempt both to locate and to prove his inner worth, which will legitimize his social and professional (not to mention economic) rise. But as he attempts to escape the external pressures that would invalidate his claims to an innate vocational worth, instead of rewriting the entire domestic and professional equation in the final scene, he stages both stasis and change, simply reinserting himself as the ultimate domestic and literary author(ity). This reading, which is particularly embodied by a reconsideration of the book's last scene, in which David inhabits the role of literary patriarch, challenges a common strain in critical evaluations of the novel. Following the conventional interpretive model assigned to Victorian novels of self-creation, most readings of *Copperfield* consider the eponymous character to be engaging in a linear development toward personal and artistic maturity throughout the course of his story. For example, Chris R. Vanden Bossche's assertion that "*David Copperfield* is a novel of destination" is not an unusual assessment.[14] Although David certainly practices an "unfettered self-making" (as Matthew Titolo labels it)[15] toward a goal of establishing his authorship and autonomy, the story of his life is less teleological than it may at first appear. It is as he attempts to dodge the "fetters" of different influences, as much in the act of writing as in the events he writes, that David's self is constituted.[16]

As an autobiographer, David exposes the processes of self-creation in his attempts to control the production and consumption of his self-image. This rhetorical awareness and attempted guidance of his audience is itself a familiar convention of European autobiography, since at least Rousseau's *Confessions.*[17] As will be discussed further in chapter 4, David becomes, in addition to a successful and self-determined author, a reimagined form of the Murdstonean patriarch in his well-controlled home with Agnes at the close of his story. This is not to suggest that readers retrospectively disbelieve his autobiographical claims or that they will determine David to be utterly unreliable. Rather, the recognition of circularity and self-shaping that this moment encourages highlights how necessary fictional narrative is to David's identity, both in his role as a "genuine" author and in his role as a middle-class paterfamilias. This conclusion to his autobiography makes visible to readers the acts of reciprocal self-shaping that define David, despite his efforts as a cautious self-narrator to prove the genuine autonomy of his inner self on which both of his major identity claims rest.

But David's is not the only identity that is frequently constructed from the pages of *Copperfield*. Dickens's own biography, of which David's is often considered a fictionalized incarnation, foregrounds the combined anxiety and ambition latent in the nineteenth-century professional writer's self-creation. Introducing Dickens here allows me to address the readerly habit (mentioned at the opening of this chapter) to attribute one's affective engagement with fiction to an autobiographical connection between text and real-world author. Addressing the question of Dickens's relation to *Copperfield* directly also brings to light some of the material conditions of Victorian authorship that inform the figure of the author as it appears in the novel and in the reading public's imagination.

As Alexander Welsh points out, "Dickens incorporated the substance and even whole paragraphs of his autobiographical fragment," a private piece of life-writing that Dickens produced about his childhood, into *Copperfield*.[18] Even upon the publication of the novel, before the similarities to the details of Dickens's own young life were publicly known, there was some speculation—as in the following excerpt from an unsigned review in *Fraser's Magazine*—that the actual life of Dickens could be read through the fictional life of David:

> This is the first time that the hero has been made to tell his own story,—a plan which generally ensures something like epic unity for the tale. We have several reasons for suspecting that, here and there, under the name of David Copperfield, we have been favored with passages of the personal history, adventures, and experience, of Charles Dickens. Indeed, this conclusion is in a manner forced upon us by the peculiar professions selected for the ideal character, who is first a newspaper reporter and then a famous novelist. There is, moreover, an air of reality pervading the whole book, to a degree never attained in any of his previous works, and which cannot be entirely attributed to the mere form of narration.[19]

This reviewer rejects the idea that the first-person telling of a life story could account for the "air of reality" that he senses in the character of David, suggesting discomfort with the notion that narrative form alone could produce such an impression of actuality. Instead, the reviewer chooses to explain the "degree" to which the narrating protagonist feels real with an autobiographical reading of the author himself. His interpretation searches for a metaphysical connection to the truths of the real world through the text's presumed alignment with certain facts of the writer's life. The details of David's and Dickens's lives are indeed parallel in some key ways, but the reviewer seems to resist what could be termed a "realist" reading of the text by refusing to accept a metaphoric or analogical relationship between these specific details and the potential real-world truths they illuminate. Instead he attempts to account for the "epic unity" the novel constructs through a more literal one-to-one connection between the fictional particulars of David's life and the referential particulars of Dickens's. In this reviewer's encounter with fictional autobiography, David's fictional identity is at once a pleasurable experience for the reader, an artistic triumph for the writer, a window onto the real world, and a possible threat to the exclusive reality of the essential self. The fact that an openly fictional self inspires such impressions of profundity asks to be disarmed by assuming a connection between this sensation of reality and the presumably innate (and thus stable) identity of Dickens.

Despite the emotional appeal of establishing some metaphysical connection between Dickens and David, Welsh is cautious about the kind of autobiographical reading of a fictional text that seeks one-to-one correspondence with the facts of the author's life. He insists that simply because *Copperfield* features parts of the "autobiographical fragment" written by Dickens, this does not ensure fidelity to Dickens's own life; any textual (re)construction of lived experience must deviate in some ways from factuality, which is not to say that it loses value by this fact: "Dickens alters, suppresses, and above all invents his life, but always within the bounds of trying to make sense of it to himself and his readers."[20] By this account, Dickens's understanding of his life and his self was unequivocally (if unsurprisingly) narrativized. After all, it is not just the similarity to the facts of Dickens's life to which *Copperfield* bears a striking resemblance, but more precisely to Dickens's written representation of his life. Mirroring his real-world creator, David-as-autobiographer also reformulates his past through his own literary creation of it. The role of authorial anxiety and the desire for self-manufactured success factors further into Welsh's characterization of the relation of Dickens to *Copperfield* when he says that "the early fame of Dickens obviously did not satisfy *his* ambition as a writer, and he was still carefully trying to control and account for it in *Copperfield*."[21] Thus, Welsh reads the fictionalized autobiography of Dickens within the fictional autobiography of David as both a justification for and an attempt to increase Dickens's own authority. These same concerns are reflected in the textual maneuvers and cyclical structuring of his life story by David-as-narrator.

With this correlation in mind, Dickens's messy and often worrisome business affairs, which bring to the forefront issues of anxiety surrounding the manufacture of texts and of one's literary and social identity, perhaps inspire David's own artistic angst surrounding the self-fashioning of his textual persona. Dickens's early career seems to have been marked by his practice of a kind of factory time of long and strictly observed working hours, akin to David's practice in the description of his work habits by Jennifer Ruth,[22] in order for him to meet the demands of publishers and public.[23] The raw material provided by innate ability, according to Dickens and his fictional avatar, David, "must be coupled with the time-discipline the mechanized factory exemplified."[24] Ruth's underscoring of the positive emphasis placed on self-discipline in David's autobiography brings into the discussion the other half of the equation for authorial vocation espoused by Carlyle and reproduced throughout much of Victorian culture. The heroic Man of Letters is generated not only by his inner essence of genius, but also by his willed labor to realize that genius through outward, literary expression.

The figure of the author is wrought from the two opposing yet complementary forces of industrial management and a Victorian version of "Romantic inspiration."[25] Ruth's (and, implicitly, David's) definition conforms to Carlyle's, when he defines the heroic Man of Letters as developing through the coexistence of an intense work ethic, distinctive suffering, and inherent inspiration—it is precisely this combination that qualifies him as "heroic": "[The Man of Letters] must pass through the ordeal, and prove himself. *This* ordeal; this wild welter of a chaos which is called Literary Life: this too is a kind of ordeal! There is clear truth in the idea that a struggle from the lower classes of society, towards the upper regions and rewards of society, must ever continue. Strong men are born there, who ought to stand elsewhere than there."[26] It is the cultural acceptance of Carlyle's portrayal of this struggle from humble beginnings to literary and social greatness, a struggle that explicitly fuses upward mobility and artistic advancement, that lends legitimacy to both Dickens's and David's claims of authority as heroic Men of Letters.

David's life story figures over and over again a similar if often more allegorical struggle for self-definition. The account of his early years alternates between episodes detailing his "innate" curiosity and observation as a youth, qualities that are supposed to communicate his inner fitness for authorship, and occurrences in which he must resist illegitimate external forces that attempt to shape him and pervert not only his "true" self but also the autonomy necessitated by this notion of innate identity. Authority—and particularly singularity as an indicator of an inner originality—is at issue in *Copperfield* from the very first dramatized scene. Even before David-as-character can be born into the story world, David-as-narrator is actively prefiguring the struggles with which his young avatar will have to contend: unauthorized influence, mistaken (and undervalued) identities, and the troublesome nature of "originality."

David Copperfield opens with a scene indicative of the work's characteristic thematic obsessions and cyclical evolution in which Clara Copperfield, the embodiment of benign disorder, is confronted by the forceful, controlling Miss Betsey Trotwood. In this microcosm of the novel's dynamic, in which the (for now) unauthorized, interloping figure of Miss Betsey is the most potent, the Rookery and its mistress are characterized as confused and "childish." The Rookery, having been erroneously named by the first David Copperfield (since he "takes the birds on trust, because he sees the nest" [*DC*, 6]), exemplifies the recurrent difficulty of legitimizing original identity, as the home's very name manifests the confusion of one thing for another. Clara's legitimacy as mistress is also problematic due to her cross-class, May-December union with the elder David Copperfield; furthermore, she spends much of the first scene crying, fainting, or bemoaning her soon-to-be status as "a childish mother" (*DC*, 5). The label she applies to herself indicates her recognized unfitness to preside over even her own maternity. In response to Clara's lack of authority, Miss Trotwood provides a potent dose of domination as she begins to command the family servant, Peggotty, "with as much potentiality as if she had been a recognized authority in the house" (*DC*, 7). Once Miss Trotwood leaves—outraged at the birth of a second David instead of a second Betsey (already a certain cyclicality is evident)—the residents of the Rookery are left to their congenial confusion. Miss Trotwood fails, upon her first knowledge of him, to recognize the inherent worth of the character-narrator and is only relegitimized by her later rescue of David from the malignant Murdstones and their unredeemed regime of unauthorized influence.

The confusion of one thing for another—a kind of routine blindness to the fine distinctions of identity—pervades the Rookery and its inhabitants. In addition to Clara's inability to organize her household, as she knows "not near so much as [she] could wish" (*DC*, 8) about housekeeping, Clara Peggotty, the family's servant, "is quite our companion" (*DC*, 13), openly directing or arguing with Clara Copperfield and violating normative class hierarchies.

In this domestic landscape, in which the servant is an equal to the mistress and the "threes and fives [are] too much alike" (*DC*, 8) in the account books, David achieves self-consciousness. More specifically, as an autobiographer, he chooses to depict his development amidst this mild chaos and disordered identification of distinct entities (Clara Peggotty with Clara Copperfield, the threes with the fives). Significantly, though David-as-narrator glorifies this era of his childhood, he later employs his artistic ambition and individual experiences specifically to distinguish himself from like quantities.[27] In fact, in his childhood home, the only distinctive entity that is treated as such is David himself—he is unique in being recognized as original. He is always made much of by his mother and by Peggotty, and in addition to nature's external (and saleable) distinction of having been born with a caul, his innate capacity for observation and reporting directly contributes to the implication of his authorial vocation.

Reading the episode of the caul and David's musings on memory as the two primary coordinates for negotiating external and internal factors of identity in this fictional autobiography, the question of what constitutes selfhood arises explicitly within the first several paragraphs of the tale. At the public drawing in which his caul is sold, David recounts feeling "uncomfortable and confused, at a part of myself being disposed of in that way" (*DC*, 2). This outward and vendible sign of personal difference comes to be replaced in the hierarchy of his self-narration by the singularity of his inner qualities. Interestingly, these supposedly internal characteristics will also come to have a market value in the form of saleable writing and fictions, and they first enter the narrative with David's meditation upon his remarkable capacity for observation, recollection, and recounting. At the beginning of chapter 2, "I Observe," David-as-narrator attempts to justify the intricacy of his autobiographical details. He does this by extending the distinctive "power of observation" that his character-self seems to exercise to "numbers of young children," saying that "most grown men who are remarkable" for feats of memory, which are "wonderful for [their] closeness and accuracy," "may with more propriety be said not to have lost the faculty, than to have acquired it" (*DC*, 12–13). By linking his own abilities, which in a text of autobiography may strike readers as extraordinary, to a common human potentiality for memory, David-as-narrator makes the case not only for his own memory's accuracy but for humankind's overall potential. In a literal way, David asserts that the characteristics of authorship are indicative of the latent possibilities of humanity in general. Furthermore, in a society painfully aware of the problems of history and historiography, memory is not a neutral skill to propose as one of humanity's defining qualities.[28] Through the covert discourse of human possibility and progress, David legitimizes his special power by suggesting its potential availability to all.

But his capacity for observation is nonetheless to be taken as distinctive to himself. David-as-author's symbolic importance to society rests on his ability to communicate the universality of precisely those features that also make him special; this contradiction marks one of the central paradoxes of the cultural figure of the author. In this authorial role, David performs the function of Carlyle's literary Hero in revealing—literally—the potential of others by elucidating his own externally realized inner abilities. David writes that "if it should appear from anything I may set down in this narrative that I was a child of close observation, or that as a man I have a strong memory of my childhood, I undoubtedly lay claim to both of these characteristics" (*DC*, 13). His individual originality appears as the synecdoche for the human potential to remember, report, and shape history through narrative, both of which capacities—originality and narrative creation—qualify him to assert his authorship later in life. And, reading against the grain, David's curious choice of diction, in which he "lay[s] claim" to his treasured personal characteristics on the sole basis of what he "may set down in [his] narrative," carries further implications for the nature of his selfhood. This phrasing, which seems to attribute the existence of his authorial characteristics to the mode and content of his narration, may be read as tantamount to an admission of narrative's role in constructing David Copperfield just as much as it forms *David Copperfield*.

The groundwork for the reader's understanding of his genuine authority having thus been laid, the real story of David's troubles, and of his struggle to self-define as an author, begins with the invasion of the Murdstones into Blunderstone Rookery. Mr. Murdstone is the epitome of an unauthorized power, as an insensitive, controlling husband to Clara and an overreaching stepfather to David, against which David-as-narrator can cast his own inwardly legitimate (and legitimate because inward) claims to authority. Although Uriah Heep may be said to be David's biggest hurdle to a successful self-definition in his autobiography—as the uncomfortable similarities in their social positions and sexual desires threaten the integrity of David's unique identity[29]—Murdstone is the catalyst for David's more explicitly depicted efforts toward self-authorship. He is the first external force against which David must act as an individual in order to prove himself worthy of such a label. Murdstone is also a key figure to recognizing the cyclicality of David's chosen narrative self-portrayal. David figures himself at the end of his autobiography as the potent patriarch of his family with Agnes, a position that bears uncomfortable similarities to Murdstone's reign at the Rookery and that participates in the novel's pattern of discomfiting doubling, as seen in his relationship to Uriah. While David's formula for family replaces the Murdstonean "discipline" with a benign sort of influence over his domain, and substitutes usurpation with biologically legitimate fatherhood, David seems to replicate the Murdstonean model of the paterfamilias in his construction of himself as the ultimate authority, one who creates both his own and others' identities in the combined domestic and professional space of the author's home.[30]

The arrival of the Murdstones is the first textual instance of an externally imposed "corrective" on the chaos of the Copperfields. The Murdstonean "firmness" that fatally overcomes Clara Copperfield's more "pliant nature" (*DC*, 43), however, ultimately not only proves ineffective upon David but also thereby suggests the protagonist's parallel claim to his own brand of (perhaps benign) firmness. The scenes most indicative of the temporarily deleterious effect of the Murdstones' illegitimate discipline are those of David's "lessons," which are supposedly administered by his mother but over which both Mr. and Miss Murdstone preside. In this way, both mother and son may be properly "formed" to the Murdstonean standard of comportment: the Murdstones find David's lesson time "a favorable occasion for giving my mother lessons in that miscalled firmness, which was the bane of both our lives" (*DC*, 50).

Before this unfortunate turn toward firmness, David recalls, "I had been apt enough to learn, and willing enough, when my mother and I had lived alone together. I can faintly remember learning the alphabet at her knee" (*DC*, 50). The nurturing scene of learning in David's recollection of the bygone days of the Copperfields' muddled but happy existence is directly juxtaposed with the rigid pedagogical approach demanded by his stepfather. Shifting to the present tense to focalize through the child-protagonist, David "bring[s] one morning back again" and literally "relives" his instinctive rejection of unauthorized influence:

> I come into the second-best parlor after breakfast, with my books, and an exercise-book, and a slate. My mother is ready for me at her writing desk, but not half so ready as Mr. Murdstone is in his easy-chair by the window (though he pretends to be reading a book), or as Miss Murdstone, sitting near my mother stringing steel beads. The very sight of these two has such an influence over me, that I begin to feel the words I have been at infinite pains to get into my head, all sliding away, and going I don't know where. . . . I take a last drowning look at the page as

The Author and the Reader / 81

I give it into her hand, and start off aloud at a racing pace while I have got it fresh. I trip over a word. Mr. Murdstone looks up. (*DC*, 50–51)

The runaway train of David's forced scholarship comes to a screeching halt on that remembered occasion, with his mother pleading, "Now Davy, try once more, and don't be stupid." Exhibiting the adult narrator's darkly humorous perspective of the scene but continuing in the present-tense conjugations of the boy, he says, "I obey the first clause of the injunction by trying once more, but am not so successful with the second" (*DC*, 51). His textual flourish here, in addition to making the scene less painful and more comical, further establishes the authority of the adult David—the writing David—by couching his jest in grammatical terms that underscore the medium of his creative success. The transition to present tense also calls attention to the narrative artifice that enables the narrating David to immerse his readers in the immediacy of his identity troubles through the telling, rather than the remembering, of them.

This passage featuring the imposition of knowledge onto the unwilling child, a scene that ends in emotional turmoil for both David and his mother (he "is wallowing in such a bog of nonsense" and she is "despairing" by the termination of the lesson [*DC*, 51]), dramatically engages in an almost allegorical depiction of the precariousness of the individual's right to self-author. In the case of the parasitic Murdstones, whose very presence causes knowledge to seep uncontrollably from David's mind, the application of external, unauthorized, and therefore deleterious influence results in a decided decrease of mental acuity in the disciplined subject, David. The child begins to feel "sullen, dull, and dogged" (*DC*, 52) under the sway of the usurping Murdstones; even on his school holidays he "lapse[s] into a stupid state" (*DC*, 115) of inner lifelessness when too long in the same domestic atmosphere. But this "delicate" child, of "excellent abilities" (*DC*, 149)—note the rhetoric of innate identity in these descriptors—is saved from falling entirely under the stupefying spell of Murdstonean discipline. His inborn worth is reclaimed through a literary intervention in the form of novels left to him by his biological father. David declares that the "glorious host" of fictional characters he thereby encounters "kept alive my fancy, and my hope of something beyond that time and place" (*DC*, 53).

David also engages in prototypical creation, mentally rewriting these novels by casting himself as the hero and the Murdstones as the villains: "By impersonating my favorite characters in them—as I did—and by putting Mr. and Miss Murdstone into all the bad ones—which I did too" (*DC*, 53), David indulges in his first authorial act, rejecting the Murdstones' authority in favor of shaping himself through his (absent) father's literary legacy. As Welsh characterizes the first David Copperfield, "the child's actual father appears only by repute, as a man rather gently susceptible to women and a bestower of books."[31] The façade of potency conferred upon the removed but legitimate father figure establishes a precedent of authorized power while not actually exercising any immediate influence over the shaping of young David. The figure of the father is a narrative tool employed to make more palpable, and more legitimate, the authority of David-as-narrator.

These carefully wrought passages depicting the Murdstone-Copperfield confrontation—the former element thwarting David's supposedly innate abilities, the latter enhancing them—reveal the significance of the anxiety about self-manufacture within David's autobiography. In the episode that precipitates David's removal from the Rookery to Salem House school, Mr. Murdstone's decision to stimulate David corporally to learn is predicated precisely upon his own boyhood experiences: "'I tell you Clara,' said Mr. Murdstone, 'I have been often flogged myself'" (DC, 54). Though the child David, through whom this section is focalized, purportedly does not understand the import of these words, the narrator has nonetheless effected a deliberate juxtaposition of antithetical scenes. David-as-narrator structurally and thematically contrasts the image of the young boy joyfully learning amidst the works of literature that belonged to his biological-though-absent father (a scene that emphasizes legitimate authority and unbounded autodidacticism) with a scene in which the patriarch's usurper is prepared to discipline David in his own image. The anxiety of influence is latent in this episode: in attempting to make David more like himself, Murdstone seeks any way, even by physically violent means, to (perhaps literally) reshape the boy to his own standards. This is, possibly, the ultimate undesirable consequence of ceding self-authorship: by conforming to Murdstone's system, David would be consenting to be a created product rather than a creative producer. For that reason, perhaps, in addition to his childish fear, he meets Murdstone's gesture of physical authority with an instinctive, animalistic response. To protect his highest inward potential, David devolves into the very sort of being to which the Victorians dreaded that humans were all too closely related, and to which they might return. In response to Murdstone's beating, David writes, "I caught the hand with which he held me in my mouth, between my teeth, and bit it through" (DC, 55). David quite literally leaves his mark upon the hand that intends to mark *him*. Whereas David's previous reaction to Murdstone's unauthorized attempts to shape him was to degenerate into a passive idiocy, here, through his active rejection of illegitimate authority, he almost literally seems to gain advancement in his journey of self-construction: as a result of this incident he is sent on to his next formative experience, at Salem House school. David's bite, while evoking fears later associated with theories of both evolution and devolution, also represents an externally directed act that asserts at least a modicum of agency in his character-self, a necessary attribute for the Victorian author.

But the bite that frees David, at least temporarily, from the imposition of the Murdstones imposes upon him the possibility of another, less concrete kind of influence. When David arrives at Salem House, his teacher places a sign upon his back. Although it is the holidays, and no other boys are present, David is forced to wear a board that cautions onlookers about his mordant propensities: *"Take care of him. He bites"* (*DC*, 74). When he first sees the sign lying on a desk, David believes the biting beast to which it refers is a dog; he is appalled to find out that the placard rather describes himself. But if one reads his act of self-protective biting as a prototypical gesture of authority, which resists the shaping of others and instead tries to author them, then David's experience of wearing publicly the sign that proclaims his devolved form of authorship may be indicative of how audience and readership are to be conceived in his later role as published author. David writes,

> What I suffered from that placard, nobody can imagine. Whether it was possible for people to see me or not, I always fancied that somebody was reading it. It was no relief to turn round and find nobody; for wherever my back was, there I imagined somebody always to be. . . . The playground was a bare gravel yard, open to all the back of the house and the offices; and I knew that the servants read it, and the butcher read it, and the baker read it; that everybody, in a word, who came backwards and forwards to the house, of a morning when I was ordered to walk there, read that I was to be taken care of, for I bit. I recollect I positively began to have a dread of myself, as a kind of wild boy who did bite. (*DC*, 75)

The audience for David's sign is mobile, flexible; it is composed of everyone (and most notably, those of lower status), and yet they are invisible, ubiquitous, and impossible to avoid in this space of public reading. This fictional and allegorical representation of audience gives new meaning to Robert Altick's comment in his landmark monograph *The English Common Reader* that "more and more, as the century progressed, it was the ill-educated mass audience with pennies in its pockets that called the tune to which writers and editors danced."[32] David's imaginings of readers' impressions of him do just as much to shape his ideas and feelings of self as do their actual reactions—which, except for the cruel groundskeeper who enjoys harassing the child, are actually no reaction at all. But the potential for public condemnation by this ever-changing, volatile, and imaginary readership is the bane of David's young life that summer. This idea of audience alienates David from his formerly stable sense of self by forcing him to integrate into his evolving identity the potential responses that others might have to his first "authorial" creation. This is one of the first moments in which David's sense of an essential self explicitly wavers as a result of the narrative process that Rae Greiner describes as "thinking of others thinking of us."[33]

Even the empty desks and the names of the absent students carved on the door at Salem House become animated instances of hostile individual readers declaiming David's authorial actions and misconstruing his identity. "I could not read a boy's name, without imagining in what tone and with what emphasis *he* would read 'Take care of him. He bites'" (*DC*, 75–76, original emphasis). Although this episode provides comic relief, as well as plenty of pathos, in the progression of little David's story, it is also one of the only instances in which David-as-narrator gives any indication that an ever-growing audience—of varying classes, professions, and genders—plays an uncomfortably influential role in how the author is constructed through his public texts, and how this, in turn, affects the author's understanding of his own identity and authorship. The readers' reproductions and narrative explanations of him and his authoring acts markedly affect David's self-conception. His sense of identity is (comically) skewed by the perceived critical response of his public, so much so that he begins to see himself as a "wild boy" who has devolved into the antithesis of the human rather than as the proto-author—the paradigm of human potential—who refused illegitimate influence. Of course, his narrative of identity is later redirected, as evidenced in and by the very existence of the autobiographical text; but this moment of public reading that he chooses to include in his written selfhood suggests that the trauma of being read into existence by the "many-headed"[34] lingers in the authorial identity of the David who writes.

The Reader and the Author in Victorian Fiction

The incorporation of hostile readership into the successful (fictional) author's textual identity raises once more the question of why the reader—especially the resistant reader—figures so pointedly and is given such sway in the discourses of fictional autobiography. Although in less directly allegorical ways than in the instance of the placard, David's efforts to demonstrate his independent self-authorship throughout his narrative seem just as concerned with readers' potential understanding of his authorial identity as with his own (supposedly) expressive project. The first reason for the reader's figured presence recalls Carlyle's philosophy of authorship and its relation to ideals of identity: while it is a conventional gesture to affirm one's essential self by proclaiming the difficulty of expressing that essence in words, its expression nonetheless must be, and is, attempted. Paradoxical as it may be, only external confirmation by others can affirm the genuine self. The second reason for the reader's prominent place in fictional autobiography is historical and material: an ever-increasing number and diversity of readers were subscribing to circulating libraries and flocking to book stalls in the Victorian midcentury. As Bradley Deane points out, Victorian authorship was "shaped not only by writers themselves, but also by publishers and printers, book buyers and periodical readers, reviewers, circulating libraries, bookbinders, literary agents, and legislators."[35] This fact explains the need to grapple with the figure of the reader, and it accounts for the many anxieties of authorship—the vulnerability as well as the potency of influence inherent in the position—that are so thoroughly evinced in *Copperfield* and other fictional autobiographies of author figures. Not only was widespread popularity taken as a measure of a novel's artistic worth at midcentury, according to Deane,[36] but it also could determine the future market value of a writer's works. Conceivably, the public's reception of a single publication could determine one's professional status (incompetent hack or genuine author?) and the economic prospects (starving garret-dweller or contented bourgeois?) of a writer's chosen career.[37]

In addition to the significant concerns of audience reception and economic viability, there remains the related and more ambiguous (and, perhaps for that reason, all the more terrifying) prospect of the reader's role in constructing the author himself, which is epitomized by the ever-moving but ever-present reader of young David's torturous first "publication." Dickens himself objected vociferously to conditions that similarly put him in print, as it were, against his will. He battled the American system of reprinting English works without concern for the copyright holders' wishes, using terms that marked the intersection of identity and economic concerns. In a letter to Henry Austin written during his first trip to the United States and Canada, Dickens notes sarcastically that "the existing law allows [American publishers] to reprint any English book, without any communication whatever with the author or anybody else. My books have all been reprinted on these agreeable terms." He demands, "Is it tolerable that besides being robbed and rifled an author should be forced to appear in any form, in any vulgar dress, in any atrocious company; that he should have no choice of his audience, no control over his own distorted text[?]"[38] The author and his texts become synecdoches for one another, and it is as much "Charles Dickens" as it is *Nicholas Nickleby*, *Oliver Twist*, and the like that is "forced to appear . . . in any vulgar dress" before an unauthorized public.

George Eliot, too, suffered from her position as a public, published, and, in her case, anonymous author. Having been "accused of using other people's materials and disavowing them" in her popular novel *Adam Bede*, she writes to her friend Charles Bray that "these things are painful to me, partly due to my morbid sensibility, but the pain is not the less real." She goes on, evincing a very poignant and personal dread of the invasive public, "I only wish to do something to save any other author anything like the keen suffering of various kinds that I have endured since the publication of 'Adam Bede'—I only wish I could write something that would contribute to heighten man's reverence before the secrets of each other's souls, that there might be less assumption of entire knowingness, as a datum from which inferences are drawn."[39] As these excerpts from letters of two of the Victorian era's most widely read writers demonstrate, the intrusive reader (in single and communal incarnations) was acknowledged to play an uncomfortably influential role in the publicly known and privately felt identity of the author. Complementarily, as evidenced in Carlyle's writings, individual authors were thought to exemplify the innate potential of humanity more broadly. In this way, the overt fictionality of texts that were engaged in these processes of mutual identity construction could serve as a buffer for both the writer (against the interpretive power of the reader) and the reader (against the mesmerizing and perhaps uncomfortably thought-provoking power of the writer).

Deane's monograph *The Making of the Victorian Novelist: Anxieties of Authorship in the Mass Market* contains in its title a suggestion of just such a relationship between writers—would-be authors—and the reading public. He maintains that "the social status of novelists across the nineteenth century was both more mercurial and more controversial than that of writers in any other genre" as these authors in particular "were thoroughly embroiled in the momentous restructuring of the Victorian public." Highlighting the role the author played in the Victorian imagination, Deane claims that novelists were "the figures onto which Victorians projected the hopes and anxieties of their transforming society." For Deane, the novel attempted to ameliorate the alienation of social classes characteristic of early and mid-nineteenth-century Britain. One way that this was accomplished was in the privileging of the figure of the author in the social imaginary as an end in itself—"eclips[ing]," as he says, "other ways of imagining literature's social purpose." By representing authorship as a kind of selective yet universal friendship, social turmoil was submerged in a discourse of common sympathy.[40] If achieving an authorial identity is an implicit part of the act of novel-writing, then the representation of the author as an intimate friend signals a rhetorical choice on the part of the novelist herself that works to preclude the reader's desire to read against the grain, as it were, of the writer's self-creation. At the same time, however, this tactic of implying intimate yet common friendship introduces its own problems in the equation of identity. It constructs the author in an extensively affiliative rather than an individuating way, exposing another latent contradiction in the figure of the Victorian author. While the author serves as a stand-in for the exemplary individual in society, this figure also comes to be defined by a relationship of trust forged between the singular creative self and the many interpreting selves of the reading public.

Because of the mutual influence writers and audiences were thought to have on one another, the idea of the reader in its singular and plural forms is notably contradictory in Victorian texts. This is especially so in texts of fictional autobiography, in which the reader seems to be at once the selected recipient of an intimately personal discourse *and* the necessary extratextual agent that animates whatever reality the fictional autobiographer possesses. Garrett Stewart's monograph *Dear Reader: The Conscripted Audience in Nineteenth-Century British Fiction* describes a version of this splitting of the reader's intratextual representation and her extratextual function. He writes that Victorian fiction represents readers as "the traditional *captive audience*," while also asking readers to recognize that the text is "a tale for whose realistic manifestation as scene, if not for whose telling, you the obligated reader are always in part responsible—its coauthority and its conscript at once."[41] Stewart sees these doubled roles—"coauthority and conscript"—as a particular trope of realist fiction that invites the imaginative embodiment of the written scene while encouraging awareness of the text's status as make-believe. The dual roles of the reader, pointedly emphasized in fictional autobiography, correspond to the complex Victorian understanding of authorship as both a personal attainment based on inner essence and a public role dependent upon social input, which, in turn, exercises influence on individual readers.

In fictional autobiographies, readers' participation in constructing the fictional author through the narrative of his life is disarmed of some of its most subversive implications by its very fictionality, all the while allowing the audience to actively follow or defy the "marked textualization of [reader] response" that characterizes Victorian realism more broadly.[42] As the author (fictional or actual) has imagined *them* and *their* reactions to her and her story, so too will readers, as an actual force and an imagined one, forge the existence of the author. Stewart names several ways in which novels "write" their readers: in model or allegorical scenes of reading (broadly meaning "interpretation"), in direct address to the reader, or in descriptions of reading. All of these are examples of what I have called "reader inclusion," which sometimes escalates to reader provocation. Both inclusions and provocations are rhetorical gestures that solicit and attempt to guide readers' interpretive responses, even while, as Cora Kaplan has noted, the variety of ways in which Jane Eyre and other fictional autobiographers try to engage readers evince the narrators' recognition that their texts are ultimately at the mercy of "an unknown, heterogeneous public."[43] Stewart emphasizes that the responses represented in the text are already part of the work to be consumed: "Implicated by apostrophe or by proxy, by address or by dramatized scenes of reading, you [the reader] are deliberately drafted by the text, written *with*. In the closed circuit of conscripted response, your input is a predigested function of the text's output—digested in advance by rhetorical mention or by narrative episode."[44] These readerly responses are built into the text as positive or negative models, inducements or discouragements to certain kinds of reading by different kinds of readers.

As the example of Jane Eyre's resistant narration in chapter 12 shows, in the fictional autobiography specific solicitations of the reader and pointed allusions to interpretive acts prompt audiences not just to construct the self of the narrator-protagonist but to perceive the processes of that construction. Yet all fictional autobiographers, as the model "individuals" that they are, engage readers with their own particular versions of common narrative techniques, to varied effects. In more explicit ways than David Copperfield, Jane Eyre focuses her narratorial attention on the reader's contribution to her story and construction of her self. In this way, Jane's narration encourages readers to become conscious of the collaborative self-making that constitutes her authorial identity, particularly in its function as an exemplar of human identity beyond the text.

Minding the Gap while Making Jane Eyre's "Social Heart"

One of the most well-known occurrences of reader inclusion in Victorian literature opens the final chapter of Charlotte Brontë's *Jane Eyre: An Autobiography*. Stewart analyzes Jane's triumphant declaration "Reader, I married him" as the ultimate moment that registers the necessity of reading and readership in order for narrative itself to function. Stewart claims, "What this master sentence makes clear is that second person, even in a first-person narrative, invokes the only existential grounding possible for a fictional text."[45] To push this claim further, the identities of Jane and her fellow fictional autobiographers can only be vivified and come to exist as real experiences through the reader's interpretive processes, figured through invocations of "you" and "your" reading, in partnership with their texts. For this reason, the reader is not just a source of anxiety or a force of undue influence in these texts. The reader is also the necessary corollary of authorial identity. Communication and mutual imagination are the foundations for the experience of selfhood more broadly in these texts. Through this dynamic, the figure of the author emerges as a model of fictional identity, and, because he is fictional, the author also becomes a paradigm of communal identity creation.[46]

The reader inclusions that characterize Jane Eyre's fictional autobiography, in the interpretations they prefigure and activate, literarily bridge the perceived gap between that which is personal and inward (the essential self) and that which is external and social (the collaboratively, creatively constructed self). This apparent fusion of inner/outer and essential/constructed is exemplified by Jane's most famous address to the reader as it exhibits the mutual dependence of the forces of individuality and sociability in this novel. Because "reading is read as community," according to Stewart, "'Reader, I married him' consummates two lines of desire at once, suspends two solitudes: that of the narrator as well as that of the heroine, a doubleness all the clearer in *Jane Eyre* because the two personae are interchangeable."[47] Stewart here conflates the two autobiographical selves of Jane, as character and as narrator. Though these Janes are not "interchangeable" in their separate temporalities and narrative roles (a point that will become particularly important in the following close reading), Stewart's emphasis on mutuality between character-Jane and Rochester, and on community between narrator-Jane and her readers, nonetheless illuminates the social underpinnings of Jane's seemingly independent self.

In Stewart's interpretation, Jane's fictional autobiography strives to satiate the twin yearnings of individual fulfillment and communal engagement. But the implications of this narration are even more complex than Stewart expresses. These doubled yearnings, while aligning with the actions of character-Jane and narrator-Jane, respectively, also expose the fictional dynamics of narrative selfhood that unite those dual desires. The text's features both construct an autonomous "Jane" and require the collaboration of the reader to vivify this seemingly independent "Jane"; she appears as her own author even as she both invites and resists the reader's creative impact on her selfhood. The narration's reader-inclusion strategies effectively collapse the interdependent binaries of individual realization/social engagement, auton-omy/collectivity, and author/reader by prompting the audience to recognize the gap between story and discourse. In a narrative, the "story" refers to the events and the diegesis that readers imagine based on what they read; "story" only exists conceptually, in the mind of the reader. The "discourse" of a nar-rative is the specific telling itself, the actual language and order of the text. When readers extrapolate the story from what is given in the discourse—that is, when they fill the gaps between how something is told, what is told, and what it all means—they animate the narrative world it describes and cre-ates, including the identity of the narrating protagonist. *Jane Eyre*, with its contrary urges toward independence and sociability, essential and fictional selfhood, makes the gap between story and discourse visible as part of its character-creation and reader-engagement process. While these dual levels of narrative are often difficult to perceive as separate yet mutually reliant elements, the fictional autobiography encourages readers to mind the gap, as it were: readers are asked to attend to the cognitive and affective processes required to make narrative sense (and selves) in the space between story and discourse.

Acts of reading within the world of *Jane Eyre* are instrumental to Jane's self-narration and to how she marshals her audiences' interpretations of her selfhood.[48] Yet, simultaneously, sympathetic reading and masterful life-writing are not put forth as simple or utopian solutions to the heroine's iden-tity problems. At the very start of the novel, her struggle is, like David's, to achieve the autonomy to self-author, especially as she finds herself trapped in the "uncongenial" narratives that the Reeds construct about who she is.[49] Vicky Simpson proposes that "as an adult, Jane uses storytelling to implicitly challenge social institutions," including, I argue, the institutionalized notion of an essential identity, "by gaining the authoritative position of storyteller, a position that gives her significant influence over St. John Rivers, Edward Rochester, and, of course, her reader."[50] Jane's telling nonetheless betrays a distinct ambivalence about the curative possibilities of a fictional identity that is constructed through the collaborative exercise of her narrating abilities and the imaginings of her readers. After all, as Kaplan puts it, "Telling one's story *performs* the power of the listener."[51]

Jane Eyre demonstrates even more pointedly than does *David Copper-field* the dangers as much as the productivity of selfhood generated socially through fictional narratives. Young Jane has been reared upon the language of her own dependence, and it is this, almost entirely, that cultivates in her the sense of injustice she nurses throughout her growing rebellion in the early chapters of her autobiography. Her outbursts of physical and verbal violence that rewrite the relationship between herself and the Reeds mark a distinct rejection of "this reproach of my dependence," which had become "a vague sing-song in my ears; very painful and crushing, but only half intelligible" (*JE*, 16). Here, a repeated public narrative not only structures her existence but determines the experiences that define that existence. Pain and misery and, eventually, rebellion are the hallmarks of Jane's young life, all stemming from this nearly "unintelligible" but markedly affecting narrative. This is not a story she has written for herself, or through which she has consented to be created. As with David, but more strikingly so, when readers meet character-Jane she is being shaped by unsympathetic external forces. This starting point for the novel, as I argue in the introduction, is carefully shaped to foreground and legitimize Jane's "development," thus privileging innate inwardness as the site of personal authenticity. But it is not a lack of authentic interiority that turns out to be Jane's early stumbling block. Jane's identity crisis, as it were, is due to a lack of reciprocity in her narrative selfhood.

Because the imposed narrative of her dependence lacks intelligibility for young Jane, she cannot actively participate in or revise it. Recalling David's anxieties in his search to validate his identity, to lack a role in the construction of her personal narrative would make Jane the passive product of another's creation. Even the narratives that the Reeds inflict upon her that she does comprehend at first elicit from her written self only silent "anguish," as demonstrated in her first interview with Mr. Brocklehurst of Lowood School. When Mrs. Reed accuses Jane of having "a tendency to deceit" in front of Mr. Brocklehurst, Jane-as-narrator reports that her younger self feels "transformed under Mr. Brocklehurst's eye" (*JE*, 41) by this publicized narrative about her character. Just as David's imagining of potential reader responses to the placard he must wear at Salem House causes him to fear his own wildness, the scene with Mr. Brocklehurst enacts for Jane the frightening possibilities of fictional self-making in which readers wield potent authorial power over the created and experienced self. The readers and/as rival authors must be appealed to, and contended with, in the pas de deux of fictional self-making.

Rather than avoiding the mutually influential dynamics of the shifting author-reader relationship, as David's narrative seeks to do, Jane's autobiography instead strives to attain reciprocity among these agents that collectively determine her identity.[52] Demonstrating this yearning for reciprocity in the above-quoted scene, young Jane fears how Mrs. Reed's socially authorized version of her identity will affect her potential to achieve the mutual affection she so desires; she writes that Mrs. Reed was "sowing aversion and unkindness along my future path" (*JE*, 41). In these early instances of narrative self-making it is an entire lack of reciprocity in the narratives about "Jane Eyre"—both in how they are told and in their social effects—that Jane wishes to correct. She later observes to Helen Burns that "you are good to those who are good to you," declaring, "It is all I ever desire to be" (*JE*, 68). The syntactical balance of this sentence epitomizes Jane's ideal of reciprocity: the "good" exchanged between self and others is valued equally. This declaration grammatically and thematically forecasts narrator-Jane's attempt to show, through her choices in the discourse of the closing chapter, the final realization of such reciprocity in her union with Rochester: "I am my husband's life as fully as he is mine" (*JE*, 519).

Jane-as-narrator even goes so far in her authorial search for reciprocal sociability as to acknowledge that she, in her younger years, was unsympathetic to the Reeds and failed to understand their position. She describes her younger self as an "uncongenial alien permanently intruded on [Mrs. Reed's] family group" recognizing that she was a "discord" in the story of Gateshead Hall (*JE*, 20, 19). Although Jane never fits into their family narrative, in her role as mature autobiographer she makes at least a rhetorical gesture of reconciliation. But the exact placement in the discourse of this narratorial gesture of mutual understanding is significant: it interrupts the events of chapter 2, Jane's unjust imprisonment in the Red Room, and shows that Jane also makes the Reeds' oppression fit *her* story of successful selfhood. The Reeds, after all, feature prominently as "obstacles overcome" in her generically self-aware autobiography. In this way, even as Jane seeks to demonstrate mutuality, the power to self-author remains a point of anxiety that informs her narrative choices, which, in turn, call attention to how her discourse attempts to construct her authorial self.

The imperfect separation between the roles of reader and author, and between acts of reading and acts of authorship, makes the ideal of an essential self appear to be the safest ground on which to establish personal value in the Victorian world. This explains why the rhetoric of essential identity persists throughout *Jane Eyre*. Both her unfitness to the Reeds' way of thinking, and, as she yells at Mrs. Reed, the Reed children's unfitness "to associate with me," Jane attributes to her "temperament," her "capacities," and her "propensities" that are all "opposed" to the natural dispositions of the Reed family (*JE*, 34, 19). This rhetoric suggests that Jane's problem with the Reeds is the imposition of their innate affinities, external and alien to herself, onto her inner life. But that imposition, significantly, is achieved through the public declaration of the Reeds' stories about her, as evidenced by the scene in the Red Room and the scene with Mr. Brocklehurst: Jane's self is shaped through socially contextualized narrative methods.

Jane's narration overtly explores the potential troubles of an identity founded upon such social narratives, while submerging these problems in the language of essential selfhood. Even the passages that most clearly illuminate the power of fictional narratives to rewrite one's sense of personal identity are characterized by tropes that simultaneously evoke the ideal of essential inwardness. For example, in chapter 4 Jane challenges her aunt to reimagine herself through another's counterfactual subjectivity when she demands, "What would Uncle Reed say to you if he were alive?" (*JE*, 34). Jane's provocation surprises Mrs. Reed, and, as with Jane's verbal resistance to young John Reed in chapter 1, it shocks Jane as well. Her outburst, Jane narrates, "was my scarcely voluntary demand. I say scarcely voluntary, for it seemed as if my tongue pronounced words without my will consenting to their utterance: something spoke out of me over which I had no control" (*JE*, 34). On the one hand, Jane's diction constructs the illusion of an inner essence by meditating on that inaccessible and ontologically secure inner "something," uncontrolled and authentic, that makes her speak. On the other hand, however, the accompanying parable of creative and combative self-interpretation enacted in this scene undercuts the ideal of a stable interiority from which the sense of self proceeds. Character-Jane's challenge to Mrs. Reed serves as a model of antagonistic author-reader relations, showing the precarious way those roles can shift and further demonstrating the power of fictional processes to alter one's inward experience of the self. Jane's least-sympathetic narrative collaborator, Mrs. Reed, momentarily becomes the provoked reader of her own selfhood; young Jane's proto-authorial act incites Mrs. Reed to feel herself "transformed" by "thinking of [imaginatively vivified] others thinking of [her]" (to adapt Greiner's phrase). Mrs. Reed involuntarily fulfills Jane's narrative prompt: her eye is "troubled with a look like fear"; she then lashes out at Jane physically and retreats, significantly, "without a word"— silenced, just as she silences Jane in the novel's opening paragraphs (*JE*, 34).

If, as the foregoing examples from *Jane Eyre* propose, the experience of self is constructed through narrative processes undertaken with others and/as outer forces, then that which determines who one "really is" becomes a matter of what to include, what to resist, and how to connect the various elements in the story of one's self. In the fictional autobiography, despite the cloaking rhetoric of essential identity, it becomes evident that an authentic self is not dependent on inner essences and appropriate outward expression. Rather, the experience of selfhood comes into existence as a matter of autobiographical selection, as a product of socially contextualized narrative choices. Jane's choice of linguistic narrative as the tool she must wield in her own self-creation is at last registered within the story events (though the discourse has signaled as much from the start) in the extended passage of direct discourse with Mrs. Reed that concludes the initial interview with Mr. Brocklehurst. Jane's vindication of herself—both in this scene and, later, to Helen Burns and Miss Temple—calls to mind the conditions and existential implications tied to becoming a published author of autobiography in the Victorian period:

> *Speak* I must: I had been trodden on severely, and *must* turn: but how? What strength had I to dart retaliation at my antagonist? I gathered my energies and launched them in this blunt sentence—
> "I am not deceitful: if I were, I should say I loved *you*; but I declare I do not love you: I dislike you the worst of anybody in the world except John Reed: and this book about the Liar you may give to your girl, Georgiana, for it is she who tells lies, and not I. . . .
> I am glad you are no relation of mine. . . . If anyone asks me how I liked you, and how you treated me, I will say the very thought of you makes me sick, and that you treated me with miserable cruelty."
> "How dare you affirm that, Jane Eyre?"
> "How dare I, Mrs Reed? How dare I? Because it is the *truth*. You think I have no feelings, and that I can do without one bit of love or kindness; but I cannot live so: and you have no pity. . . . I will tell anybody who asks me questions this exact tale. People think you are a good woman, but you are bad, hard-hearted. *You* are deceitful!" (*JE*, 44)

Young Jane finally realizes not only that her potency lies in her language but also that a distinctive and original "I," as a sign of her singular individuality, authorizes her narrative of self. In the passage from which the above quotation is taken, even in moments when an "I" is not grammatically necessary, Jane puts it in, insisting that it is her identity that is being constructed and actively taking narrative control of its revision. In the whole of this exchange Jane invokes her self-determined and thus authorial identity this way, saying (and, on the level of the discourse, writing) "I" a total of twenty-four times, in just four short paragraphs. The autobiographical form of this narrative, furthermore, lends this passage doubled interpretive weight. Narrator-Jane's choice to include character-Jane's lengthy outburst as quoted discourse encourages in readers a competing consciousness of the fictionality of the protagonist and an impression of her as a self-conscious and complex autobiographer.

Written Jane's eruptions of language, which call attention to the paradox of identity in this text, are her first acts as a willfully self-authored being. As with David, these proto-authorial acts earn her the accompanying anxieties of readerly misprision. Mrs. Reed's story of Jane's deceitful nature—as "published" (*JE*, 79) to the community of Lowood School—results in the feared devaluing of Jane's words: if she is believed to be a liar, then no one will give credence to her most cherished narrative, the rewritten story of her young life at Gateshead. Her wrathful style of telling is already a liability to her authority, as Helen Burns's remarks upon first hearing Jane's tale suggest: "How minutely you remember all [Mrs. Reed] has done and said to you! What a singularly deep impression her injustice seems to have made on your heart! . . . Would you not be happier if you tried to forget her severity, together with the passionate emotions it excited?" (*JE*, 69). Not only is the amount of detail that Jane relates suspicious to Helen as a mark of Jane's heathen, unforgiving character, but the "passionate emotions" with which Jane relates the tale put the validity of Jane's interpretation into question as well: can she reliably produce her own story within the accepted conventions of self and genre?

Helen's response to Jane's first attempt at autobiography suggests a recognition in the text that it is suspicious to insist on "minute" details in life-writing without naming either a source or a method for accuracy. "Mindful of Helen's warnings" about what makes an autobiography seem accurate and genuine, Jane retells her life story to Miss Temple to clear herself of Brocklehurst's charges. "Having reflected a few minutes in order to arrange coherently what I had to say, I told her all the story of my sad childhood. . . . I infused into the narrative far less of gall and wormwood than ordinary. Thus restrained and simplified, it sounded more credible: I felt as I went on that Miss Temple fully believed me" (*JE*, 84). Jane's revision process is tantamount to a methodology for writing a classical autobiography: she "arrange[s] coherently" the events she is going to tell and selects to tell "all" the events that will allow her to present the unified narrative of a "sad childhood." Further, she chooses more temperate diction to communicate her tale so that the resulting message about her identity is clearer and, most importantly, "credible." Her new narrative meets her listeners' expectations of genuine autobiography, directing those listeners to interpret "Jane" favorably. Jane is successful in this inset model of autobiographical self-making: Miss Temple absolves her of the imputation of deceit, restoring to the child her hope to "win affection" (*JE*, 85, 81) from the Lowood community.

In a text that features the telling conventions—temporal, formal, and thematic—of autobiography, it is no mere coincidence that the protagonist learns through the enacted events of the story that the effect of authenticity is derived as much from how a life is told (its discourse) as from what is told of that life (its story). Jane's incorporation of Helen's perspective into the discourse construction of her autobiographical statement to Miss Temple demonstrates the intersubjective dynamics of specifically autobiographical self-making. Carol Bock remarks on this episode, "For the first time, Jane has not been blindly preoccupied with her need to validate herself and her experience but has considered the perceptions of those whom she has invited to participate in the unfolding of her story."[53] Helen and Miss Temple, as young Jane's intratextual audience, model for readers the communal dynamics of self-making that must take place extratextually as well. By asking readers to pay attention to the intersubjectivity inherent in her style of narration, Jane is directing them to precisely the attributes of the text that will also invite them to recognize the creative narrativity undergirding the "reality" of Jane's identity.

Jane-as-narrator also engages the reader more directly, anticipating, representing, fulfilling, and sometimes undercutting the audience's imagined reactions to and constructions of her tale. By including in the discourse the attention-grabbing invocations of the reader, Jane writes with the anticipation that one day her autobiography will be a published and publicly read text in her own world: she will be an author. Despite its significance, however, Jane's explicit engagement with the reader does not begin until chapter 9. In a novel where reader address becomes so pronounced, this building up to an enacted relation with the reader performs in the discourse the same kind of linear development that Jane constructs for her character-self on the level of the story. Before the initiation of direct address, Jane mentions explicitly only once the actions of the imagined reader, using the subjunctive to suggest how one could complete a portrait of Miss Temple, directress of Lowood (*JE*, 57). In other words, Jane does not ignore the reader until chapter 9, but rather crafts the appearance in the discourse of a linearly maturing authorial voice.

From the very earliest passages of the novel, Jane's narration progresses to an explicit relationship with the reader through indirect appeals to what readers "already know" or what "fiction readers . . . are ready to imagine"—a tactic Stewart calls "reader positioning." According to Stewart, this "positioning," a form of reader inclusion, seems to differ little from direct address in its effect,[54] which may be true of the realist novel more broadly. However, as argued in the introduction, the fictional autobiography operates differently than most of its novelistic siblings, sharpening readers' focus on questions of self-making. In the case of the fictional autobiography, explicit appeals to the reader more blatantly expose the gap between story and discourse through which narrative meaning comes to exist. Direct second-person address in the discourse interrupts the seamless flow of the story's progress while simultaneously asking readers to attend to the guiding subjectivity of the fictional teller as she appeals personally (or so it seems) to *you*, the reader. This doubled effect—which stems from and reinforces the doubled reading stance solicited by fictional autobiography—reveals the nuts and bolts of narrative, its artifice, and its efficacy as a mode of naturalizing experience and engendering intersubjective connection through fiction.

There are myriad examples of Jane's overt discursive appeals to the reader. The variety of attitudes with which narrator-Jane approaches the reader and the variety of actions (usually on the continuum of imaginative or interpretive work) that she encourages the reader to perform have been noted by Stewart and other critics.[55] I have selected an example that, rather than insisting on certain mental activities or readings for her readers to follow, temporarily converts them into her embodied companions within the narrative world, enacting—almost to the point of parody—the intimate friendship Bradley Deane highlights as the primary trope in the representation of the author-reader relationship at the Victorian midcentury.[56] In this scene from chapter 25, Jane awaits Mr. Rochester's return to Thornfield the night before their ill-fated wedding. She yearns to disclose to him the secret of the mysterious appearance in her room of a violent, disheveled female figure that on the previous night had torn her wedding veil. At this point in the story, character-Jane does not know the apparition's provenance, identity, or import, but it gives her intense "trouble of mind." As she anticipates Rochester's return she contemplates the chestnut tree that was struck by lightning the night he proposed to her. Her description of its wrecked life but still unified form— "though community of vitality was destroyed . . . they might be said to form one tree—a ruin, but an entire ruin" (*JE*, 318)—prepares the reader for the similarly imperfect sundering of Jane and Rochester soon to come.

As character-Jane waits for Rochester, narrator-Jane entreats, "Stay till he comes, reader; and, when I disclose my secret to him, you shall share the confidence" (*JE*, 318). By lapsing into the present tense, Jane creates a situation that at once represents narrative artifice for Jane-as-autobiographer and the current reality of the reader's unfolding experience of the story world. Narrator-Jane offers intimate knowledge of her self to her readers—she will "disclose [her] secret" and confide in them as much as in her future husband— and plays with the perception that the discourse (the telling) is somehow simultaneous with and identical to the events of the story. By addressing the reader in the present tense, Jane (and, on the extratextual level, Brontë) re-purposes a narratorial device made popular by her eighteenth-century prede-cessors, such as Sterne and Fielding. But, as Stewart remarks, she achieves much more than a mere "latter-day revamping of eighteenth-century formu-las."[57] Unlike the comedic conflations of story and discourse time in *Tristram Shandy*, for instance, which discourage a reading of the characters as compli-cated, real-feeling beings, the effect of Jane's present-tense direct address does not derail an understanding of her selfhood into pure satire or mechanical literary artifice: Jane's narration replaces satire with self-aware sincerity.

In this moment of dread and longing at the level of the story, narrator-Jane's discourse solicits readerly investment by seeming to promise personal revelations and communal confidence. At the same time, she reminds readers of the story's status as story, as fiction, whose "reality" is the product of the gap between the invented events and their telling, which can only be ani-mated through the contribution of readerly imagination. Nor is this scene in chapter 25 the only episode in which Jane conflates story and discourse time to construct self-conscious intimacy with the reader. As Mr. Rochester looks at her drawings in chapter 13, she writes, "While he is so occupied, I will tell you, reader, what [the drawings] are" (*JE*, 147). Although this kind of present-tense reader address occurs only three times in *Jane Eyre*, Jane's self-conscious diction and careful placement of these moments at emotion-al crossroads between herself and Mr. Rochester contributes to a doubled awareness of Jane-as-autobiographer and Jane-as-fiction.[58] In each of these cases, by calling the reader's attention to both the narrative artifice and the emotional significance of the passage, Jane highlights how an openly fictional identity achieves its sense of actuality through affective potency.

Enhancing the emotional impact of her text, then, is one way in which Jane achieves fictional self-realization. The story's fixation on Jane's relative social worth and relationships both echoes and enhances the necessarily col-laborative structure of self-making in the fictional autobiography. In the pas-sages of direct address in which Jane petitions or provokes the reader to vivify her individual authorial identity, she is almost always writing about her life as a social being as well. Jane's reader inclusions exercise her authorial voice while they enact the need of her "social heart" (*JE*, 362) for mutual self-making. The fact that it is Rochester who recognizes Jane's "social heart," and that Jane authorizes this reading of herself by including it as quoted dialogue, only further underscores the importance to Jane-as-autobiographer that her audience reads her thus. Her first direct appeal to the reader, for instance, bears on her behavior to her school companion Helen Burns, anticipating and then revising the notion of her self that her narrated events might create for the reader. During the description of Jane's first spring at Lowood, when typhus rages among the underfed orphans and the healthy ones are let to roam the woods at will, Jane interrupts her narration of past events to pose questions that, she implies, are identical to the ones being asked by readers: "And where, meantime, was Helen Burns? Why did I not spend these sweet days of liberty with her? Had I forgotten her? or was I so worthless as to have grown tired of her pure society?" (*JE*, 93). No, reader, Jane is not so bad as this. She consents to Helen's excellences as if they were her reader's suggestions: "True, reader," she assents, "though I am a defective being, with many faults and few redeeming points, yet I never tired of Helen Burns; nor ever ceased to cherish for her a sentiment of attachment as strong, tender, and respectful as any that ever animated my heart" (*JE*, 93). With this passage as both its inception and its prime example, a pattern emerges throughout the novel in which Jane's inclusion of and address to the reader often corrects, specifies, or meditates on her feelings for others and their influence on her. As in chapter 12, when she resists the "many" who might "blame" her for her restlessness, Jane often dares the reader to misconstrue her; her text is marked by such resistant narration and reader provocation. As the present example demonstrates, it is no accident that the affection that "animates [Jane's] heart" should frequently be the subject of the utterances that similarly engage the reader in most explicitly "animating" Jane as an affecting fictional presence.

And the animating nature of fictional identity construction is, structurally at least, a fully reciprocal process in *Jane Eyre*. That is, it is not only Jane's identity and the identities of her fictional companions that are subject to collaborative creation. After all, it is the reader who is figured, addressed, challenged by, and asked to respond to Jane's textual advances. Jane's prose registers an approximate portrait of the reader that one may strive to embody or to resist but that nevertheless incites the reader to recognize Jane as an affectively potent agent that has at least some measure of influence over how we think about our own identities as they interact with hers. For instance, in the above passage on her attachment to Helen Burns, the reader whom Jane anticipates—and thus constructs—is a reader who judges quickly and cynically. Jane's use of free indirect discourse to focalize (and effectively to invent) the sentiments of the audience implies that it is the reader who would describe Jane as "worthless" and Helen as "pure" in the same breath. This kind of reader is at once very much like Jane's first rival author, Mrs. Reed, with her hypocritically aggressive piety, and, paradoxically, somewhat like Jane herself in her quickness to evaluate others according to a personalized code of morality. By portraying the reader as both her adversary and her other self, Jane's narration performs a consciousness of identity's required reciprocity, one that functionally reaches across perceived ontological boundaries even as it evinces a discomfort with the role this mutuality allows others to play in her acts of self-making. Nonetheless, she continues to goad her readers, inviting and provoking them to participate in the construction of her identity as well as their own.

By repeatedly highlighting the gap between story and discourse so that readers more readily perceive their imaginative role in *Jane Eyre* and "Jane Eyre," Jane-as-fictional-autobiographer temporarily bridges the gap between modern subjects, at least in the lived experiences of the interested reader. Her modes of overtly fictional and autobiographical self-making construct her identity in the chasm that separates self and other in the modern world by bringing the external inward: she makes the "other," the reader, a recognizable coauthor of her self, even as she "authors" them in turn. Stewart claims that these narrative methods elicit feeling: "Apostrophe does less to disrupt than to propel narration if the force of that narration has largely to do with the isolated subject humanizing otherness in the form of an audience for her own otherwise untold desire."[59] An invested reader might come to realize that without a cocreator in her audience, Jane's desires, and the sense of her fictional self, would not only be unfulfilled (as Stewart suggests) but would be virtually nonexistent. One might say—if, reader, you will allow the pun—that Jane's autobiography reveals to readers that, without us, there is no "Eyre" there. Whether by encouraging readerly investment or by seeming to resist participation, the fictional autobiography suggests that without the allied processes of fiction and feeling, our own experiences of self would be as unintelligible, as static, and as unrealized as an unread novel.

CHAPTER THREE

Domestic Interiors and the Fictionality of the Domestic

Esther Summerson Writes Home

Esther Summerson, the primary embodiment of domesticity and feminine interiority in Charles Dickens's *Bleak House*, has rarely been considered an iconoclastic figure. But that is precisely what I argue in the present chapter: that Esther Summerson, domestic fictional autobiographer, challenges her readers to perceive as constructed the fictional mechanisms that undergird the cultural assumptions about gendered plots and gendered identities that, at first glance, her narration seems to endorse as "natural." As with all fictional autobiographers featured in this study, Esther's unmasking of the narrative, imagined, and social dynamics of selfhood proves complicated and ambivalent. In her doubled existence as narrator and protagonist, Esther seems to demonstrate a poignant desire to achieve social and familial acceptance through her fulfillment of an idealized bourgeois femininity. Whether Esther's attachment to the gendered role of domestic autobiographer engages readers' sympathies, or piques their curiosity, or pointedly annoys them, audiences often have a strong response to "Esther," and this affective engagement both stems from and calls attention to the structural similarity between her identity and selves beyond the text. Even negative feelings about Esther make her identity feel like a self that exists separately from and beyond readers' minds. Certain Victorian readers noted such an effect of intra- and extratextual parallelism when reading *Bleak House*. John Forster observes in his unsigned review in the *Examiner* that all of Dickens's characters must be "filled up by the reader or the spectator," just as we attempt to do for the characters of people outside the novel, since "we see nobody minutely in real life."[1]

But Esther in particular—as a domestic fictional autobiographer—makes this structural likeness-to-life an uncomfortable experiential reality for Forster, whose own attachment to an ideal of essential selfhood is implicit in his discussion of knowing real-world selves. For this reason, Forster struggles to reconcile Esther's "naïve" persona with the self-consciously autobiographical form of her tale. He quibbles with her "tone" in certain passages, insisting that its seeming "self-consciousness" would not be "used in her narrative by a person of the character depicted." Indeed, he tries to consider Esther's supposed "graces and virtues" separately from the "method" of communicating them.[2] What he presumes to be the natural inheritance of a modest middle-class woman, in other words, is complicated by the autobiographical narrative mode that brings those same "virtues" to life. It is this sensed disjunction between the "what" and the "how" of her narrated selfhood, and the constructivist interpretations of identity it engenders, that makes Esther Summerson so iconoclastic.

As evidenced by Forster's review and others, it seems that in reading *Bleak House*, the sensation of Esther-as-authentic coexists with the pointed impression of Esther-as-artifice, making some readers uncomfortably aware of the way the latter enables the former. Whether the reader finds Esther's self-conscious selflessness emotionally appealing or not, it is constructed through complex narrative processes that her narration puts on display for readers to examine. This chapter explores how her discourse—full of gaps, hesitations, and inconsistencies—constructs the impression of a lifelike inwardness, first, by exposing the fundamental absence of interiority that underlies her selfhood and, second, by revealing that the conventions of domesticity are both arbitrary and, like Esther's fictional selfhood, still potentially productive.

Domesticity: Analogizing Interiority

In the present chapter, the desire for mutually recognized self-authorship in *David Copperfield* and the affective community of identity in *Jane Eyre* will be extended to consider the persistent trope of interiority in its symbolic evocation in representations of domesticity. The invention of interiority as a crucial element in understanding human subjectivity, as Nancy Armstrong argues, derives at least in part from literary constructions of it in eighteenth-century novels, such as Samuel Richardson's *Pamela*, which notably allows its protagonist to tell her own tale in the first-person form of letters and diaries. The public reads *Pamela* and other first-person novels, Armstrong posits, as "representing an enclosed and gendered self rather than" recognizing these fictional discourses of the inward self as "a form of writing that helped to create this concept of the individual." By the nineteenth century there was a strong cultural attachment to the belief both in innate gender difference, which Armstrong highlights as one key to the novel's "feminine" mode of disguising political power, and in the enclosed, inward nature of personal subjectivity.[3]

And subjectivity—particularly "feminine" or novelistic subjectivity—is ineluctably connected to feeling in the Victorian period.

As Audrey Jaffe describes it, interiority is inseparable from feeling, and feeling, in turn, is foundational to nineteenth-century notions of femininity and domesticity. Jaffe argues that "ideologies of feeling draw their power from feeling's presumed self-evidence: feeling, ostensibly emerging from the deepest interiority, seems by definition beyond the reach of social regulation, and its cultural value depends on that inaccessibility."[4] Jaffe's remarks not only reflect the seeming "self-evidence" of the value of an unreachable interiority but also suggest how interiority functions as a necessary characteristic of an idealized essential self. Essential identity and interiority are mutually dependent concepts, with the latter serving as the imagined space in which the core "something" of personal selfhood resides, unreachable and stable.

The Victorian domestic ideal replicates, in many senses, the conditions of this ideal of individual selfhood as it exists in a modern society of individuals.[5] The home is to public and political institutions what the individual is to the social world in general: a single unit that is defined as private and inward, both by and against that which is external. But much as the individual or authorial narrative of self requires auditors, audiences, and coauthors for its existence, so too does the space of the home and the domestic sphere in general require a vaster, supposedly external public in order to make it the sanctuary that it is in the cultural imagination. In this way, the home—or its human incarnation, the family—is also a site in which safely to acknowledge and work through the larger social issues of the time period, whose conventions create that same domestic grouping. Susan Johnston cautions against ignoring the ideological commitments that inform Victorian representations of domesticity, claiming that interpretations that "necessarily see the resolution of the romance plot in marriage as nonoppositional, fail to capture the ways in which domestic fiction could and often did function as a mediator in cultural debates."[6] Exemplifying Johnston's claim, Esther's domestic autobiography disrupts the easy naturalization of the marriage plot. Her familial world is anything but nonoppositional, and her marital settlement is anything but organic. The novel's conclusion even goes so far as to challenge readerly attachment to that latter value, and in the process emphasizes the flexible potential of the domestic sphere as its own kind of cultural fiction.

Throughout this and the following chapter, which also examines the ideals and practices of the domestic in fictional autobiography, domesticity appears as a network of shifting values that functions analogously to and symbolizes the singular individual in a society of individuals. As such, the figure of the domestic autobiographer operates similarly to the cultural touchstone figure of the author discussed in chapter 2. At the same time, the domestic is treated as a privatized social space (literal, mental, and affective) in which to negotiate the very conditions of society that help to write the individual's sense of personal identity. Because the homemaker, as the keystone figure of the domestic, is believed to guide the moral education of younger generations, and because she authorizes the heteronormative practices that lead to marriage and procreation, her importance in popular Victorian imaginings about the progressive development of society should not underestimated.

This is yet another reason why the fictional autobiography of a character like Esther Summerson in *Bleak House* has a profound connection with the fictional autobiographies of more explicitly authorial characters like David Copperfield and Jane Eyre. As is the case with the figure of the author, the homemaker's inner genuineness—her "natural" inheritance as a female, rather than as a (Wo)Man of Letters—has to be expressed in her work as a creator of the ideal domestic community and to be guarded from the influence of those external to herself. In this sense, interiority of the self is almost more important to the cultural figure of the homemaker than it is to the figure of the author, whose recognized medium of creation is language and, often, fiction. In contrast to David Copperfield, for instance, as a specifically domestic (fictional) autobiographer, the medium of creation for Esther is communal feeling. Making sense of the self through collective affect—Esther's mode of identity construction for herself and others—reproduces on the level of the story the potential for experientially real connection among readers and across ontologies that the fictional autobiography draws attention to more broadly.

But despite the parallel functions of fiction on both the intratextual and extratextual levels of this novel, it is still harder to recognize Esther's creations of self and home *as creations* than it is to perceive the constructedness of the authorial self. Unlike the figure of the author, whose defining works of imaginative writing mirror the creation of the authorial self, Esther's conventionally "feminine" identity, the following close reading demonstrates, may be more readily naturalized by readers into the perception of an essential self, one based in inward emotion. This is one of the reasons that Esther is rarely credited with the iconoclastic interpretive possibilities latent in her narration: she is a homemaker, a domestic autobiographer who explicitly embraces her very Victorian femininity, so readers have trouble seeing beyond these identities of hers that are doubly defined by ideals of essential inwardness. Indeed, it can be difficult for readers to disentangle Esther's acts of imaginative creation (which are nonetheless signaled in her discourse) from the traditional value placed upon the supposed stability of family, feeling, and interiority in reading the figure of the homemaker. These are the ideals through which the homemaker achieved and maintained the cultural capital with which Victorian readers invested her. While Esther's practices of domesticity and identity are demonstrably fictional in nature (narrative, imagined, and social), their fictionality remains masked by language and tropes that explicitly privilege the inward and/as the natural. Reading Esther as revolutionary, in this way, requires close attention to the rifts in her narration that signal the space of creation in which self, home, and gender come to exist as socially potent, if perceptibly constructed, fictions.

The Problem with Esther: Sympathy, Self-Awareness, and Domestic Authority

Esther has often been dismissed by critics of *Bleak House* either for being too unselfconsciously upright to be a credible character or writer (Victorian reviewers) or for being mere gendered propaganda (recent critics). As George Brimley commented in the *Spectator* in 1853, Esther is such a "model of unconscious goodness" that she quickly "bore[s] one with her goodness till a wicked wish arises that she would either do something very 'spicy,' or confine herself to superintending the jam-pots at Bleak House" rather than writing an autobiography.[7] In an unsigned review from *Bentley's Miscellany* in October of 1853, the writer finds Esther's seemingly strict adherence to the feminine domestic ideal almost parodic, opining, "We should like to have substantial faith in the existence of such loveable, self-merging natures. . . . But we cannot say that we have." The review situates the most implausible and objectionable traits of the text in the curious domestic settlement of its protagonist as she is handed off from Mr. Jarndyce to Dr. Woodcourt at the novel's close:

> Indeed, the final disposal of Esther, after all that had gone before, is something that so far transcends the limits of our credulity, that we are compelled to pronounce it eminently unreal. We do not know whether most to marvel at him who transfers, or her who is transferred from one to another like a bale of goods. Neither, if we could believe in such an incident, would our belief in any way enhance our admiration of the heroine. A little more strength of character would not be objectionable—even in a wife.[8]

The ironic closing remark—that the reviewer should like to see some self-assertion "even in a wife"—suggests a discomfort with the model of domestic diligence and selflessness that Esther enacts throughout the text. And yet, this reviewer acknowledges the appeal of "such loveable, *self-merging natures*" as Esther's appears to be (emphasis mine).

The difficulties these reviewers identify have continued to plague certain readers of *Bleak House*: Esther's "unconscious goodness," as Brimley calls it, her extreme modesty and selflessness, and what is taken to be either her total lack of self-awareness or the incongruity of a woman such as Esther being self-aware at all (per Forster's review) prove troubling to some Victorian and more contemporary readers alike. Robert Newsom, expressing a common critical perspective, notes a sort of duplicity in Esther's self-presentation, claiming that she is not "reliable when it comes to describing her own character" because she "is keener and less deferential than she indicates—that is a main reason she irritates readers, after all."[9] Alison Case reads Esther's conflations of character emotion with narratorial choices as evidence of Dickens's own assumptions about gender, arguing that she is a character-narrator "who is relatively unreflectively *immersed* in the feelings and experiences she recounts, because female credibility in the period tends to be linked to a lack of the kinds of rhetorical self-consciousness and critical distance retrospectivity enables" in male fictional autobiographers like David Copperfield.[10] In a well-known attempt to account for the extremes of Esther's character and the irritations produced by her narration, Alex Zwerdling recuperates Dickens's artistry and what critics have called Esther's "coyness" by reading Esther's self-effacing narration as the product of childhood neglect and emotional abuse. Zwerdling proposes that, "deprived of the sense of her own merit from earliest infancy, [Esther] is never sure that she is worthy of love and respect," and her discourse manifests this self-doubt.[11]

But neither the cultural nor the psychological approaches to Esther fully account for the continuing challenge of her character as an affecting and specifically fictional presence. When one considers the fictionally autobiographical form of her chapters in *Bleak House*, Esther's "self-merging" tendencies seem less the result of "nature" or Providence and more the result of producing the self through fictional processes. Furthermore, the marked fictionality of Esther's account permits readers to participate in her self-creation, and to accept this revelation of the self's fundamental fictionality, by couching it safely in an imaginary—if affectively real—framework.

Sympathy for Esther's world and sympathy within Esther's world are crucial to redefining the intersection of identity and domesticity in this book. In this, too, fictionality plays a role as an enhanced mode of sympathetic understanding of others. Sympathy itself has recently been theorized as a sort of fictional process, one that operates through the structures of reciprocal, imagined narratives. Rachel Ablow defines sympathy as "the experience of entering imaginatively into another's thoughts or feelings,"[12] and Rae Greiner highlights sympathy's "formal" existence, building on Martha Nussbaum's work on the essentially narrative nature of emotion. Greiner further asserts that the realist novel "depicts the sympathetic consciousness," which operates through imagined narratives about ultimately unknowable others, "as the basis for reality itself."[13] In this way, Esther's pronounced need for sympathy within her world, her eagerness to experience sympathy with her fellows, and her narratorial maneuvers to cultivate the sympathetic understanding of her audience can all be read as gestures to make her self feel real to her readers. And if, as Greiner suggests, gestures of sympathy and the "fellow-feeling" they engender generate the primary sensation of reality in things,[14] then both Esther's autobiographical project and her domestic mission must dovetail in the narrative evocation of sympathy in order to be fully realized, and fully real.

The sympathetic (i.e., social, imaginative) method and affective focus of Esther's chapters of *Bleak House* are evident from their very inception. Communal feeling is both the aim and the impetus for Esther's writing. Twice in her first chapter, Esther explicitly links her penchant for observation and "cleverness"—two necessary traits for a successful Victorian autobiographer—to her domestic affections, writing that "when I love a person very tenderly indeed, [my understanding] seems to brighten."[15] Her affections are the key to her identity as a person and as a writer, a point that is repeated in her first chapter but is often overlooked in the criticism. These claims are essential to comprehending her later ironies and wit, which can otherwise prove unpalatable or incongruous to some readers—recall, for instance, Brimley's, Case's, and Newsom's insistence that Esther is either "coy" or lacks self- and aesthetic awareness. According to her own account, Esther's sometimes mordant cleverness and the distinctive artistry in her writing are a direct result of her domestic affections, and thus she represents her autobiography and her authority to write as a product of collective, rather than singularly individual, success.

In Esther's version of domestic autobiography, contrary to more binary models in which individualism and collectivity are at odds, she makes individuation and difference a key to her hybrid family group's cohesion and affective intimacy. In this way, Esther's version of family seems to realize the aspirational ideal of realist fiction as articulated by Rebecca Mitchell in her work on alterity in Victorian novels. That is, Esther already embodies the idea that "empathetic extension" and "effective connection between people," even and particularly "those closest [familial] relationships that abound in Victorian texts," "[arise] from the recognition of difference." In the fictional autobiography of Esther Summerson, acknowledging difference in others and "limits" in the self become part of the process of reciprocity, which is essential to the flexible and self-conscious fiction of the domestic woman.[16]

"I Seem to Be Always Writing about Myself"

When Esther Summerson complains that she "seem[s] to be always writing about [her]self" and that she is always finding herself "coming into the story again" (*BH*, 137), it is not the first time that she somewhat paradoxically bemoans her own persistent presence in a text that nonetheless closely follows an autobiographical form and conventions. After all, she begins her tale with her formation of consciousness, and she relates her progression from friendless orphan, to dear friend, to domestic deity and companion, to loving and beloved wife. There could hardly be a more predictable and perfect path for the figure of the Victorian homemaker, instantiated by her role as housekeeper and advisor at Bleak House (the first) and fully realized by her marriage of mutual attraction with Dr. Woodcourt at Bleak House (the second). But Esther's domesticity, like her domestic autobiography, is more complex than this pattern implies at first glance. Even the spaces through which she progresses register development: from her godmother's truly bleak house, to the inviting but tragically coded Bleak House, to her very own Bleak House, Esther's life story refuses stasis as the only model of being for the domestic woman. Through the very real differences that characterize each of these settings, Esther's autobiography manages to allow domesticity to signify change and development through the idiom of the domestic fiction itself.

Furthermore, while Esther's role as homemaker and its autobiographical representation on some level seem to fit (almost too precisely) the conventions of the domestic marriage plot, there are structural incongruities in Esther's discourse that disturb a reader's ability to naturalize that plot as unproblematically organic. These isolated but self-aware moments of inconsistency in Esther's narration suggest the plottedness of her story, and not just through the agency of the real-world author, Charles Dickens, but also—crucially— through the portrayal of critical awareness on the part of the fictional autobiographer herself. Esther repeatedly reflects on her efforts to write her life, registering her explicit self-consciousness as an autobiographer and thereby encoding the specific choices she makes as a narrator into the reader's construction of Esther as a character. This is not to say, however, that Esther-as-narrator declares an overt suspicion of the socially created role of "homemaker" that she so fully inhabits and redefines. Instead, the discourse points repeatedly to the fact that readers' responses to Esther as an affectively real presence stem from the form of the fictional autobiography itself. When Esther's narration is read as the product of a fictional autobiographer whose identity is in the process of emerging as an effect of the same narration for which she is also the fictional cause, it breaks through the illusion of "naturalness" encoded in the domestic novel's plot conventions and illuminates the interpretive reciprocity that fictionality both requires and encourages.

From the commencement of her tale, emotional reciprocity is Esther's expressed goal. Her chapters are even wrought as her share in a larger commission, requested by a nameless but seemingly specific source to whom she alludes.[17] In their affective interest, Esther's first words stand in sharp contrast to the style and content of the first two chapters of anonymous present-tense narration, which lay bare the motions of both the Court of Chancery and Sir Leicester and Lady Dedlock as cogs in the same impersonal and archaic system of power. Esther's opening declaration establishes the predominant patterns of her narration overall, being at once self-effacing and highly self-aware: "I have a great difficulty in beginning to write my portion of these pages, for I know I am not clever. I always knew that" (*BH*, 27). As does her fellow narrator, whose discourse focuses heavily on observable facts and provides little definite internal focalization of the characters, Esther relies on her remarkable powers of notice to authorize her narrative agency. But unlike the anonymous narrator of alternating chapters, she attributes her abilities to her emotional investment in those she observes: "I have always had rather a noting way—not a quick way, Oh no!—a silent way of noticing what passed before me, and thinking I should like to understand it better. I have not by any means a quick understanding. When I love a person very tenderly indeed, it seems to brighten" (*BH*, 28).[18] In this description of herself, Esther implicitly solicits a companion consciousness to join in her interpretive efforts to "understand [what she notices] better," inviting the reader to participate as her intersubjective collaborator in the story she tells. At the same time, the traits she ascribes to herself model a specifically communal type of understanding that privileges generous feelings for others as the key to telling and reading with authority. Esther further reinforces the significance of affective attachment to the success of her autobiographical project when she writes that "my comprehension is quickened when my affection is" (*BH*, 29). She reminds readers that her right to tell is founded upon her capacity not just as a storyteller or a participant but as a narrator who has a deep emotional stake in the narrative she creates. Without Esther's love for others to incite her observational powers and thus authorize her authorial abilities, there would be no discourse. This also means, in the case of the domestic fictional autobiographer, that without mutual affection as the guiding principle of her pages (for Esther's heart is always engaged by those who show her genuine affection), there would be no story at all.

After all, while the drama of the Court of Chancery and its various victims might still be able to trudge along without Esther's personalizing account to enrich it and fill in certain gaps, the anonymous, taciturn, and occasionally heavy-handed narrator of the alternating chapters does not produce in readers the same kind of active curiosity about the teller's identity as does Esther. In fact, it almost seems as if Dickens attempted a curiously fictional version of the autobiographical split of personae when he put his most scathing satire and criticisms in the mouth of the anonymous narrator and all his most tender and sentimental fancies in the writings of Esther. While the two modes of narration do not remain wholly divorced—many readers have noted Esther's own tendency to slip in rather incisive observations on the hypocrisy and social absurdity with which she is often faced—the surprising moments in which Esther's voice shows her similarities to her fellow narrator only further foreground the reader's impression of knowing, or at least wanting to know, Esther. Just as Jane Eyre manages to surprise herself with her rebellious declarations and, by writing about her surprise, to imply that the depths of her inner self are the source of these outbursts, the appearance of Esther's mordant wit proves unexpected to readers precisely because it at first seems "out of character" for her. Such inconsistency in the manner and content of her narration adds complexity to the reader's developing idea of "Esther," which in turn enhances the sensation of reality produced by her character: what extratextual human, after all, is ever perfectly consistent with herself? In this way, Esther's perceptive and critical commentary not only enriches the construction of her identity but also, by surprising them, encourages readers to be aware of the narrative means by which her selfhood comes to produce its various affective impressions.

The necessity for reciprocity dominates the thematic content of Esther's life narrative as well as its structure. When the godmother who raises her (who we discover is her "aunt in fact, though not in law" [*BH*, 33]) decries Esther's very existence, Esther writes of that memorable birthday: "I knew that I had brought no joy, at any time, to anybody's heart, and that I was to no one on earth what Dolly," her beloved toy and companion, "was to me" (*BH*, 31). As with Jane Eyre's selection of a seemingly unusual starting point to her life story, Esther's self-effacing and even awkward commencement to her tale only more fully throws into relief the final realization of her overarching desire. She expresses her yearning for mutual affection as a personal prime directive: "to try to be industrious, contented, and true-hearted, and to do some good to some one, and win some love if I could" (*BH*, 39). In this imagined economy of emotional exchange, while the goal may be to win love to herself, it is earned first through acts of giving, making, and sharing "good" with another.[19] In this way, if one reads autobiographically, Esther's choice to begin her tale here appears much less spontaneous and much more consciously selected; it bespeaks her narrative competence. She is crafting her story toward emotional fulfillment within her own world and sympathetic satisfaction in ours.

The good that Esther works, first at the school at Greenleaf, then in the Jellybys' disastrous home, and finally at Bleak House, is all "domestic" in nature in the sense that it builds and cultivates a community through affective connection, though none of it falls under the strictest notion of domesticity as exclusively pertaining to an ideal home and a nuclear family. All that Esther's domesticity requires, in fact, is a desire for and a return of affection. As Ada Clare notes in her report to their mutual guardian, John Jarndyce, Esther does not bring order to the Jellybys' highly neglected household and its herd of near-feral children; instead, she provides care and attention: "Esther was their friend directly. Esther nursed them, coaxed them to sleep, washed and dressed them, told them stories, kept them quiet, bought them keepsakes, . . . and, cousin John, she softened poor Caroline, the eldest one, so much, and was so thoughtful for me and so amiable!" (*BH*, 84–85). And while they may be distinctly nurturing in nature, Esther's actions are far from conventional. For instance, her illicit washing of one of the youngest (and dirtiest) of the Jellyby children, Peepy, is "a liberty" in standard domestic practice but one that Esther reconciles herself to taking since the child desperately needs it, and furthermore, "nobody in the house was likely to notice it" (*BH*, 64). Her attention, both as a form of noticing akin to the keen observation of the acute autobiographer and as a form of active compassion, is what makes her the productive homemaker that she is. In this way, the conventions of referential autobiography that privilege observation and accuracy are expanded by and incorporated into Esther's distinctively domestic and flexibly fictional autobiographical practice.

The flexibility of Esther's domesticity, however, often goes unnoticed in the criticism. Monica Feinberg even designates Esther's "fictional" (here meaning both inventive and mystifying) construction of Bleak House as a space of "stasis" and fixity, a "private, insular dream," claiming that Esther's "narrative moves to circumscribe an intangible ideal with set parameters."[20]

But the domestic pattern that Esther creates through her discourse and embodies in her story, as suggested above, is far from a restrictive model that imposes a single mode of domesticity or that seeks to exclude others. Already from the first chapters Esther registers her willingness to adapt her domestic care to the needs of those whom she wishes to help (*BH*, 62–63). This capacity to alter the pattern of familial and communal relations so that the real "pattern" is established only in the lack of any set standards beyond a goal of reciprocity implicitly exposes the flexibility of an idea—domesticity—that in other texts (critical and fictional) is construed as something either natural, rigidly fixed, or both.

I choose to continue to classify these relationships as domestic precisely because Esther never distances herself from the role of homemaker; instead she fully embraces it. She eagerly accepts, along with the housekeeping keys and a primary share in the decision-making of the house, even the dubious slew of nicknames that Jarndyce, Richard, and Ada lovingly bestow on her. The names that accrue to her ("little woman" and "Dame Durden," among others), and that almost performatively instantiate her domestic authority, do not erase or supplant any more authentic selfhood marked by her official name. The name Esther Summerson, one must remember, was given to her by an unloving aunt who viewed her existence as a curse. Rather, these affectionate nicknames construct for her a place of security, reciprocity, and undoubted power in the world of Bleak House (and *Bleak House*), including an unmistakable influence over the orbiting community of its many human satellites (Caddy and Peepy Jellyby, Harold Skimpole, Mr. Boythorn, the orphaned "Coavinses" children, and the street-sweeping urchin, Jo—just to name a few).

This moment of Esther's renaming, however, gives many readers of *Bleak House* pause when they assume that Esther is being reduced to, or equated with, her functions as housekeeper and general family companion.[21] Yet it is significant that Esther's rebirth as the domestic genius of Bleak House is directly followed by Jarndyce's request for her advice on what should be done with Richard Carstone—Ada's cousin and their fellow ward—to secure him a career and a future outside the family's accursed Chancery suit of Jarndyce and Jarndyce. The fact that Esther's is the voice that rules here shows that her role is not one that necessarily conforms to a strict conception of the "separate spheres" ideology so often associated with Victorian domestic practices. That her judgment prevails in this instance, and everywhere else she chooses to give it in the universe of Bleak House, certainly counteracts the reading of Esther as in some way suppressed beneath her role rather than happily constructing herself through that role.

Her quiet repudiation of wholly separate spheres for male and female duty is established even more firmly when, upon detecting Harold Skimpole's parasitic practices on the declining Richard and his betrayal of the dying urchin Jo to the police (an act that has resulted in the boy's removal from Bleak House and, subsequently, his death), Esther goes to Skimpole's home to confront him with her knowledge and to state her desire that he cease his visits to Richard. Although he "perverts" her reasoning and her requests in his standard (and implicitly put-on) "childish" manner, she gains her point, and "it so happened that I never saw Mr Skimpole again" (*BH*, 932–35). His infamous slander, published posthumously, that John Jarndyce is the "Incarnation of Selfishness" confirms for us that her persistent unease with Skimpole is wholly justified by his inability to function in the community of mutual care she assembles and superintends. In this exchange, Esther is the defender of the home and its most helpless and least conventional members; her perceptive accuracy, authority, and potency exceed those of Richard and even Jarndyce himself. Not only is her notion of domesticity, and her place within it, flexible, it is also inherently inclusive.

In witnessing the effects of Esther's self-selected and supple model of domesticity as something both "conventional" and openly creative, there is little doubt about the motivating fictional principles behind her notion of productive domesticity. To make her position even clearer, she explicitly articulates it early in the novel.[22] Esther sets out—timorously, hypothetically, but in no uncertain terms—a paradigm of openness and adaptability as the essence of "genuine" domesticity in her conversation with Mrs. Pardiggle, a so-called telescopic philanthropist (like Mrs. Jellyby), whose model of goodness is heavy-handed and imperious. In the scene directly following Esther's institution as Bleak House's housekeeper and presiding genius (both its guiding spirit and its source of wisdom), Esther and Ada are visited by Mrs. Pardiggle and her "young family" of wildly discontented, and hardly contained, children. Evincing her sharp wit and explicit recognition of her status as author, Esther describes Mrs. Pardiggle as one "among the ladies who were most distinguished for [their] rapacious benevolence (if I may use the expression)" (*BH*, 124). But to Mrs. Pardiggle's request that Esther regularly accompany her on her visits to the poor, which readers discover more resemble brow-beating than anything charitable, Esther recounts, through indirect discourse of her written self, the following rebuttal:

At first I tried to excuse myself, for the present, on the general ground of having occupations to attend to, which I must not neglect. But as this was an ineffectual protest, I then said, more particularly, that I was not sure of my qualifications. That I was inexperienced in the art of adapting my mind to minds very differently situated, and addressing them from suitable points of view. That I had not that delicate knowledge of the heart which must be essential to such work. That I had much to learn, myself, before I could teach others, and that I could not confide in my good intentions alone. For these reasons, I thought it best to be as useful as I could, and to render what kind services I could, to those immediately about me; to try to let that circle of duty gradually and naturally expand itself. All this I said, with anything but confidence; because Mrs Pardiggle was much older than I, and had great experience, and was so very military in her manners. (*BH*, 128)

Not only is this passage an indictment of the kind of "charity" that consists of bullying the destitute, impoverished, and soul-sick, but also it substitutes a more humane, more nuanced, and precisely more domestic version of charity, animating (as Newsom points out) the well-known phrase that charity begins at home.[23] And if Amanda Anderson's observation that "the Victorian domestic angel was often described as making her presence and influence felt without any element of deliberation, calculation, or even self-awareness"[24] marks a distinct pattern in Victorian representations of domesticity, then Esther distinctly breaks from this pattern by her doubled awareness and expression (on the level of both story and discourse) of her own domestic philosophy. *Bleak House*'s fictional autobiographer maintains that subtlety, adaptability, and openness alone can benefit others and thereby build a community. Knowing that she "could not confide in my good intentions alone," Esther suggests the inappropriateness of a project that imposes emotions, conventions, and interpretations on others. At the same time, through a "gradually and naturally expand[ing]" "circle of duty" that accounts for the realities of difference, Esther's identity as a homemaker is reinforced by the mutuality she insists must be part of any community-making process. Esther's statement is furthermore a direct declaration of a specifically imaginative narrative method. Only by "adapting [her] mind to minds very differently situated, and addressing them from suitable points of view" can a truly communal and creative reciprocity take place. Tellingly, this is also precisely the act in which a writer of realist fiction engages in her creative process.

Esther's apparent lack of self-confidence before Mrs. Pardiggle does not shake the reader's faith in her competing vision of a productive domesticity that seeks to adapt to, understand, and include difference. Rather, her hesitance only serves to remind readers that Mrs. Pardiggle's "military manners" are lacking precisely the imaginative and "delicate knowledge of the heart" through which Esther encodes her valued reciprocity as the basis of the domestic community that defines her identity. And while Esther's model of a slow increase of loving influence is far from radical—because domestically based and conservative in its initial aims—it resists Mrs. Pardiggle's mode of imposing strict bourgeois standards upon people for whom such principles are alien, unworkable, or simply undesirable. In glorifying her own adaptable version of middle-class domesticity, Esther also makes the case for resisting the urge to naturalize this model as appropriate for all individuals and families.

In this way, Esther's narrative suggests that it is the creativity and flexibility that inhere in the fictionality of social conventions—such as domesticity—that comprise the truly authenticating features of those conventions. Esther's domesticity is valued in *Bleak House* not because it conforms to a strict or naturalized model of domesticity, but rather because of its fictional integrity that recognizes and accommodates difference (of situation, of choice) even as it builds community. It is no coincidence that Esther-as-narrator chooses to include immediately after this polite conflict of methodologies a description of the unvoiced sharing of grief between Jenny and the brickmaker's wife on the loss of the latter woman's baby. She comments, "I think the best side of such people is almost hidden from us. What the poor are to the poor is little known, excepting to themselves and God" (*BH*, 135). This reminder of the reader's ignorance of the meaningful practices of others once more underscores the way in which domestic conventions, when strictly conceived, are limiting in their rigid, Pardiggle-esque righteousness. Whatever truth inheres in human relations, Esther implies, does so through their ability to be adapted by the creative, affective agency of individuals.

Building Inwardness by Leaving Things Out: Gaps

Taking adaptability and reciprocity, then, as the basic tenets of domesticity sketched out in Esther's portions of *Bleak House*, it is clear how fictionality, as a correspondingly flexible and affecting medium, becomes the foundation for her defining role as a homemaker. But Esther's rethinking of certain key points in the Victorian mythos does not stop with the denaturalization of a more conventional kind of domesticity. Esther shapes her discourse to construct a reading of herself and her story that will undermine the naturalization of the Victorian marriage plot. Just as this novel, when one looks closely, does not present a rigid ideal of domesticity, but rather celebrates the flexible practices of it, Esther's is not the standard recounting of the cultural myth of the natural inevitability of the heterosexual union.

One factor that complicates this tale of love, (submerged) desire, and marriage is the way in which Esther's interiority, as the substrate for love and longing, is constructed. Her self-conscious writing and her alternations between identity with her past self and detachment from that self demonstrate the openly fictional nature of the conventions of the marriage plot. It may seem contrary to insist that the marriage plot is exposed as a cultural fiction simply because its constitutive teleology is so strongly represented as such in this novel. But there are two characteristics of Esther's discourse that encourage readerly consciousness of the artifice of the domestic novel's conventions and of her fictional agency in adopting these conventions as her selected means of self-making. First, the marriage plot is the only element among Esther's network of affections that is evinced exclusively through gaps and anachronies[25] for most of the novel (she first explicitly confesses her affection for Woodcourt in chapter 36 and then selectively omits him and her feelings about him until chapter 64). Second, these gaps are made possible by the doubled identities of the autobiographical writer, of which Esther is a self-conscious example. When the particular gaps in Esther's discourse are read as the products of a cleverly self-aware domestic autobiographer, not only does her narration reveal the marriage plot's artifice but also her selective omissions lay bare the mechanisms through which her (fictional) interiority comes to possess its imaginative and affective potency for readers.

As with any autobiographer, Esther occupies two roles in the text: she is the temporally distanced character and the actively writing and selecting narrator. The distinction between Esther-as-character and Esther-as-narrator becomes complicated, however, when Esther engages with the varying feelings and knowledge(s) appropriate to each of her separate autobiographical selves. While a strict separation of these selves and a clear delineation of their functions would be impossible in any text of autobiography, the emotions of her doubled identities nonetheless dictate how and what she tells at distinctly different moments in a highly patterned way. The fact that there is a pattern to her narratorial inconsistencies only increases readerly curiosity about such stark discrepancies. Once more, this key inconsistency hinges upon her deep affections for others, though how and what she tells about these affections depends entirely on the kind of affection she is representing or, notably, not representing.

The representations of her companionable affections seem to be inflected by the knowledge and feelings of Esther-as-narrator in the present scene of writing. In these instances, she is careful to acknowledge the difference between her current understanding and what she knew and felt in the past.

Her explicit recognition of the moments in which her emotions as narrator shape the recounting of her past self suggest not only a consciousness of her doubled role as both character and narrator but also an appreciation for the conventions of storytelling that ensure readerly interest. To foreshadow too heavily or explicitly Richard's tragic end, for instance, is prohibited for an effective storyteller, and Esther carefully avoids saying too much, even when she focalizes her present sadness as she writes about his innocent courtship with Ada. Recounting the young couple's hope for their future, she notes, gives her pain in the present, "having what I have to tell" (*BH*, 215) about its actual result. While this dire warning proleptically suggests a tragedy to come, she restricts her commentary to an appropriate amount of foreshadowing without wholly disclosing the events she dreads to tell ahead of their chronological story order.

In a similar fashion, Esther is unable to prevent her persistent affection for Ada from entering her discourse at moments anachronous to the current position in the story. For instance, Esther apologizes for referring to Ada as "my darling" as she re-creates the scene of their first meeting, excusing her conflation of present emotion with past experience by writing that "it is so natural to me now, that I can't help writing it" (*BH*, 45). The recurrent foreshadowing of what is to come, whether events or emotional states, suggests that Esther's depth of affection is such that it cannot be kept out of her telling. Once more, feeling is the guiding principle of her authorship, and the suggested profundity of her domestic affections only further reinforces her identity and her authority as a domestic writer. But, distinctly breaking from this pattern, Esther manages actively to omit her emotions as they regard one person, who, readers learn, proves to be at least as dear to her as her darling Ada. This discrepancy in how she narrates her emotional attachments incites readers to reconsider to what extent all that which is left unsaid—the gaps—makes up their impression of "Esther." Such a reconsideration brings into focus the narrative of self that Esther and the readers have jointly constructed, thus foregrounding her identity as a kind of self-sustaining narrative fiction.

Dr. Allan Woodcourt, described by the anonymous heterodiegetic narrator as the "dark young surgeon" (*BH*, 167) who attends the sick and destitute, usually victims of Chancery's machinations, is the one character consistently omitted from Esther's discourse. He is always reinstated, but always as an analeptic, or after-the-fact, correction to an earlier gap. Gaps in themselves are not a sign of narratorial irresponsibility or authorial oversight. Rather, all literary texts necessarily contain gaps through which, and not despite which, the complex meanings of a work are forged. Gaps occur, according to Meir Sternberg, "from discontinuities between the order of narration," or discourse, "and the order of occurrence," or story, "with its straight chronology." Some gaps are temporary, and some are permanent; Sternberg points out that "it makes a considerable difference" in our interpretations "whether what happened at a certain point in the action emerges in the narration later or not at all," especially when we are not always aware of a gap until the unnoticed absence of information is filled in,[26] as is often the case with Woodcourt. Most of Esther's significant gaps are temporary, and very pointedly confined to Woodcourt and her feelings about him, although the novel ends on a marked permanent gap that will be discussed at the end of this chapter.

Generally, Esther is excessively conscientious about her sources of information and her inclusion of events and people in their chronological places, even (usually) including those elements that discomfit her, for instance, all the compliments given to her by others, which she immediately dismisses as evidence only of the giver's own goodness.[27] But the repeated inconsistencies surrounding Woodcourt in her otherwise chronological and conventionally complete mode of narrating call attention to the gaps that do persist. In addition to eliding and replacing Woodcourt belatedly in the narrative, Esther also permanently omits her motivation for these elisions and, relatedly, refuses to give an explanation for the loss she feels after she becomes engaged to Jarndyce. Their engagement takes place in the latter half of the novel, after she contracts smallpox and is severely scarred by the disease. Only then—when she no longer considers herself conventionally attractive—does Esther's narrator-self finally confess the love that her character-self feels for Woodcourt.

Taking into account, then, the number and the magnitude of the gaps that structure Esther's narration, it is particularly interesting that the effect of most gaps, according to Wolfgang Iser, is a deeper imaginative engagement of the reader with the text. Using the example of what is left unspoken in the dialogue of Jane Austen's novels, Iser posits that missing information "stimulates the reader into filling the blanks with projections."[28] The fact that Woodcourt, as readers discover only in the last few chapters of the novel, is Esther's husband in the moment of the telling makes these gaps and omissions even more complicated to explain adequately when the reader considers Esther's project in retrospect. Why does such reticence persist in the narration of her courtship with her present husband? Nonetheless, it is precisely these interpretively challenging gaps that most engage the reader, both emotionally and cognitively, with Esther's story and Esther's self.

Esther's first exclusion of Woodcourt from and belated replacement of him in the discourse is one of the most striking and representative examples of the many times this occurs, though to different extents, throughout the novel. One of the reasons for its striking nature is that we cannot detect this marked gap until she decides, hesitantly, to fill it in later. After describing in detail an evening spent dining with Richard's future mentor, Dr. Bayham Badger, and his wife, in which her humorous representation of the couple's joint obsession with the two previous husbands of Mrs. Badger remind us of her observational and rhetorical prowess, Esther closes the chapter with a passage that diverges drastically from the flowing subtlety of her previous narration. I also include here the comment that directly precedes (and perhaps inspires) the analeptic revelation of Woodcourt's presence at this dinner, which, tellingly, features Jarndyce requesting that Esther not become wholly "consumed in care for others":

> "Care? My dear Guardian, I believe I am the happiest creature in the world!"
>
> "I believe so too," said he. "But some one may find out, what Esther never will—that the little woman is to be held in remembrance above all other people!"
>
> I have omitted to mention in its place, that there was some one else at the family dinner party. It was not a lady. It was a gentleman. A gentleman of a dark complexion—a young surgeon. He was rather reserved, but I thought him very sensible and agreeable. At least, Ada asked me if I did not, and I said yes. (*BH*, 214)

Esther here seems conscious that by reporting Jarndyce's hint about "some one" who would hold her "in remembrance above all other people," she implicitly acknowledges Jarndyce's recognition of Woodcourt's admiration of her (and possibly his own), even on this first meeting. Her omission of Woodcourt in his chronological place, her odd description of him by negatives ("not a lady") and short, declarative statements ("It was a gentleman"), and her reticence even to give her opinion of him, all indicate that her character-self's attraction to Woodcourt influence the way in which her narrator-self tells the tale. If one reads fictionally and autobiographically, one realizes that she is altering the emotional logic of her discourse so that it registers her character-self's reserve about her amorous feelings.

Although her emotions seem to be the driving force behind this drastic anomaly in her narration, it is not only Esther's emotions for Dr. Allan Woodcourt that she omits from her discourse. She excludes the fact and presence of the doctor himself repeatedly, having to replace him in the correct story time analeptically and with evident traces of embarrassment, and not just about the omission but also implicitly about her unspoken desires, which are signaled by the gap. The complexity of the interpretive consequences of these elisions remind the reader that storytelling conventions, especially in a first-person tale, affect (and effect) the construction of a narrating protagonist's inwardness through particular discursive techniques: in Esther's case, through absences. Furthermore, these gaps, which on the surface appear to be precisely the opposite of Esther's earlier inclusions of present emotion in past scenes, curiously tend to produce a similar impression on the reader. Namely, these omissions suggest Esther's profound inwardness and depth of feeling. Where her earlier inability to keep her present feelings out of the story implied their authenticity by their unbidden resurgence, in the case of Woodcourt—her future husband—her inability to write about him for half the novel suggests the overwhelming depth of her love for him, but in a way that constructs our sense of Esther-as-character, rather than Esther-as-narrator. This kind of telling through gaps asks readers to interpret "genuineness" from a marked absence that signals inwardness.[29] In the case of Esther, the particular effect of these gaps also relies on the autobiographical form, insistently drawing our attention to the patterned continuities and differences of emotion between her writing self and her written self. After all, Esther-as-narrator chooses to omit Woodcourt and her feelings for him, and chooses to replace him in the discourse as she does. The confluence of the autobiographical form with the construction of domestic feeling at these moments indicates, yet again, how much each of these Victorian conventions—autobiography and domesticity—privileges interiority as a key to genuine truths.

Even four hundred pages after her "revelation" of the "secret" of her affection for Dr. Woodcourt, Esther still refuses to name her emotions and motivations in relation to him. Late in the novel, when Jarndyce suggests that Woodcourt's mother stay with them in London to make it more convenient for Woodcourt to see her, Esther narrates, engaging first in indirect discourse and then, possibly, in free indirect discourse of her written self: "Yes. That [it was most convenient] was undeniable. I had nothing to say against it. I could not have suggested a better arrangement; but I was not quite easy in my mind. Esther, Esther, why not? Esther, think!" (*BH*, 919). While the exclamation of "Esther, Esther, why not?" could be a result of Esther-as-narrator's focalizing her younger self without indicating that the thoughts she reports belong to that younger self (in other words, while this could be construed as free indirect discourse), this moment can also be read as the present confusion of Esther-as-narrator in the moment of writing. In the first reading, she is re-creating her written self's distress through present-tense language that focalizes her past emotion. In the second interpretation, her writing self continues to be so troubled by her sexual feelings for Woodcourt, and his mother's less-than-subtle objections to Esther's illegitimate birth, that even in the moment of writing—in which both her desires and her personal worth have been "legitimized" by her marriage—she is yet unable to name to the reader the source of her unease. In these two parallel readings of this passage, readers can detect the marked but still ambiguous distinction between Esther's written self and her writing self, making them particularly aware of her status as a fictional autobiographer. Esther's exclamation, about which both interpretations are viable based on what is present in the discourse, encapsulates the striking and persistent manner in which Esther's narration registers its own autobiographical artifice while simultaneously enhancing the audience's sense of the depth of her emotions.

Throughout Esther's discourse, the possibility that her writing (re)produces in the present her past timidity and discomfiture performs two functions along the doubled axis of fiction and autobiography. On the one hand, it asks us as readers of fiction to construct Esther's inward integrity through the absence of explicitly expressed emotion. On the other hand, it asks us as readers of autobiography to recognize (at least in retrospect) the artifice of representing her past experiences as if they were occurring in the present moment of her writing. Although the gaps of Woodcourt allow readers to experience for themselves, as it were, Esther's developing emotions, from embarrassment, desire, and admiration, to regret and gratitude, and finally, to mutual love, the constructed nature of the technique—more common to fictional texts—is nonetheless highlighted by its contrast with her treatment of the other relationships in her life. Because romantic love and Woodcourt are the anomalies in her discursive creation of her life, the marriage plot seems to acquire more importance than her other relationships, but only through a mode of telling that we recognize as distinctly fictional.

The reader's ability to naturalize Esther's romantic experiences and her resulting union, told as they are in this anomalous way, may be challenged or disrupted when one reaches the end of the novel and is given the chance to mirror Esther's retrospective view of her life and perceive the seemingly illogical persistence of her narratorial reserve when it comes to Woodcourt. Although Esther's ongoing relationship to Ada in the time of narration influences how she narrates her in the past, in the story, with Woodcourt, there is no indication that she will eventually become his wife and bear his children.

In fact, the readers have believed, as has Esther-as-character, for much of the novel that she will marry Jarndyce. Jarndyce's proposal and Esther's acceptance are framed by her implied resignation of any romantic hopes with respect to Woodcourt, once she believes she has lost her good looks. When all is known by the reader at the end of the novel, however, her overly timid omissions of Woodcourt begin to seem doubly contrived, not just in her abject reticence about him but also in her contrary treatment of the other close relationships in her life. As I suggest above, this can indicate, on the one hand, that the so-called marriage plot is still predominant in the way that Esther (or Dickens) tells her story. While knowing that Ada will become and ever remain her darling friend will not decrease readerly interest in the story, and can even enhance the audience's identification with the caring reciprocity of the women's friendship, knowing that the dark, young surgeon will become Esther's loving husband and the father of her children would certainly decrease the plot-driven curiosity about her *bildung*, inasmuch as a happy marriage based on love is (still) coded for many readers as the ultimate satisfaction of female development in Victorian domestic novels. On the other hand, however, as much as this manipulation of discourse for the enhancement of the story's effect on readers' curiosity speaks to the importance of marriage in the construction and "completion" of the homemaker character, it also allows readers to interpret Esther as a savvy author of autobiography, shaping her telling to keep the "greatest secret" for last.

What I earlier termed "inconsistencies" in Esther's narration can now be read as functioning on a level beyond that which is merely concerned with intratextual coherence. The myriad interpretive avenues these anomalous gaps open up to readers put into practice at once all of the many ways in which fictional autobiography permits readers to perceive identity and fiction as similarly creative narrative processes. Let me trace some of these interpretive outcomes. The gaps through which Esther constructs the profundity of her love for Woodcourt solidify Esther's self and her narrative. This happens by giving readers a sense of her inner authenticity of feeling through absences, and simultaneously by signaling her active narrative shaping (the present reproduction of past emotion) toward a conventional "closure" that features not only productive homemaking but also reproductive romantic marriage. At the same time, however, the essential plottedness of her narrative's resolution in her marriage, which is further underscored by the highly unconventional way in which the union finally transpires, reminds readers that while her narration's gaps help increase our curiosity and add to our surprise,[30] they also reveal the artifice through which this resolution must be brought about.

In turn, Esther's mode of telling challenges readers to perceive the narrative mechanisms of, and therefore to question the naturalness of, the marriage plot itself.

The climax of this particular narrative design demonstrates the plottedness of Esther and Woodcourt's union, which is brought before the reader in the final filling in of a gap. This time, however, it is a gap produced in the world of the story by Jarndyce's silence about his plans to abdicate his place as Esther's fiancé to Woodcourt. Esther's careful retention of this gap on the level of the discourse ensures, once more, that readers are able to feel with and through the experiences of Esther-as-character. When Jarndyce asks Esther to marry him, she registers happiness and gratitude, but also, when writing of it, an additional sense of loss that she refuses to name (*BH*, 692). This loss of the possibility for passionate love and desire in marriage, rather than affectionate, platonic companionship, remains always implicit, representing a second level of motivational gap that Esther maintains only in reference to the Woodcourt plot. However, when Esther fixes a day for her marriage to Jarndyce, he rejoices over the "day on which I give Bleak House its little mistress" (*BH*, 943). As the day approaches, he arranges to take Esther to Yorkshire, ostensibly so she may see and superintend the installation of Dr. Woodcourt into his new medical practice there. However, when they arrive at the house, Esther sees "in the arrangement of all the pretty objects, *my* little tastes and fancies, *my* little methods and inventions which they used to laugh at while they praised them, my odd ways everywhere" (*BH*, 963, original emphasis). She grieves that this material, domestic incarnation of herself all around him will burden Woodcourt, who has confessed his love for her "too late" (as she guiltily reports thinking) (*BH*, 937). However, when Jarndyce shows her the name of the new home—Bleak House—she begins to understand his contrived, if beneficent, confounding of one thing with another to obscure his engineered plot twist. His eagerness to make her "the mistress of Bleak House" was an eagerness to correct that "mistake" that he saw "caused [Esther] some distress" (*BH*, 966). That is, by wishing to be "restor[ed] to [his] old place in [Esther's] affections," Jarndyce corrects an error in judgment, and an error in plot. He reverses the confusion of the father-figure with the fiancé by replacing himself in the latter role with the man who will make her "happier" and, he says, who can receive no higher compliment than that he "know[s] [Woodcourt] deserves her" (*BH*, 964, 966).

The handing off of Esther as a literal "gift" (*BH*, 966) from one man to another evokes plenty of connotations to make any reader today—and, as we saw in the review from *Bentley's*, some Victorian readers as well—uncomfortable about the role of Esther as an object of sexual exchange. But while this moment has been much remarked upon in scholarship, ironically, Esther's own reaction is rarely considered valuable in an analysis of this scene. Her response to these events is one of unqualified joy and consent; she calls herself "the happiest of the happy" (*BH*, 986). The fact that her powers of homemaking, and "the little home she brings" to Woodcourt (rather than the other way around), are valued for the traits earlier established as those of fiction's adaptive reciprocity suggest that privileging the protagonist's happiness, and a recognition of how this is brought about—literally—by the processes of fiction, might yield a more productive reading. When readers consider Esther's own efforts to enact the artifice of literary and domestic conventions, Jarndyce's scaled-down model of the contrivances that go into any domestic novel's realization of the idealized marital union make this scene an appropriate crowning moment for the breakdown of the appearance of the natural inevitability of the marriage plot, though not for its total devaluation.

At the end of this scene, Esther's declaration "My husband—I have called him by that name full seven happy years now—stood at my side" (*BH*, 965) forces us to reread retrospectively all of her earlier omissions of Woodcourt. Even as the novel concludes, readers are busy remaking, animating, and reconsidering Esther's narrative and/as her identity. That this statement's diction and content parallel her earlier invocation of Ada as "my darling" but come sixty-one chapters later only further underscores the effect of her narrative inconsistencies in teaching readers to perceive the artifice, as well as the potential productivity, of the domestic novel's marriage plot. It is productive because the reader, like Esther (if he is an emotionally identifying reader), can experience the fulfillment of a reciprocal love in which the growth of one partner is enhanced by the love of the other through the shared authorship of one another's narratives of identity. This possibility is established earlier in the novel, when Woodcourt declares his love for Esther and she implicitly confesses her own, finally achieving the romantic mutuality she has sought. Both gratified and regretful at this newly shared knowledge, Esther attributes all that she might become, any improvement in herself, to knowing that the man she loves loves her in return (*BH*, 939). Woodcourt echoes her sentiments, saying he will strive to fulfill his humanitarian duties in remembrance of her, as if he held a "sacred trust" (*BH*, 940). Once her engagement to Jarndyce is dissolved, however, her union with Woodcourt can be brought to fruition. In the novel's overtly contrived realization of the marriage plot, instead of a gendered play for power the reader can alternatively see the happy fulfillment of a reciprocal, and therefore productive, affection. This creative reciprocity extends to Esther's emotionally identifying readers as well. By reading Esther as a fictional autobiographer, we are empowered to perceive in her chapters the flexibly social processes of identity and domesticity that structure her fictional life narrative in *Bleak House*.

And yet, while Esther's narrative asks readers to perceive and to value the potential flexibility of such cultural constructs as gender difference and class distinction, her narration also refuses to enforce a compulsory sense of completion in the ongoing negotiation between self and other, individual and collective. Ending her narrative on a permanent gap that declines to construct through language her own self-image—other than as it is reflected in her persistent care for her loved ones—Esther's narration suggests the impossibility of avoiding the narratives imposed on the individual by the social world. In the last scene she narrates, which takes place the night before the moment of her writing, she puts off responding to a question posed by her husband that prompts her to consider whether her smallpox scars have faded, returning her to "[her] old looks, such as they were." He fondly asks her, "Don't you know that you are prettier than you ever were?" Instead of answering she lists the beautiful traits of her friends and family, concluding her autobiography by writing that her loved ones "can very well do without much beauty in me—even supposing—" (*BH*, 989). Her refusal to complete her manuscript, her thought, and her self-image by failing either to accept or to reject her husband's representation of her restored beauty hints at (and encourages) the ongoing role that others must play in fashioning one's necessarily dynamic sense of self.

This final, permanent gap in a novel so marked by strategic gaps suggests that Esther is aware that there is never a complete solution to the intersecting challenges of subjectivity and community. The resolutions offered, including the marriage plot, are never perfect. And thus, despite Esther's productive outlook on the flexible, communal artifice of the marriage plot, she nonetheless must leave her own narrative of self unfinished, invitingly open to the interpretations of her readers. Esther's refusal to integrate her husband's image of her into her own fictional self is thus not just an act of agency or modesty, but also a gesture toward the difficulties of achieving, and indeed, the undesirability of possessing, a unified and finished self in the modern world. As a narrator who values the dynamic and adaptable nature of the fictional self, in this final authorial act Esther refuses perfection as a static—and therefore unsocial and unprogressive—mode of being.

CHAPTER FOUR

"No True Home"

Difficult Domesticity and Controlling Collaboration in
David Copperfield and *Villette*

NOT ALL NARRATIVES OF DOMESTICITY are as open, or as flexible, as Esther Summerson's. It may be unsurprising that making a home, much like making an identity through imagined narratives, must in part depend upon the participation of one's fellows. Yet both David Copperfield from Dickens's novel and Lucy Snowe from Charlotte Brontë's *Villette* register their discomfort with the prospect of collaborative domesticity, especially as an element of and an analogue for self-making. The implicit anxieties about the necessary reciprocity entailed by identity construction using the processes of fiction are enacted in these two novels through more overt anxieties about the making, and breaking, of homes. Both novels pointedly reveal the ambivalence that characterizes the Victorian engagement with fictional selves. As discussed in chapter 2, David's authorial self-making uncomfortably discloses the required reciprocity between fictional autobiographer and reader as an instance of the intersubjective nature of personal identity creation. His self-construction in moments and spaces of difficult domesticity most poignantly evinces a desire to avoid the insecurity of collective self-creation, while, in the process, undermining his attempts to demonstrate his autonomy.

The ambivalence about collaborative self-making also resonates in Lucy Snowe's laboring domesticity, divorced as she is from the potential for mutual love within her own world. In *Villette*, Lucy's extreme methods of reader inclusion, paradoxically, help to facilitate the audience's active realization that the self-making procedures that create "Lucy" are, in fact, the same as those that make extratextual selves feel so real. Lucy's homelessness (literal, emotional, and social) foregrounds her lack of a fixed identity and stable position in the Victorian world, making her fictional self-making at once freer and riskier. Having no set conventions with which to anchor herself in the face of society's, and the reader's, potential misprisions, Lucy seeks in her discourse to control the necessarily collaborative construction that animates her. Her rhetorical antagonism toward her potential collaborators in self-making, both those within the story world (e.g., M. Paul) and those addressed by her discourse (i.e., the readers), proves partially ameliorative of her homeless state, however. Readers are discursively forced to become the "careful friend[s]" M. Paul identifies as Lucy's greatest need in the absence of a home (an origin, an essential locus) to which to return.[1]

"The Centre of Myself": David Copperfield and the (Unintentional) Author-ization of the Domestic Laborer

In *David Copperfield*, Dickens's first fictional autobiographer struggles between the poles of authorial self-definition as a professional whose work, by necessity, must be conducted in the home and as a self-made man attempting to create himself free from the interference of outside forces. Ironically, even though he is a successful novelist in his fictional world, David is often unable to perform the act that Esther Summerson suggests is so necessary to reciprocal intersubjectivity, namely, to "adapt [his] mind to minds very differently situated" (*BH*, 128). In this David fails to fulfill the aesthetic and ethical mandate of realist fiction through which he defines himself as an author. David's self-conception marks a distinctly more rigid ideal of identity than that modeled by the domestic autobiographer, Esther. It will prove to be the strictness with which David attempts to maintain the separation of domestic roles—masculine professional writing and feminine amateur housekeeping—and their respective values that ultimately betrays the extent to which his own authorial identity relies on the relationship he constructs with his "child-wife," Dora, and, extratextually, on his readers' imaginations.

Just as David insists on the exclusivity of domestic roles, even as his creative homebound profession seems to break down those same traditional expectations, he also strives to maintain a strict surveillance over his own narrative in its treatment of fact and fiction. Because David is a well-known creator of fictional works within the diegetic world, his autobiography seems to sit uncomfortably close to the generic dividing line between reference and imagination. Of course, it is his desire to control the construction of his tale, and himself *through* his tale, that produces problems for this author of fiction who also writes autobiography. The idea of the self as a fictional construct is something that David's narration seems to register, but also to reject, in his dealings with the two kinds of writing (fiction and autobiography) with which he defines his authorial identity.

In a primary example of this implicit unease, David reflects on Mr. Micawber—an instance of a rival "author" within David's text[2]—and his petition while in debtor's prison, a memorable event witnessed by young David. Micawber's writing of the petition to Parliament, begun as a response to his imprisonment for debt near the end of chapter 11, has a literary influence on David's own fancy. By introducing Micawber's rhetorical creation within framing references to his own imaginative life, David obliquely signals a fear of external influence by trying to structurally contain Micawber's work within his own. However, because Micawber's petition fires young David's latent creativity and serves as the segue through which David's autobiography can again discuss his own artistic progression, Micawber's effect on David's authorial identity (on the levels of both story and discourse) is evidently an influential one. David describes his reaction to the petition-signing ceremony as "an instance to myself of the manner in which I fitted my old books to my altered life, and made stories for myself, out of the streets, and out of the men and women; and how some main points in the character I shall unconsciously develop, I suppose, in writing my life, were generally forming all this while" (*DC*, 163). David-as-narrator here claims that, even as a desolate, laboring child, he was effectively already narrating this literary autobiography and his authorial self into being. Additionally, he suggests that any fanciful elements he generates by means of this textual exercise are unintentional as he "unconsciously develop[s]" his "character" in this work. This assertion implicitly attempts to connect his past creative self with his present one, all the while disowning any inorganic—that is, textually rather than existentially based—changes in himself from the moment of living to the moment of writing. Though he highlights his inherent creativity, he explicitly disavows any intentional fictionalizing of the self that he creates through the autobiographical act.

There is a palpable tension in David's narration between veracity and creativity, particularly as the two modes are associated, respectively, with the "authenticity" of a continuous identity and the instability of fictional self-fashioning. He treats these possibilities as if they were mutually exclusive, though careful reading shows how intimately intertwined they are. In David's rhetoric the ideal of an essential self struggles to dominate the fictional practices of identity creation that surface throughout his text through those same rhetorical choices. David-as-narrator attempts to reconcile the conflicting urges of veracity/creativity, essence/artifice in his autobiography by underscoring the possible but avowedly unintentional fictions that comprise his text, saying, "I wonder how much of the histories I invented for such people hangs like a mist of fancy over well-remembered facts" (*DC*, 164). Here he actively guides the reader to perceive innate authorial skills in his childish self, while simultaneously privileging the referential requirements of an autobiography by emphasizing "well-remembered facts." David attempts to negotiate the conflicting ideals and practices that characterize his dual roles as authentic autobiographer and fictional creator by legitimizing his "novel" profession and his (reclaimed) status as a rising middle-class gentleman. Significantly, for David, both of these roles must be enacted in the domestic, rather than the public, sphere.

David lays claim to the identity of a legitimate literary laborer by representing his past self at work in the evenings, after the regular working day, in the parlor of his home with Dora, his domestically inept wife. As John Picker points out, "Workers whose place of rest doubled as their place of labor" had no "separate, official workplace" in which to conduct their business, thereby eliciting, in some cases, questions of their legitimacy.[3] Questions of legitimacy, and, in David's case, authority, are therefore inherently bound up in the space in which one carries out the tasks by which he defines himself. Although David's precarious professional and personal position might seem to pose obstacles to his self-fashioning as an author, Dora and the instability she produces instead become the necessary catalysts to David's self-definition—one that coincides with almost parodic literalness with Carlyle's description of the "Hero as Man of Letters," discussed in the second chapter. David's attempt at an identity that privileges the insular individual over a communal identity ultimately shows its vulnerability—its implicit need for mutuality—in the narrative's reliance on Dora's domestic failures for the instantiation of David's authority.[4]

In Carlyle's writing on the subject, one characteristic that distinguishes Johnson, Burns, and Rousseau (his literary "Heroes") from "not genuine" men of letters is that "their business and position was such a chaos."[5] In a very literal fashion, this is also a description of David's domestic situation with Dora, which, because he is a newspaper reporter and an aspiring fiction writer, becomes not only a refuge from the working world but itself a space of literary labor and production. Though when Carlyle mentions "chaos" in the writer's professional world he is making a case for increased economic viability and social standing for truly qualified men of letters, the novel's literalization of the alienating experience of artistic production in the Copperfields' household is nonetheless evocative of what, to David at least, characterizes the artist's unique situation. As narrator, David spends vastly greater portions of the discourse describing his and Dora's domestic misadventures than he does detailing the actual act of writing. And yet, most of the scenes that occur between the spouses begin or end with a mention of David's working at his craft, which structurally, thematically, and spatially links the two seemingly contradictory subjects. "Sometimes, of an evening," David tells his audience, "when I was at home and at work—for I wrote a good deal now, and was beginning in a small way to be known as a writer—I would lay down my pen, and watch my child-wife trying to be good" (*DC*, 628). Dora's attempts to make heads or tails of the account book (echoing Clara Copperfield's earlier problems with threes and fives) pain David; his "child-wife" is not meant for the hard work that he does: "I had a great deal of work to do, and had many anxieties," but, in thinking of Dora's bewilderment at anything remotely practical, "the same considerations made me keep them to myself" (*DC*, 629). Dora's ineptitude at "her" portion of the domestic work, failing to fulfill what David expects of the upwardly mobile middle-class homemaker, seems to place his own professional abilities and increased responsibilities in stark relief. While he upholds his role of providing for them financially, and exercises his writerly potential to achieve ever greater fiscal and social potency, Dora's failure to keep pace domestically, and his resulting self-indictment for his folly in marrying her, suggests a very strict interpretation on David's part of the purpose of domestic partnerships. There is none of Esther's flexibility of conception in David, as there is none of her competence in Dora.

At first glance, it would seem that Dora's inability to be an effective domestic laborer is a source of strife for David and a threat to his success as a professional writer in the domestic space. The isolating effect of secret-keeping on David's part is compounded both by his love for Dora and by the regret of realizing, in Annie Strong's words, that "there can be no disparity in marriage, like unsuitability of mind and purpose" (*DC*, 678). This "old unhappy loss or want of something" (*DC*, 629) separates him emotionally from his domestic partner, making their relationship, and their home, less of a joint venture and more of an individual endeavor. Tellingly, in one of David's attempts to institute some much-needed order in his anarchic home life, he takes the Murdstonean tack of trying to "form Dora's character": "No matter how incidentally or naturally I endeavoured to form my little wife's mind, I could not help seeing that she always had an instinctive perception of what I was about, and became a prey to the keenest apprehensions. In particular, it was clear to me, that she thought Shakespeare a terrible fellow. The formation went on slowly" (*DC*, 675). He does not berate his "child-wife" as cruelly as Murdstone did Clara, though he does call her "ridiculous" and enjoin her to be "reasonable" (*DC*, 674), as well as making a point to impress upon her his own preferences—significantly, literary and intellectual ones.

In this way, David, who has so studiously avoided narrating his character-self into the position of a created product of someone else's influence, is quite prepared to be the creative producer of another human's mind, particularly in the fields of literary taste and intellectual self-control. He "persevered, even for months," "looking forward through this intermediate stage, to the time when there should be a perfect sympathy between Dora and me, and when I should have 'formed her mind' to my entire satisfaction" (*DC*, 676). And yet, this attempt at "determination" and discipline is an utter failure: Dora is "already formed" (*DC*, 676). If readers take David at his word, there is no sense of mutuality in this marriage, as there is between Jane and Rochester, and Esther and Woodcourt. David explicitly wishes to form Dora to *his* standards of sympathetic union in the most Pardiggle-esque manner, rather than permitting a mutual process of becoming to take place between them. When his plan miscarries, the unsuccessful household authority declares, "I could not endure my own solitary wisdom" (*DC*, 677) in domestic matters; it is this final failure that leads to "the old unhappy feeling pervad[ing his] life" (*DC*, 678).

But Dora proves to be more essential to David's sense of authorial identity than his writing self seems to wish to concede, and her role in his fictional autobiography attests to the necessity of others in the creation of the self. The form of the fictional autobiography, which draws attention to the difference between the written and the writing selves of the narrator-protagonist, helps the careful reader to perceive the requisite sociability that underlies David's identity creation even as he attempts to avoid such external influences on his authorial self-construction. While David's disharmony with Dora marks a disappointment on the level of the story, the dynamic it establishes on the level of the discourse permits David to present himself as a successful author. The Dora episodes allow David implicitly to invoke Carlyle's definition of authorship as chaotic isolation. In alluding to Carlyle, David strikes a chord that would resonate with many Victorian readers, asking them to connect David to the cultural touchstone figure of the author. Relying on the doubled selves of the autobiographical structure, David-as-character's failure to create the perfect wife and home allows David-as-narrator to describe himself as the silently anguished yet wise and prophetic author direct from Carlyle's writings. Though David "labored hard at [his] book . . . and it came out and was very successful" (*DC*, 671), the physical space of his production is in chaos, which is in turn evidence of the motive for his secret emotional turmoil: Dora. Because Dora is the key discord in his domestic-professional situation, she becomes essential to David's self-presentation as the Carlylean author. In this way, his marriage to Dora is not merely a step in the representation of his psychological maturation (as Mary Poovey suggests),[6] but rather provides a necessary element in the construction of the characteristically isolated figure of the original Man-of-Letters Hero.

Further, David's choice to confess to readers both his folly in marrying Dora and his failure to correct her character represents open criticism of his younger self. By readily admitting his youthful errors—drawing attention to his once-flawed and now-matured authority—David-as-narrator encourages the reader to see him as a strictly truthful autobiographer and, therefore, to validate his account as authoritative. Even more significantly, admitting to such errors in his personal actions invites readers to judge young David, to consciously experience disapproval of his decisions. His confessions lead readers to sense just how different their judgment is from his, implicitly developing a sense of his singular individuality in the process. David's errors establish a likeness-through-difference with the novel's audience, just as Jane Eyre's rhetorical provocation of the readers who may "blame" her for her restlessness in chapter 12 reinforces the impression she gives of possessing a unique subjectivity. David's choice to narrate his unwise behavior toward Dora (and, in a parallel example, toward Uriah Heep, when he slaps him) curiously promotes a sense of the autonomy and singularity of his identity.[7] His missteps mark him as distinct from his readers—the same readers whose imaginative input his fictional identity uncomfortably requires. Furthermore, his gently comic and sometimes rueful narration suggests that his tendency to make these individualizing errors has now been reformed by the older, authoritative David.

In the above example, Dora becomes a productive prop to David's confessional construction of a singular, authorial self. The fictional autobiography contains even more literal illustrations of Dora's importance to David's processes of self-creation. Consider, for instance, the scene in which she fails as a household manager and David enlists her in reproducing his artistic work: "The next time I sat down to write, and regularly afterwards, she sat in her old place with a spare bundle of pens at her side. Her triumph in this connexion with my work, and her delight when I wanted a new pen—which I very often feigned to do—suggested to me a new way of pleasing my child-wife" (*DC*, 631). This new way to please her consists of the futile rote copying of manuscript pages, which appears to have no functional purpose other than making her happy. However, not only is Dora suddenly employed in (re)producing some *thing* of value, an activity that controls and channels her energy, but, assuming that "writing and copying [are] analogous activities," Alexander Welsh points out that "the second is also the multiple extension of the first."[8] Therefore, Dora's work of copying multiplies and extends David's literary work and his self-construction contained therein. This scene, on the surface of it, is a literal representation of the symbolic fruitlessness of Dora and David's joint labor, which simultaneously underscores the solitary success of David-as-author. But, with this double effect, the scene also suggests the crucial importance of Dora to David's self-definition, both as character and as narrator. So while David declares that his marriage to Dora was the "mistaken impulse of an undisciplined heart" (*DC*, 647), his particular portrayal of this relation implies that it is not despite this failed domesticity, but rather because of it, that David becomes a productive and well-known author during this period. Dora's importance in this way is rather ironic: David, in this construction of himself, has managed to elude the artistic and intellectual influence of his aunt Betsey Trotwood, Mr. Murdstone, James Steerforth, and Mr. Micawber, only to be supported in his textual self-creation by the figure of his incompetent child-wife. Seemingly despite his own best efforts, David Copperfield's narration of his failed domesticity and successful authorship enacts the communal dynamics of identity creation in the very attempt to resist the appearance of anything short of autonomous self-making.

Agnes, David's second wife, also becomes a figure of influence, and in the representation of this relationship David-as-narrator almost seems to embrace, perhaps even too whole-heartedly, the practice of reciprocal identity creation. However, unease with the idea of a fictional self—an identity at once narrative, imagined, and social—persists in this text. Agnes's beatific influence is emphasized more for the effect of narrative closure than for David's actual self-fashioning as an author (at least to the extent that those two aims may be separated in this novel). Poovey, arguing that Agnes is the final female through whom David defines himself, points out that "in Dickens' final representation of Agnes, she might as well be David's mother, so perfectly does she make him what he is."[9] While Poovey stresses a more general ideal of maternity in the foregoing statement, she overlooks the textual specifics of David's and Agnes's relationship, and of Clara Copperfield herself. First, Agnes is, in many ways, the anti-Clara: she is intelligent, independent, and domestically capable—even running a school for young girls in her father's home (*DC*, 815). Further, though Poovey cites the fact that David's ultimate union with Agnes links "effortless housekeeping with effortless writing," David's authorial success was already achieved by this point in the story,[10] and it is important to note that effort itself is far from being demonized in this novel. Truly, effort and work are essential factors in David's self-definition throughout his autobiography; hence their disappearance from the discourse is more problematic than ideal for his identity. Poovey, however, points to an interesting phenomenon: although he "had advanced in fame and fortune" (*DC*, 844) at the start of chapter 63, there are no more direct references to David's writing, or to his highly valued literary work(s).[11] Most of his writing—at least, most of his textual representations of his writing—occurs around periods of psychological or physical exile from those he loves, whether during his marriage to Dora or at the end of his sojourn in Europe following her death. This trope of isolation reinforces the productive nature of failed conventional domestic labor in generating conditions for the success of literary labor.

Though David's story ends with his marriage to Agnes, and with his declaration that Agnes is "the source of every worthy aspiration I had ever had; the centre of myself, the circle of my life, my own, my wife" (*DC*, 844), this claim of perfect intersubjectivity between them sits uneasily with both the fictional facts of his world and the ideals of essence and autonomy that his narration has previously tried to uphold. Although he credits his union with Agnes for his professional success, far from marking the beginning (or the "source")[12] of his literary career, it is at best the midpoint of his rise as an economically viable artist. Further, as Poovey notes, he ceases to write about his writing at this point in the discourse, suggesting a lack of progressive development (perhaps even a stagnation) in his creative resources. The perfect harmony in the marriage of Agnes and David, rather than providing fascinating fodder for the autobiographer's text, merits no more than a passing line: "My domestic joy was perfect, I had been married ten happy years" (*DC*, 844). In this brief gloss of his married life, David's narration more closely mirrors the reticence on personal matters often seen in nonfictional autobiography in the res gestae tradition; in this statement, his life story diverges from the more intimate and exciting content conventions characteristic of the fictional autobiography. Indeed, the unity of David and Agnes is represented as so complete that his autobiography must come to a close—either because there are no more worthwhile stories to tell or because the narrator finds it safer to exclude the active reader from his domestic kingdom. The Copperfields' mutual "suitability of mind and purpose" may create domestic bliss, but it hardly provides the ideal proving grounds for the workings of a heroic man of letters.

The strict standards of authorship and rigid definition of domestic duties that David's narration has previously enacted make this abrupt change toward utter surrender in the interpersonal dynamics of his text feel uneasily contrived. David's superficial absorption into Agnes's saintly influence can be interpreted not so much as a failure to be a completely self-manufactured author, nor as a frank negotiation with the reciprocal (if risky) processes of fictional self-making, but rather as a narratorial technique that institutes an artful narrative closure. This happy, seemingly "self-less" ending foregrounds David's, and not Agnes's, authorship of their story. Appearing at first to be an act of narrative self-effacement, this rhetorical maneuver only further reinforces his singular, authorial identity. After all, David's perfunctory summary of his domestic contentment does introduce one new personal element to the story: it produces his self-representation as the paterfamilias of a hybrid professional household.

This final scene underscores the cyclical nature of the novel by locating in David the ultimate (pro)creative authority. David's home environment at the novel's close features a top-down model of patriarchal production in which he rules his partner and his progeny fully, if also benignantly. Notably, this is an only slightly altered version of the arrangement of the Murdstones' reign at the Rookery. The scene in which Mr. Peggotty reenters the narrative, in chapter 63, is especially interesting for the representation of David as author and patriarch. Though the narrator begins the chapter asserting purely narrative motives for writing this final scene (the last chapter is merely reflection, rather than action), explaining that "there is yet an incident conspicuous in my memory . . . without which one thread in the web I have spun would have a ravelled end" (*DC*, 844), this chapter also provides the reader's only glimpse of the home life of David and Agnes. In this scene, then, David-as-narrator foregrounds his authorial consistency and autobiographical conscientiousness as well as his position of domestic authority. The commands he gives, "Let [the visitor] come in here!" and "Let these dear rogues go to bed" (*DC*, 845), establish his as the voice that manages the living spaces and the movements of household members. Though the children cheerfully play at hiding and running, their father's commands gently bring their childish chaos under firm, if affectionate, control: they disappear from the room and from the discourse immediately.

Yet this happy ending that so closely resembles an idealized version of David's beginnings cannot help but evoke the anxiety of stasis. As John Stuart Mill makes clear in *On Liberty* when he critiques the supposed stagnation of Chinese culture, an absence of progressive development implied to the Victorians all sorts of potential losses of value—from the imperial to the personal. Stasis raises the specter of illegitimate and explicitly "foreign" intervention as the only remaining remedy for those who do not develop themselves.[13] Despite the fear of unprogressive sameness, however, the belief that one could surpass one's parents in economic as well as social standing was still relatively new and often troubling to Victorians. And, as David's early "fall" from the Rookery to Murdstone and Grinby's warehouse makes clear, at the other end of the scale from social improvement is the equally possible reality of the loss of social standing. For this reason it is no wonder that the Victorian self sought refuge in contradictory ideals of essence and practices of fictionality. After all, even security itself becomes sameness and stagnation, as Mill implies, and the alternatives—that is, personal development and social mobility—always come attended by the threat of downward, as well as the promise of upward, movement.

David's one-line description of his married life with Agnes, in its very brevity, strives for security yet evokes the threat of stasis: such marital perfection looks a lot like an absence of progressive development. This lack of narrative material for his autobiography—the very need to tie up its loose ends and complete it—contains its own haunting suggestion that the author's originality (in its many senses) has its limits. In *David Copperfield*, domestic bliss and upward mobility represent not just tempting Victorian ideals but also a threatening kind of static stability that, for the figure of the "original" author and his reclaimed status as gentleman, is attended by the familiar specter of illegitimacy. David Copperfield's attempt to control his self-production, which concludes with the glorification of a conventional domestic situation and a carefully absent, though novel, professional status, at once evokes the possibilities of Victorian selfhood as a mutual fiction and endeavors to reestablish the expected domestic, authorial, and gendered realities that David has privileged throughout his text. In other words, David's fictional self remains redolent with the tensions of the Victorian world, its essentialist ideals and its constructivist practices.

In *Villette*, there is a similar cyclicality of plot that also suggests a fear of downward social mobility and personal stagnation. Lucy's trouble is her initial fall from gentility through the unspoken loss of her family and her inability to regain the traditional position of domestic bourgeois womanhood. As with David, the particular melding of the seemingly separate spheres of domesticity and labor dictates the dynamics of Lucy's self-construction. But her textual struggles to represent herself both as consistent over time and as progressively developing leave Lucy's doubled autobiographical personae in a state of limbo between past and present, home and work, existentially being and fictionally becoming. Whether to attempt the isolating (and fractured) individualism of David, or to embrace the sociability of identity of Jane and Esther, remains undecided in *Villette*. This ambivalence is recorded not only through Lucy's exposure of her fictional self-making and autobiographical self-authorization but also through her unresolved position in the domestic and professional spheres, which, increasingly, cannot be easily distinguished from one another. Lucy's resistant narration and perpetual homelessness construct a fraught relationship of mutual meaning-making between her text and her reader. Her narrative ultimately exaggerates the readers' role in determining her reality to such an extent that they may more readily recognize the animating entanglements that create all fictional selves.

"I Must Hurry Home": Lucy Snowe's Perpetually Postponed Homecoming as Fictional Provocation in *Villette*

Lucy remarks in a passage in volume 3 that she "must hurry home" (*V*, 543) from the festival in the park of Villette, but the home to which she refers is her stark bed in the dormitories of the *pensionnat de demoiselles* in the Rue Fossette. There, she is both inmate and instructor. Even though she arrives at her destination that evening, she does not then, nor ever, reach her *home*. The only place she consents to treat as truly homelike is not a space, per se, but a relationship. Only when she is at last embraced by her beloved and tempestuous Monsieur Paul Emmanuel does she tell the reader that she has been brought "home" (*V*, 567). This homecoming is short-lived, however, and her ambiguous ending—her refusal to confirm or deny M. Paul's death at sea—perpetually puts off the one partnership that she (and the reader) perceives as a truly mutual one, with the potential to provide the reciprocity she has yearned for throughout her life and/as narrative.

Homelessness for Lucy is an emotional state as well as a socioeconomic problem. If the domestic sphere is an analogue in Victorian literature for the sanctity of the idealized inner self in a chaotic social world (as I argue in chapter 3), then Lucy's exclusion from an exclusively domestic home life has serious repercussions for her identity.[14] Lucy's lack of a home signals her lack of a defined and stable place in the Victorian social structure and, further, signifies her lack of belonging among others: she has no community with whom she can reciprocally create her fictional self. Her self-making is at once freer for this fact and more subject to the whims and misconstructions of potentially hostile interpretive forces.[15] For this reason, it is more important for Lucy than for other fictional autobiographers, on the one hand, to insist upon her identity's essential self-permanence as a means of rhetorically resisting undue external influence. On the other hand, in a bid to maintain such power over the reader's imaginative construction of her inner self, Lucy's controlling narration more forcefully draws attention to the collaborative, creative dynamics of selfhood that she simultaneously resists.[16] Lucy's frequent narratorial insistence on her solitary authority demonstrates that, despite the teleological story of emotional development she attempts to invoke—consonant with the expectations of a Victorian autobiography and a Victorian ideal of self—the mutuality she seeks is never fulfilled by her relationships within her fictional world. The frustrated reader of Lucy's discourse, rather than the beloved within her story, is at last the only entity who can engage her legibly fictional selfhood in any animating way.

Lucy Snowe has commonly been read as a controlling narrator: she overtly regulates what her readers know and when.[17] But it is rare to see these moments of control analyzed as moments of invitation to the reader.[18] It is rarer still to see these narrative choices associated with Lucy's explicitly embraced role as an autobiographer.[19] These two interpretive possibilities inform how I read Lucy and her narration. Lucy participates in specifically autobiographical forms of authorial self-creation. She highlights her extraordinary powers of observation and memory, accounts for her knowledge of fictional facts, and denounces overly "fanciful" modes of telling—except, of course, when she engages in explicitly creative narration in order to obscure the facts about herself that she hesitates to surrender to her readers. Furthering her (selective) identification with the genre of autobiography, Lucy's narration draws attention to the reciprocal self-making that occurs between her two autobiographical personae: her written and her writing selves. This type of identity creation between protagonist and narrator—specific as it is to the autobiographical form—is familiar from, if also less visible in, the other fictional autobiographies examined in the foregoing chapters.

This intratextual form of "reciprocity" between Lucy's selves is not the type of exchange that proves sufficient truly to animate "Lucy Snowe" or to satisfy her audience, however. She requires a reader, and not just in the functional sense that the other narrating protagonists in this study have needed a reader: to imagine them into being across a perceived ontological boundary. Rather, Lucy's provocations of the reader, while seeming to represent gestures of control over her narrative, also invite more active readerly creation of her story world. Garrett Stewart argues that the reader in *Jane Eyre*, and even more so in *Villette*, is "able to exercise a certain editorial control over the course of the plot, the reader is made to intervene," especially in the "suspensive conclusion" to Lucy's story.[20] These readerly interventions happen despite, and in Lucy's case because of, the concurrent resistance of the narrator-protagonist. By omitting crucial moments, motives, and memories from the discourse and by making those same omissions the focus of her discursive self-fashioning, Lucy's narration prepares interpretive gaps that invite more extreme readerly engagement, at last asking her audience to decide the (undecidable) fictional

facts of her world.[21] The power of the reader becomes so inflated by the closing lines of *Villette* that, compared to that in other fictional autobiographies,
it makes the audience's role in Lucy's identity creation all the easier to accept
as an instance of the same processes they collaboratively enact in their own
acts of fictional self-making.

"I Will Permit the Reader to Picture Me" Maneuvers for Circular Self-Making

As a self-conscious autobiographer, Lucy strives to fulfill the reader's expectation of her selfhood by demonstrating both its consistency over time and
its progressive development into its fully realized potential. For Lucy, who
begins her story by losing family, security, and status, full self-realization
would include the achievement of an improved social position as an external
recognition that she has successfully developed her inner essence. By shaping
the story around these cultural and generic coordinates, her narration implicitly attempts to conform to the standards of authentic individuality laid out by
Mill and Trollope (discussed in chapter 1), in which the inward self requires
concerted cultivation through engagement with the social world to bring to
fruition one's innate essence. Lucy's project to evince both sameness with
and difference from her past self coincides with the structural doubleness of
the self in autobiographical narration, but to an almost parodic extent. Her
past and present selves reciprocally construct one another so completely that
they demonstrate her exclusively discursive nature, even as her very resistance
to other influences within and beyond her story world makes her isolation
as a real-feeling self a provocation to sympathetic extension by her readers.
Further, the marked lack of reciprocity she experiences within her diegesis is
an unresolved obstacle to the success of her narrative of self-realization in a
social world, and it draws the reader into active engagement with her identity
construction.[22]

Lucy's distance from other characters is a constant throughout her narrative, to the point that she almost seems to elide her own presence at the
beginning of her tale. Karen Chase remarks that "Lucy scarcely exists at the
novel's opening."[23] However, rather than an actual absence, Lucy is instead
a force of pure observation, becoming a minimally embodied invocation of
the stereotypically all-seeing nineteenth-century narrator. Her powers of
perception also underscore her autobiographical authority to tell the truth
of her world. Lucy's character-self is often constrained to watch the events
around her rather than live them, marking both her chronic alienation from
others and her uniquely conditioned authority to narrate. In this way, her

observant character-self permits her fastidious narrator-self to report, thereby epitomizing in the beginning of her tale her fragmented autobiographical selves, characterized by the examining eyes and the writing hand that represent her being(s). And yet, these fragmented selves are united in their joint life-writing project. By representing her consistently superior powers of sight, insight, and (narrative) order, Lucy-as-narrator attempts to construct an organic development of her younger self into the actualized writerly incarnation of herself producing the autobiographical discourse. Janice Carlisle articulates the essentialist logic underpinning the need to show one's consistency over time: "The connections between past and present selves . . . are proof of the organic growth of a distinct identity."[24] Only some level of continuity can make development appear to be a natural, rather than an artificial—or fictional—process.

The paradoxical aim to evince both consistency of the self over time and diversity from earlier versions of the self exemplifies the active tension between Victorian ideals and practices of identity in *Villette*. The Victorian ideal of selfhood requires the innate self to be the source and at the same time the product of one's lived identity, and such circularity of cause and effect becomes evident in Lucy's life story. Demonstrating the circularity of Lucy's global narrative patterning, volumes 1 and 2 trace the beginning of Graham Bretton and Paulina Home's love story and its movement toward conventionally successful closure. This does not mean that those two traditional lovers ever rob Lucy of her starring role in her own life story. Rather, it is through and between the bookend examples of genteel domestic love provided by the pair that Lucy's yearnings for, and against, mutual adoration and reciprocal self-making like that of Graham and Paulina is obliquely revealed.[25] Carlisle similarly suggests that "the events of Volume II recapitulate the events of the first three chapters," wherein Paulina figures as both Lucy's double and the usurper of her position in the Bretton family.[26] In volume 3, Lucy and M. Paul's less traditional love story rewrites the conventions of volumes 1 and 2. In her self-consciously unconventional romance, Lucy's representation of her long-withheld expression of emotion to M. Paul (and his responding "fountain" of feeling for her) in chapter 41 constructs her experience of reciprocal love to fulfill the cultural ideal of female *bildung* as the realization of her innate self. Through this relationship of mutual attraction with M. Paul, she seems to grow from the isolated yet independent teacher in Madame Beck's school into the autonomous (yet still possibly isolated) directress of her own. But Lucy's partial embrace of the fictional principles of collaboration and adaptability at the close of her story—her hybrid domesticity, and her unusual if requited romance that mixes business with passion—proves insufficient to secure her a defined place within her world, and her combative narration registers this persistent existential homelessness.

Despite her best narrative efforts, Lucy's attempt to demonstrate the progressive development of her written self of the story into the writing self of the discourse ultimately remains problematic precisely because of the marked similarity that persists between those temporally separate selves. This continuity between her character and narrator selves is problematic for two reasons. First, like character-Lucy, narrator-Lucy remains controlling and repressive. In addition to instances where she frankly refuses to tell or interpretively overdetermines through a metaphoric mode of telling, Lucy's often acerbic tone as narrator replicates the "sarcasm" and "raillery" her character-self employs to control her "rebellious" students in her role as teacher—thereby aligning her readers with the "mutineers" of the classroom (V, 89–91, 93). In this way, her self-consistency uncomfortably resembles a static, unprogressive self, which (per Mill) evokes anxieties about the need for external influence to achieve development. Second, and generically speaking, the suppression and manipulation of information that Lucy continues to practice in both story and discourse becomes troublesome because her writing takes the form of autobiography. Whereas David Copperfield's conception of himself as an author is based primarily in the conventions of fiction (about which, nonetheless, he remains rather cautious), Lucy is primarily an autobiographer, supposedly depicting herself, as Robyn Warhol claims, "as [she] really was."[27] But her continued habits of control expose the recursivity of her self-creation rather than an organic forward trajectory to an improved emotional and social state: her development and thus her self are legibly textual in nature. Lucy's narrative maneuvers, which flout the conventions of autobiography while embracing them, consistently draw attention to the absences that sustain her existence. Her narration employs fictional techniques to construct, and to expose the impossibility of, the ideal of essential identity that undergirds conventions of reference.

Lucy's fictional autobiography commences not with a description of the child she was, neither her looks nor her temperament nor her experience, but rather with a succinct history of her godmother, Louisa Bretton of Bretton, and her family. The only information immediately available about the narrator-protagonist is why she is fond of staying at her godmother's house: "The house and its inmates pleased me well. The large peaceful rooms, the well-arranged furniture, the clear wide windows, the balcony outside, looking down on a fine antique street, where Sundays and holidays seemed always to abide—so quiet was its atmosphere, so clean its pavement—these things pleased me well" (*V*, 3). *Peaceful, well-arranged, quiet, clean*: these are the words Lucy uses to laud the atmosphere of the house of Bretton and the town of Bretton. Initially, readers associate Lucy's preferences, and her character, with the calm, comfortable space of the bourgeois home. Even the street on which the Bretton house sits seems always to exhibit an air of "Sundays and holidays," scorning the bustle of public commerce. By opening her life story with an image of this exclusive domesticity, Lucy-as-narrator acquaints readers with the ideal that her character-self will strive to regain, in fits and spurts, resisting her own urges all the way, throughout the first two volumes.

Drawing together the complementary traits of her written self and her writing self, Lucy's early narration highlights her observation at the story level and her knack for description at the discourse level. Further, these moments that attempt to evince both continuity and development of her identity also tend to foreground Lucy's social isolation—her implicit need for the kind of reciprocity she aims to create between her layered selves. When little Paulina Home arrives in Bretton, desolate at the separation from her father, she seats herself away from Mrs. Bretton and Lucy, who is told to take no notice of her. "But I did take notice: I watched Polly rest her small elbow on her small knee, her head on her hand; I observed her draw a square-inch or two of pocket handkerchief from the doll-pocket of her doll-skirt, and then I heard her weep" (*V*, 7). In this moment, Lucy's act of observation is also an act of vicarious feeling. As the little girl weeps, despite the narrator's attempt to distance herself from this quaint child through the repeating modifier *doll*, Lucy's attention highlights the loss of family that she herself, as both narrator and character, refuses to express but must experience.

While this moment foreshadows Lucy's own grief and hints at submerged emotions, it also bolsters her authority in another way. Both Lucy-as-character and Lucy-as-narrator display those traits upon which their separate yet dependent selfhoods are founded. This combination of privileged, even transgressive, surveillance (sometimes not unlike the kind Madame Beck performs later in the novel) and written accounts of what is seen, notable for their detail as well as their poetic language, occurs no fewer than nine times in the first three chapters. Each of these occurrences of the observation motif distinguishes the protagonist's withdrawn role with phrases such as "I observed," "I perceived," and "I witnessed" (*V*, 7, 9, 12). In none of these events—usually involving the deep emotional bonds of the other characters—does Lucy participate except by vivifying them through her retrospective telling. The production of the discourse is Lucy's way of gaining intimate access to these turbulent but tender interactions among people. Through her acts of observation and narration, she can be protected from *and* participate in the implications of these scenes—much like the reader of a fictional autobiography, in fact.

Lucy's time in Bretton, and her later temporary residence in the remade Bretton household outside Villette, are the only epochs of her narrated life in which she exists in exclusively domestic territory. In both cases, however, she is no more than a visitor. Her position as a chronic if warmly welcomed outsider characterizes her persistent homelessness and the identity problems that accompany such a lack of status for the downwardly mobile Victorian woman. The instability of identity that her homelessness creates on the level of the story is met with attempts to control her reader's interpretation of "who she really is" through what she includes and markedly leaves out of the discourse.

Lucy's first textual separation from the Brettons and the loss of her remaining kin are effected in three brief paragraphs that are more remarkable for how Lucy avoids revelation than for what she reveals. After "quitting Bretton," Lucy ventures to speculate on what readers' expectations of her life will be (*V*, 37). Specifically, she charges readers with constructing in their minds a conventional upbringing for her:

> It will be conjectured that I was of course glad to return to the bosom of my kindred. Well! the amiable conjecture does no harm, and may therefore be safely left uncontradicted. Far from saying nay, indeed, I will permit the reader to picture me, for the next eight years, as a bark slumbering through halcyon weather, in a harbour still as glass. . . . A great many women and girls are supposed to pass their lives something in that fashion; why not I with the rest? (*V*, 37–38)

Lucy's challenge to the reader is thinly veiled and recalls Jane Eyre's rebuffs to unsatisfactory readerly interpretation. As with Jane Eyre, such antagonism vividly marks out Lucy as a singular individual. She is *not* like "a great many women and girls," safe in their domestic harbors; both her precarious personal situation and her demonstrated authorial abilities set her apart. In resisting the readers, Lucy implies that it is not up to her audience to determine her fate. Her story, she suggests, will go forward in its determined way with or without their imaginative, and mistakenly conventional, contributions. Yet Lucy has no intention of refraining from contradicting her naïve (if also necessary) readers. She continues her extended metaphor, commenting that "it cannot be concealed that, in that case, I must somehow have fallen overboard, or that there must have been a wreck at last" (*V*, 38). Highlighting the (fictionally) referential nature of her story and her role as a selective autobiographer, her phrase "it cannot be concealed," though facetious in tone, implies that she will not omit anything she judges appropriate to her topic. While Lucy seems to conform to the basic autobiographical imperative to report a meaningful change in her personal circumstances, she leaves out the significant contextual elements that would allow readers to understand this turn of events. None of the causes of the tragedy are specified, only oblique outcomes. But even the ambiguous telling through omission enhances the reader's imaginative construction of "Lucy Snowe": her deep distress is signaled by the very absence of details, hinting at her unspeakable interiority.

Lucy's selectivity as an autobiographer is marked by a reluctance to confess her own secrets while being ready enough to discuss the less personal details of her world that might surprise or displease the reader. Indeed, she is most eager to supply such (fictional) facts when they will explode a conventional understanding of reality. In the episode in which Lucy-as-character receives her unsought promotion to English teacher at Madame Beck's school, Lucy-as-narrator declares of her rebellious students, "Then first did I rightly begin to see the wide difference that lies between the novelist's and the poet's ideal 'jeune fille,' and the 'jeune fille' as she really is" (*V*, 89). This claim to know and fearlessly to tell the truth about the *jeune fille* furthers her project to authorize her writerly identity by explicitly calling to mind what readers expect from a legitimate autobiographical undertaking: accurate, firsthand telling. While undermining clichés about the angelic nature of the young bourgeoise—a role from which Lucy's gapped misfortunes have excluded her—is a different thing than giving readers complete access to the most intimate elements of her life story, both are acts of narratorial control. Lucy's replacement of fictional fact with creative metaphor in the passage about her loss of family both fulfills and resists autobiographical conventions, privileging a method that is imaginative and opaque rather than empirical and expressive. Such reader provocations regarding her personal identity taunt the audience with what they wish to know but, thanks to her telling, cannot know, and reinforce Lucy's role as both a selective autobiographer and an imaginative author.[28]

Lucy's text, as with many fictional autobiographies, but more markedly, exhibits opposing urges: to conceal and to reveal, to express and to suppress, to show development and to demonstrate the permanence of her self-defining creative passions. This last desire, to evince both change and continuity between her selves, illuminates Lucy's narrative struggle to form a progressive writerly identity that, by definition, must both advance and return. Lucy's character-self is frequently distinguished for her self-control and her ability to control (or at least manage) others; Lucy-as-narrator similarly exercises interpretive mastery over her readers. As seen in the foregoing examples, Lucy-as-narrator frequently corrects her readers, and she temporarily withholds and permanently censors information on a regular basis. She even orders the reader to revise her discourse, staging a controlled collaboration that foregrounds her struggle for both continuity and development. In chapter 6 she narrates an extended flight of fancy that her character-self experiences aboard the *Vivid*, eagerly anticipating a new life in Europe, over which continent she imagines seeing an "arch of hope" (*V*, 55). The passage poetically demonstrates the "natural" creative capacities she usually takes pains to disavow. Yet despite having included these musings in the discourse, Lucy-as-narrator nonetheless rejects them once written. The retention of the passage juxtaposes her selves' conflicting perspectives, thus constructing in the space of the page both her imaginative propensities and her development of a wiser, narratorial point of view. Her mode of censorship here is also one of her more extreme reader inclusions. She directs readers first to cross out the poetic passage and then, instead, to add an alternative interpretation to the discourse, which is positioned on a separate line in the printed text of the novel:

> Cancel the whole of that, if you please, reader—or rather let it stand, and draw thence a moral—an alliterative, text-hand copy—
>
> *Day-dreams are delusions of the demon.* (*V*, 55, original emphasis)

Lucy-as-narrator marshals readers' participation by forcing them to become her coauthors (or at least her imagined amanuenses) in an almost literal manner. The fact that she already supplies the requested "text-hand" revision within the printed page stages the dual and contrary urges to include and to preclude the reader's participation in her narrative.

A slightly less extreme "collaboration" between narrator-Lucy and the audience takes place in chapter 14, when she mocks the "polite tact of the reader," asking him "to please leave out of the account a brief, secret conversation" she reports between Madame Beck and another teacher, which exposes the hypocrisy of Madame Beck's "disinterested" façade regarding her birthday celebrations (*V*, 147). Whether the reader reads this passage with more relish, or feels galled by being made privy to what Lucy could only know through eavesdropping, depends on the reader. Despite Lucy-as-narrator's sardonic invitation, leaving the dialogue out of an already printed book is impossible;

this moment of reader-provocation reminds the audience of Lucy's authority even as it directly contributes to how "Lucy" takes shape in the audience's construction of her.

More common in *Villette* than such blatant reader inclusions, though with similar repercussions for Lucy's contradictory self-making, are the gaps for which this novel is so well known. In one of the most notable instances of a temporary gap, Lucy-as-narrator unveils an important resemblance between her past and her present personae by repeating at the discourse level a suppression of information also practiced on the story level. Whatever progression toward social mutuality her character-self might achieve, these repeated narratorial suppressions indicate that Lucy-as-narrator is still repressive, and the depicted progress of the self is less literal and more literary. In chapter 10, Lucy recognizes Dr. John, the physician who attends Madame Beck's children, as her godmother's son and childhood acquaintance, John Graham Bretton. When Lucy-as-character first realizes there is something even more familiar about him than their brief meeting on her first night in Villette would explain, her narrator-self is careful to report her actions very distinctly, and even some of her perceptions, but none of her conceptions. In this selective reporting, Lucy-as-narrator walks a fine line to maintain both her text's autobiographical conventions and its limited communicativeness. Looking on Dr. John, she says that "an idea, new, sudden, and startling riveted my attention with an overmastering strength and power of attraction" (*V*, 111–12). Disturbed by this gaze, Dr. John asks with a "shade of annoyance" why she stares, to which the protagonist does not respond; the narrator remarks, "I might have cleared myself on the spot, but would not" (*V*, 112). Once the secret is finally revealed—to readers and to the Brettons alike in chapter 16— her assertion that she could "clear" herself begets a double meaning. Not only could she be absolved of any rudeness through this revelation but also she could make "herself" clear to Dr. John by disclosing her identity. But she wills it otherwise: indeed, she is "rather soothed than irritated" by his possible "misconstruction" of her (*V*, 112). When the disclosure must come, she justifies the delay at the story level by citing her "habits of thought," saying that she likes to have privileged knowledge of the man she admires while he continues to be unable to "see through" the "cloud" with which her unobtrusiveness covers her, blind as he is (her story implies) to the truth of her inner passions (*V*, 203).

No corresponding motive is expressly given for the delayed revelation at the discourse level, but it is evident that Lucy-as-narrator understands the literary effect—increased readerly interest—that results from such blatant withholding of information. Indeed, the reader's experience of piqued curiosity and delayed satisfaction parallels Dr. John's. Through this parallel, Lucy-as-narrator seems to court the reader, likewise, to "misconstrue" her: will her reader, like Dr. John, be so imperceptive as to fail to recognize the "real" Lucy Snowe?[29] These withholdings thus also function as assertions of her personal autonomy, playing into the ideal of essential selfhood by triggering readers' desire to know precisely what she is concealing about her story and herself. But this episode is also prime evidence that what "suits" Lucy has not altered from her younger years, and in fact, her control is doubly inscribed in her literary remaking of her life. She has not changed, and thus even as her narration tries to indicate the permanence of an inner essence, she must fail to fulfill the concomitant expectation of development. Given such a conceptual bind, "successful" self-making for Lucy is displaced onto her readers, who must practice the cognitive dissonance of using fictional means to construct an openly textual self that also answers to Victorian ideals. Ivan Kreilkamp identifies such moments of withholding as "[opening] up a new space of interiority" through which narrators like Jane Eyre and Lucy Snowe connect with a "mass readership," "[constructing] an authorial identity through writing." Through this lens, Lucy-as-narrator's actions of interpretive control are positively related to her project of establishing a seemingly autonomous writerly identity, even as they privilege her readers (both imagined and actual) as her recognized—and authoritatively managed—cocreators. As Kreilkamp puts it, Lucy's tendency to avoid disclosure in fact "acquires value by refusing to narrate. . . . She resolves difficulties not by talking her way out of a jam but simply by shutting up."[30]

Despite her methodical censorship at the discourse level—her tendency to "shut up" rather than to share—there is nonetheless an important enacted release of emotion at the story level. This outward expression of Lucy's deepest domestic desires, in turn, catalyzes a romantic denouement in her modified marriage plot and models the kind of reciprocity Lucy seeks with others, particularly with her readers. M. Paul—her sometime-antagonist, unconventional lover, and eventual business partner—serves as a stand-in for the perceptive reader throughout much of the text. His privileged recognition of Lucy's inner potential motivates the audience to follow his lead (and her narratorial guidance) to animate her identity as the developed writerly persona her discourse strives to create. M. Paul's vehement assertion to Lucy "I know you! I know you!" (*V*, 177) is the exemplary utterance of his role as a model reader of her artistic interiority: it tempts the audience to imagine and thus to create this "knowledge" of her identity they wish to share. By serving as her reason to express the inner depths she guards so zealously, her reciprocal relationship with M. Paul allows Lucy-as-narrator to stage development into an improved personal and social state, and (discursively at least) to escape the threat of stasis.

Lucy-as-character's refusal to control her passion for M. Paul comes only upon his imminent departure from Villette. As he turns to leave her, Lucy-as-character cries out to him that her "heart will break," in an episode of feeling that "defied suppression" (*V*, 557). In expressing that which her narrator-self has shown to be ever present but restrained, Lucy-as-character's outburst elicits a corresponding gush from M. Paul, which reciprocally begets even more feeling: "The seal of another fountain yielded under the strain: one breath from M. Paul, the whisper, 'Trust me!' lifted a load, opened an outlet. With many a deep sob, with thrilling, with icy shiver, with strong trembling, and yet with relief—I wept" (*V*, 557). This moment is a release not only for Lucy's written self but also for the reader, her constant companion and potential sympathizer. The long-sought and hard-won satisfaction of this moment enhances the reader's emotional investment in Lucy's story and smooths the interpretive difficulties her narration presents.

Significantly, however, including in her discourse this moment of irrepressible desire is just as much an act of interpretive control (for the narrator) as it is a gesture of release (for the protagonist). As aware readers of fiction, the audience may recognize that Lucy's represented liberty from internal control merely relinquishes that function to the narrator, who in turn forms this episode into a scene of developmental culmination. Only by showing her written self finally "letting go" can Lucy construct through her narration the progressively developing self that will fulfill her genre requirements as an autobiographer. In this gesture, both at the level of the story and at the level of the discourse, Lucy fashions her passionate character-self as well as her authorial writing-self, managing in her dual roles to achieve what might feel like autobiographical authenticity through the imaginative participation of her readers.

"I Betook Myself Home": The Reader and Reciprocity

Villette's denouement progresses from the moment of Lucy's performed self-actualization, leading her to a (temporary) homecoming. Though the new dwelling M. Paul gives her is not the conventional scene of bourgeois domestic bliss and procreation, it is a place of increased independence and hybrid domesticity. M. Paul, in the "proved reality" of his "silent, strong effective goodness," brings Lucy to a "neat abode" where "silence reign[s]," recalling

Lucy's initial description of Bretton (*V*, 563, 561). After he shows her a small schoolroom and hands her a card naming her the "directrice" of the present "externat de demoiselles," it becomes clear that her long-standing plan for liberation from Madame Beck's establishment has finally come true, although it is a romantic attachment rather than the anticipated solitary struggle that wins her this "advance in life" (*V*, 418–19). While M. Paul's devotion seems to promise a welcome deviation from the lonely future Lucy had expected, and dreaded, her situation nonetheless departs from both a conventionally secure domestic settlement and the solidly independent destiny of individual "labour" that was to "prove" to Lucy her "right to look higher" for emotional satisfaction in life (*V*, 419). She is neither able to "lay down the whole burden of human egotism" by becoming M. Paul's wife nor to claim to be wholly self-sufficient (*V*, 419). The hybridity of her situation keeps her in limbo between the sphere of the domestic-romantic and that of the professional-independent.

But Lucy's desire to develop her own identity through communion with someone "dearer to me than myself" (*V*, 419) seems at least temporarily within her grasp, and the language character-Lucy employs and narrator-Lucy reports throughout this scene emphasizes this possibility. M. Paul's directions to Lucy are to "live here and have a school," and to "employ yourself while I am away," and she assures him, "I will be your faithful steward. . . . I trust at your coming the account will be ready" (*V*, 564). In their exchange, while M. Paul's language of business encodes an expression of his love for her, Lucy's messianic treatment of her lover performs an apotheosis of her beloved benefactor. In this moment of mutual felicity, Lucy shows her audience what could have been, through this rhetorical assignation and acceptance of roles, brought about by joint recognition and emotional reciprocity. Just as Esther and Woodcourt promise to become their own best selves through the love of the other, and just as Paulina and Graham both interpret and develop one another to best advantage (*V*, 491–92), so too Lucy and M. Paul gladly accept each other's imagined expectations to direct the actions and identities of their projected future selves.

Lucy-as-narrator characterizes her feelings and actions toward M. Paul in language that is at once typical of idealized domestic connections between husband and wife and oddly worshipful of his supposed godliness, saying, "I pressed [his hand] close, I paid it tribute. He was my king" (*V*, 564). In these juxtaposed passages, the hybridized working and living space parallels the divine yet commercial gloss given to the aspiring domestic relation between the new directress and her "benefactor-guest" (*V*, 564): the space reflects their personal dynamic. In this fusion of employment and homemaking, business, religion, and passion, Lucy's repressed yearning to regain a place among the classes of exclusive female domesticity is not fulfilled but is redirected into an alternative mode of satisfaction that is no less reciprocal in its dynamics. Her evening with M. Paul, in which she "[accepts her] part as hostess," and the touches of domestic comfort she lingers over (such as her "gold and white china service"), must be sufficient for her (*V*, 565). In his new role as Lucy's explicit personal savior, M. Paul thus "saves" her from a purely commercial life. Although she does not achieve this independence alone, she is the sole administrator of its success or failure; though she reaches no permanent domesticity, in her peaceful new house the balance of the space's purpose has shifted. No longer does she reside where she works, but, finally, she works in her home.

Overwhelmed by this unexpected and unconventional offering, Lucy-as-character feverishly narrates all of her fears to M. Paul. Highlighting the sensually affective experience of narration to a sympathetic ear, she writes, "I spoke. All escaped from my lips. I lacked not words now; fast I narrated; fluent I told my tale; it streamed on my tongue" (*V*, 567). As he "[incites her] to proceed" with her revelations of passion and doubt, she says, "I was full of faults; he took them and me all home" in an embrace (*V*, 568). At last, despite her circular progress, Lucy-as-narrator creates with this description a metaphorical homecoming that is based not on her environment but on the intersection of two kindred beings. Chase, reflecting the Victorian interest in and ambivalence about communal identity creation, says this sort of interdependence cannot be maintained, however: "It is not final; [instead] it makes possible a further return to self and self-sufficiency."[31] Replicating her earlier challenges to the contributing reader, Lucy proves that this zenith of personal development—toward love, openness, and the sharing of self-making—cannot last. Lucy's "king" is rapidly displaced in the story, traveling to Guadaloupe for three years. According to Lucy, he continues to serve as her symbolic inspiration to pursue a "persevering, a laborious, an enterprising, a patient, and a brave course" (*V*, 571). She even asserts that "the secret of my success did not lie so much in myself" (*V*, 571) as in him. This statement gestures at the Edenic moments of reciprocity she shared with M. Paul before his departure, and yet the very act of writing it in his (potentially ongoing) absence suggests that Lucy-as-narrator—within the fictional world, and contrary to her expressed wishes—continues to be her own solitary producer. As with David's attribution of his success to Agnes, the apparent "selflessness" of Lucy's declaration functions more as a narrative device of authority than a relinquishment of it. Although her "new state of circumstances, a wonderfully changed life, a relieved heart" (*V*, 571) seem to offer a temporary sense of narrative closure as the result of the mutuality she anticipates from M. Paul's return, the perpetual postponement of his fate is likewise a perpetual deferral of Lucy's fictional self-realization.

For three years her partner is removed from a sphere of direct influence over her life except as her imagination actively involves him through letters, memory, and hopes for their future. In his absence, M. Paul becomes even "more my own" (*V*, 572), she writes: he is most real to her when he is gone precisely because her communion with him during these years is primarily experienced in her imagination. Through five paragraphs she highlights the preparations she makes for his return, repeating the refrain "—but he is coming" as the motivation that determines her actions and perceptions of the world (*V*, 572–73). The repeated phrase marks at once his literal absence and the resulting imaginative potential of such a partnership for Lucy. But her hopes for domesticity and reciprocity are not to be fulfilled in the flesh. M. Paul's more permanent removal from the story is effected through the same metaphoric language and self-conscious narrative artistry earlier used to communicate the loss of her family without expressly revealing the same. The circularity of Lucy's life story manifests itself in the recurrence of sorrow, her precise representation of it, and her continued solitary existence as a laborer in the home.

Revisiting the stormy sea images she first described in the passage on the loss of her family, Lucy tells of a great storm that strikes M. Paul's homebound ship.[32] Significantly, Lucy chooses to narrate both her anticipation of M. Paul's return and the "frenzied" tempest in the present tense, temporarily conflating her past experience with the present moment of the telling through her grammar. Dorrit Cohn posits that a passage such as this "creates the illusion of a fiction that 'tells itself.'"[33] Bringing the past into the present in this manner, Cohn suggests, provides a feeling of emotional immediacy, obscuring the retrospective selection and shaping that characterize the act of narrating a fictional autobiography. However, as witnessed in the narratives of Jane, David, and even Esther,[34] the proximate return to a grammatically marked retrospection (in Lucy's telling, with the paragraph beginning "That storm roared . . ." [*V*, 573]) calls attention to the act of narrative crafting rather than obscuring it. Shifting between tenses, and between temporally distant "presents," illuminates the gap between the events and their telling and demonstrates the extent to which this foundational gap of narrative form—the distinction between story and discourse—causes the impression of emotional immediacy. The potency of this emotionally fraught passage, and the complicated fictional self from whom it seems to issue and whom it characterizes, is thus shown to be the result of a carefully wrought narrative.

The force of this passage, significantly, is not dimmed by the overtly fictional methods that it illuminates and from which its power derives. Narrating in the present tense as if she were (re)living the dreadful moments of suspense awaiting M. Paul's return, Lucy declares, "The wind shifts to the west. Peace, peace, Banshee—'keening' at every window! It will rise—it will swell—it shrieks out long: wander as I may through the house this night, I cannot lull the blast. . . . That storm roared frenzied for seven days. It did not cease till the Atlantic was strewn with wrecks" (*V*, 573). As she did with her description of the weeping Polly in the first chapters, Lucy imagines and describes the sorrows of others as a veiled method of expressing her own; she at once sympathizes with others through creative narration and attempts to avoid readerly pity. She writes, "Oh! A thousand weepers, praying in agony on waiting shores, listened for that voice, but it was not uttered—not uttered still, when the hush came" (*V*, 573). But she does not complete her description of the storm's consequences, not even in poetically descriptive terms: "Here pause, pause at once. There is enough said. Trouble no quiet, kind heart; leave sunny imaginations hope. . . . Let them picture union and a happy succeeding life" (*V*, 573). Her continually uncommunicative narration, in saying she has said enough, rather tells her audience only that there is *not* enough said to determine M. Paul's fate.[35]

Stewart writes of M. Paul that "his fate is actually left up to you as a narrative event itself in the first place, a death yours to activate, to believe in, if you so choose." What Stewart does not say, however, is that for all of Lucy's "lures of rhetoric" that, he claims, leave the audience "no real choice" in the matter,[36] readers do indeed have a choice to make, though it is not about whether M. Paul is at last dead or alive. We may try to imagine M. Paul now dead and now alive, and we may conjecture how Lucy's life and narrative might be in each case (extending, of course, her potential identities through these mental mini-narratives). However, the two options open to the reader seem equally impossible due to their absence from the discourse and their mutual exclusivity. It is a narrative bind for readers. The choice we have is to try to fill the gap (necessarily unsuccessfully) or (and) to realize it is a gap never to be fully filled despite our ongoing imaginative additions. In this way, in her final act of withholding, Lucy-as-narrator exercises the ultimate control over her narrative world by allowing M. Paul both to live and to die at once, trapping both her lover and her audience in a state of interpretive limbo. This final narratorial gesture epitomizes the ambivalence with which Lucy Snowe has engaged with and resisted her own fictionality, and her readers' participation, throughout the novel.

However, it is also this final gap that most overtly insists on the reader's intimate entanglement with the realities of the fictional world, and on the way that fictional processes construct the sense of "reality." While the marked absences and reader inclusions that are distinctive of the subgenre of fictional autobiography usually register an attempt to engage readers in imagining the inner depths of the fictional characters, Lucy's narration goes one step further. In demanding that readers try unsuccessfully to fill in the major fictional realities of the protagonist's world, Lucy enshrines her audience as the cocreators not just of her discourse (recalling her "revision" in chapter 6, where she tells readers to cancel the poetic passage), and not just of her personal identity, but also of the foundational events of the story world. The implications of this exaggerated appeal to the reader's power are extreme: if the facts of the diegetic world can be made to feel potent and immediate—that is, real— through imagination's overt intervention, how much more reliant upon such fictional processes must be those "realities" that are already acknowledged to be subjective and social, such as the self?

Lucy's insistence on her personal difference from readers' expectations, her refusal to write her own tragedy, and her unresolved emotional turmoil— made vivid by its very concealment—literally and literarily realize "Lucy": the reader's imaginative response to these tropes makes her identity into an experiential reality. Lucy's narration foregrounds the readers' outsized role in determining the (eternally indeterminate) realities of her world and, in the process, makes their role in animating Lucy's self seem at once more logical and potentially—by comparison—less threatening. Through the provoking conclusion, Lucy goads readers to sense her influence on them (whether affective, cognitive, or both) even as she stages through the permanent gap their creative construction of her. In the final lines of *Villette*, then, the circle of fictional reciprocity is temporarily complete, though never closed. Every rereading becomes another self-making interaction, constantly expanding and changing the selves involved. *Villette* demonstrates that neither Brontë, nor "Lucy," nor the readers are the source of the sensation readers have of the narrating protagonist's reality; it is rather a joint, if also a fraught, venture among them. Fictional self-making, thus, is no utopian solution to the identity crises of modernity: Lucy remains "homeless" after all, by her society's standards of idealized identity and conventional domesticity. But in staging selves as fictional processes, the fictional autobiography exposes such ideals as unnecessarily limiting while proposing a narrative, imaginative, and social method for their perpetual revision. In confronting our collaborative and contended role in vivifying Lucy's provocatively fictional identity, we come face to face with the possibilities of our own fictional selves.

Coda

Fiction and Selfhood in the Twenty-First Century

THE SUBGENRE OF THE FICTIONAL autobiography is not an exclusively Victorian form. But in the nineteenth century, once fictionality and referentiality were implicitly understood as distinctive modes of literary truth-telling and "autobiography" was a recognizable genre with attendant conventions and expectations, the marked phenomenology of reading characteristic of the fictional autobiography became possible. In the Victorian period most especially, these texts illuminate and mediate conflicting cultural urges: the fictional autobiography adheres to the rhetoric of essential selfhood while overtly engaging the reader in the fictional practices of self-making. In the preceding chapters, I have argued that these conflicting urges stem, at least in part, from the momentous changes underway during the Victorian period. The extensive modifications in the lived experience of people's daily realities made fictional identity practices both more legible and more productive in this period, and they simultaneously made the ideal of an essential self—some ontologically stable ground, ultimately unknowable though it may be—a persistently seductive belief.

Despite the profound changes that took place during and after the Victorian moment, the cultural belief in a core self has followed us into the twenty-first century with very little alteration. The evidence of an ongoing attachment to the ideal of an essential self as the basis for human identity is everywhere; the rhetoric of this ideal saturates cultural texts of all kinds, from literary works to daily conversations to advertising campaigns. Consider a 2016 episode of the popular podcast *Invisibilia*, hosted by Alix Spiegel and Lulu Miller. In the episode entitled "The Personality Myth," the hosts explore the belief in essential selfhood that continues to guide some of the most significant social interactions one can experience and to play a role in one's personal decisions. After interviewing several recently married couples, Spiegel sums up their predominant assumptions about identity this way: "These people had searched the world and finally found a person—an entity with a very specific set of characteristics that resided deep within them and made them who they were. And they were pretty sure that their loved one's essential them-ness—their personality—would endure."[1] Although the terminology has shifted somewhat, the idea is largely the same: Americans in the twenty-first century still seem to believe that people are "who they are" thanks to a "deep" inward something that is "essential" and permanent.

Why does a core self, with all its attendant social problems and personal anxieties, continue to characterize our ideals of identity? The answer might reside not just in a cultural persistence of certain Victorian values and attitudes but also in a recurrence of similar lived conditions of change. As many scholars have recently pointed out, in the catastrophic political rhetoric and in the revolutions taking place in communication technologies, the first decades of the twenty-first century closely resemble—at least in the scale and the focus of the changes—the transformative conditions of the Victorian period.[2] For this reason it may be unsurprising that many American and British cultural texts exhibit an ongoing fixation with essential selves in this brave new digital world. After fleshing out the claim of similarity between these two different moments in time and culture, the rest of this coda will explore one key question that this hypothesis raises: If the classical fictional autobiography in the Victorian period mediated the rigors of constant change with the desire for stability, all while illuminating the productivity of selves that are narrative, imagined, and social in nature, how do the literary trends of today adapt the form of the fictional autobiography to address similar paradoxes of lived experience?

To augment the historical context offered in the introduction of this book, the following paragraphs give a broad-strokes account of just some of the changes that reshaped the lives of British Victorians in the first half of the nineteenth century, highlighting the parallels between then and now. People and their daily patterns of life began to move much more quickly in the early Victorian period, both literally and metaphorically. In just fifteen short years between 1835 and 1850, Eric Hobsbawm notes, the railway system "transformed the speed of movement—indeed of human life—from one measured in single miles per hour to one measured in scores of miles per hour," simultaneously regularizing timekeeping across the nation.[3] The commercial growth and personal mobility that the railways enabled "revealed the possibilities of technical progress as nothing else had done, because [the railway system] was both more advanced than most other forms of technical activity and omnipresent."[4]

In conjunction with the exponential increase in mobility, the Victorian periodical boom, the laying of transatlantic telegraph cables in the 1850s and 1860s, and the growing standardization of postal services (particularly the penny post, beginning in 1840) transformed communications. By midcentury, personal mail and the most recent periodicals could be distributed to even the most far-flung reaches of the island nation—and even to some corners of the empire—in a time frame unheard of less than a generation before. Robin Gilmour notes the proliferation of information via newspapers and other print media, which gave the increasing number of Victorian readers access to an unprecedented quantity and breadth of information, ranging from politics to literature to science to theology.[5] The sudden accessibility of this vast range of subjects to an increasingly literate and linked society sounds eerily similar to the way in which the internet and handheld digital technologies have expanded the availability of information for many inhabitants of the globe since the 1990s, especially in countries such as the United States and the United Kingdom. The rapid advance of digital technologies has drastically altered the way we learn, conduct business, communicate, and subsist on a daily basis. The Victorians' similarly massive shift into a recognizable modernity influenced not just the major structures of society and the economy, but, as Sally Mitchell explains, even the most quotidian experiences: "The texture of daily life—the physical and technological surroundings in which people lived, the patterns of their education and work and recreation and belief—were utterly transformed."[6] Mitchell's words seem both predictive and descriptive of the present digital age: the "texture of daily life" will never be the same.

While the specific technologies of change are distinctly different, some of their effects point to an unquestionable parallel between the present moment and the Victorian period. As so many people are experiencing new iterations of the same kinds of transformation the Victorians underwent, how are the literary forms of today dealing with the questions of progress, history, the individual, and the contingency of truth that these changes make so perceptible and so pressing? To rephrase the central question of this coda: How are we negotiating our contemporary ideals and practices of identity in and through specific literary forms? A comprehensive answer to these questions would ideally consider texts from television and film (which are undergoing their own transformations), the internet, and particularly social media. But such an answer is beyond the scope of this coda, which will only skim the surface of the broader conversation this book invites; for that reason, I limit my consideration to parallels in printed and electronic books. Within these parameters, I take bestseller lists and media attention to be reasonable if partial indications of widespread interest. Looking at those resources, it is evident that there is a twofold, parallel trend in the reading preferences of the general public that indicates what might be called the ideals and practices of our current, postmodern identity crisis.

On the one hand, autobiographies and memoirs represent a much-discussed portion of the texts read by the general public. While the bestseller lists do not always register the popularity of autobiography or (more broadly) life-writing in sheer numbers, this is mainly because *Publisher's Weekly* and other publications often place autobiography in the "nonfiction" category with texts of distinctly nonliterary appeal, such as cookbooks, self-help manuals, and politically charged analyses of historical figures. Nonetheless, personal life-writing[7] has managed regularly to appear in the nonfiction top ten lists over the last decade (in Amazon.com's, *Publisher's Weekly*'s, and the *New York Times*' lists).[8] The appeal of life-writing is noticeable in both the United States and the United Kingdom; there is a brisk business in celebrity tell-alls as well as triumphant survival stories of "extraordinary subjects," people whose experiences seem to place them on the margins of the presumed normative conditions of American and British life. (As an example of the latter trend, think of Dave Eggers's novel *What Is the What*, which is marketed as "based on the life of Valentino Achak Deng," one of the "Lost Boys" of Sudan, or Malala Yousafzai's popular personal account *I Am Malala: The Girl Who Stood Up for Education and Was Shot by the Taliban*.)[9]

Millions of general readers prefer these personal texts of life-writing, sometimes (at least in my anecdotal experience) to the complete exclusion of fictional texts. As Ross Posnock declares in his review of Terry Castle's autobiographical collection *The Professor and Other Writings*, "As everyone knows by now, we are living in the Age of Memoir."[10] In both the United States and the United Kingdom, infamous incidents of "false" memoirs or "fake" autobiographies' being exposed—Oprah's live-television confrontation of James Frey about his book *A Million Little Pieces* is the most notable example of the present century, but there have been many more—demonstrate the implicit but firmly enforced standard that many audiences apply to these genres. For today's general readers, the value of life-writing depends substantially, if not entirely, on its empirical, factual accuracy. And this notion that factual accuracy can somehow bring a reader closer to the truth of a subjective individual life is bolstered by the attendant perception that a story told in the first person, a tale that comes straight from the horse's mouth, as it were, is more likely to present the "real story." The public's desire for easy access to strictly demonstrable facts as the foundation for personal truth represents an intellectual commitment that is oddly reminiscent of the early eighteenth-century epistemological position that Michael McKeon calls "naïve empiricism." This mode of knowing assumes that truth and measurable fact are entirely synonymous—that, indeed, truth without fact is nothing, it is impossible.[11] I explore this contemporary version of naïve empiricism later in the coda.

On the other hand, and adding a complicating if complementary dimension to this equation of factuality with personal truth value, certain kinds of fiction have nonetheless retained a hold on the attention of the general reader. There has been a rise recently in the number of fictional texts that have a first-person narrator, often one who tells her tale in the present tense. The blogosphere is buzzing with writers who, whether they love this kind of narration or hate it, address this trend of first-person, present-tense narration. Joseph O'Brien writes in his blog on literature, "I'm partial to present-tense narration whenever possible, since it makes me feel more immersed in the story."[12] Vicky Smith, writing for the *Young Adult* blog on the *Kirkus Reviews* website, complains that "although the present tense in the hands of a skilled author does grant a bit of immediacy to a narrative, not every new book demands it, which is sometimes how it feels."[13] Despite their divergent evaluations, both of these literary bloggers assume, and overtly value, the immediacy that first-person, present-tense narration supposedly grants to a story.

Nicola Morgan, a Scottish writer, goes so far as to suggest that, while telling stories in the past tense is a long-accepted convention of narration, "it introduces a peculiar extra level of artificiality, an extra mental hurdle to leap" for the reader. Contrary to the position I have argued throughout this study, Morgan's critique assumes that "artificiality" in fiction is not only a bad thing, but (perplexingly) an avoidable one; she implies that the reader's awareness of the constructedness of the narrative situation is not only unpleasurable but undesirable. She believes that "the cognitive processes for the reader ought to be easier," and that, therefore, "the present tense would often be a more magical way to tell the story."[14] Indeed, Morgan's assumptions align uncannily with Nicholas Paige's description of eighteenth-century aesthetic theories that insisted artifice was a necessary evil of invented literature.[15] It seems that Morgan would be happiest with writers like Daniel Defoe and Samuel Richardson, who actively sought to shield their readers from consciously recognizing the necessary imaginative crafting that undergirds the effects of their texts.

The resurgence of first-person fictions amid the continuing popularity of personal life-writing in the market can be explained by the fact that "immediacy" is the name of the game in both forms. This feature of both kinds of literary text indicates that numerous present-day readers prefer books that seem to operate under the value assumptions that inform eighteenth-century literary conventions. These assumptions are characteristic of naïve empiricism: the belief that unmediated and verifiable facts constitute "truth" and that language and narrative form are transparent media for relating that truth. Even in the context of the recent recuperation of fictional texts' popularity, today's readers tend to be resistant consumers of self-conscious fictionality. This resistance suggests that contemporary general readers may be overlooking the fundamentally fictional practices of modern selfhood in an attempt to find stable ontological ground. In the current moment of existential uncertainty, readers' appreciation for fiction's role in constructing the experience of self and reality seems to be slipping.

Consider Lee Child's contribution to the *New Yorker* in May of 2016 in which he proposes that we "uninvent" fiction. Despite being a novelist himself (an irony he acknowledges), Child places novelistic production, political misinformation, and outright lying in the category of the fictional.[16] Just as McKeon describes its development in the eighteenth century and before,[17] "fiction" in the twenty-first century no longer indicates a type of literary invention that is easily and intentionally recognizable by readers (as it was for the Victorians); rather, the word now seems once again to signal a form of malicious deception. These two types of fiction—overtly creative invention and malignant attempts to deceive—are, judging by the examples Child gives in his essay, utterly indistinguishable from one another or, curiously, not worth distinguishing. In the context of such a perspective, it seems that, much like Victorian ideals of identity, contemporary discourses of reality and selfhood remain fixated on essence. Simultaneously, and less like the Victorians', contemporary practices of identity in a rapidly changing world perform—yet simultaneously strive to ignore—the highly fictional processes that constitute our impressions of permanence and stability. In this way, the naïvely empirical stance reflected in Child's article and in the rhetoric applied to texts of personal life-writing suggest a modern-day resistance to all types of fictionality. We may be losing our grip on the significant value of metaphoric (and not just literal) connectivity between text and world, self and other.

Curiously, I am arguing (in part) that a rise in the popularity of certain fiction texts might in fact reflect a decrease in our culture's tolerance for fictional—narrative, imaginative, and social—modes of meaning-making. Although first-person, present-tense novels have been appearing (if infrequently) for decades, the increasing visibility and number of novels featuring such narration have only come to be remarkable since the turn of the present century.[18] Popular examples include *The Time Traveler's Wife*, by Audrey Niff-enegger; *Aleph*, by Paulo Coelho; the immensely popular *Hunger Games* se-ries, by Suzanne Collins; and many more-recent novels, such as *The Girl on the Train*, by Paula Hawkins, and parts of *The Nightingale*, by Kristin Hannah, and *The Widow*, by Fiona Barton (both of which feature sections of such nar-ration intercut with third-person or first-person, past-tense telling). Victorian readers preferred to see character development in history and over time, but this trend in fiction suggests a preference today for immediacy, for the illusion that the tale being read is unmediated, unshaped, and unselected.[19]

Despite the referentiality of memoir and life-writing, and the fictionality of the first-person, present-tense novel, both of these movements in literature betray a common contemporary investment in forms that provide the illusion of an unmediated connection between the life, the story, and the subjectiv-ity of the narrating protagonist, whether fictional or not. For many readers, while life-writing seems to elide the communal, imaginative processes re-quired by fiction, the first-person, present-tense novel seems to bypass the processes of selection and shaping that construct the trajectory, and the self, of the narrating protagonist in a retrospective life account. In this way, both forms cater to contemporary culture's hunger for the impression of unmedi-ated and empirically true connections. Having explored what fiction could mean for a Victorian audience in the foregoing chapters, I would now like to pursue some potential consequences of these literary trends in the newly Victorian world of today.

Life-Writing and Its Expectations in the Twenty-First Century

Nonfiction texts, and particularly autobiographies, have gained both critical and popular attention over the last few decades, occupying a privileged place in book clubs, libraries, and other forums of reading. In my own discussions about book preferences with general readers, the inclination to read texts of personal nonfiction derives in large part from the idea that memoir and autobiography—texts of personal life-writing, more broadly—promise their readers that "this really happened." To paraphrase one woman to whom I spoke about her preference for autobiographies, readers like to know how the protagonists did it: how they survived, or succeeded, or were redeemed. Since life-writing texts claim a referential relationship to the real world, many gen-eral readers gravitate toward them as blueprints or road maps for accomplish-ing something, whether that is personal fulfillment or success in business.[20] The ambiguity of truth that plagued the Victorians persists today; in our postmodern world, it is difficult to find anyone who does not acknowledge at least some level of subjectivity and contingency in lived experience. But, as the attitude of today's general reader suggests, that does not mean we like or embrace the concept. The gap between language and reality so firmly insisted upon by Victorian and postmodern philosophers alike appears to have been dissolved, or buried beneath a new kind of naïvely empirical faith in the representation of objective reality and absolute truths. In other words, we seem to cling to Victorian ideals of self without the Victorians' more overt commitment to fictional practices of identity creation.

What seems to be absent from the current popular-reading culture is the recognition, implicit or otherwise, that fiction conditions the personal experience of everyday life and that its imaginative mediations are not mystifying some essential truth that inheres in referential representation. But that is what so many readers seek: empirical and direct knowledge of another person (preferably a successful or particularly unique one), which, by dint of this information's supposed factuality, will guide the reader in her own experience of the real world. Though her work primarily examines the phenomenon in relation to reading fiction, Lisa Zunshine's explanation of "mind-reading" can also shed light on the continuing readerly insistence upon, and the general appeal of, factuality in autobiographical writings. Zunshine, building on the findings of cognitive psychology, explains "theory of mind," or what she calls mind-reading, as "our ability to explain people's behavior in terms of their thoughts, feelings, beliefs, and desires." She further specifies that "attributing states of mind [to others] is the default way by which we construct and navigate our social environment, incorrect though our attributions frequently are."[21] The appeal of life-writing as a referential genre is twofold, then. Since it refers to the "real world" of the reader, the writer's experience seems more directly applicable than that of a fictional character as a model for the reader to use to navigate that same reference world. And by seeming to provide direct access to the mental states and motivations of another person—something Zunshine suggests is a necessary, often unconscious, and generally imprecise exercise in social existence—personal life-writing seems to deliver unmediated contact with the most difficult kind of information to acquire: knowledge of the inner life of another human being. This is why factuality in texts of life-writing remains the most crucial feature of the genre to many of its dedicated fans.

One has only to read the reviews section for books on Amazon to see this hypothesis played out in the main themes that general readers seek in their reading of life-writing. A key characteristic that is often linked to a work's factuality is its motivational potential, which is maximized when the protagonist is represented as successfully "overcoming obstacles." One can see this ideal repeated throughout the reviews of Jeannette Walls's memoir, *The Glass Castle*, in which the author details a difficult childhood in West Virginia and the quirky parents who shaped her trying experiences. A British reader by the handle of "JohnBrassey" on the Amazon.co.uk site describes the memoir in just these terms, writing, "As an example of triumph in the face of adversity this is an uplifting book."[22] In the public reviews sections on Walls's work, there is also the parallel trend of "witnessing," or readers attesting to the accuracy of the memoir's events as a way to prove the authenticity, and thus the value, of its most "uplifting" elements. One reviewer (signed as "beckybramer") writes on the American Amazon site, "I grew up in Welch, WV and was acquainted with Jeannette. . . . For those of you who doubt things could not [*sic*] have happened like it was written, don't. I knew it and I saw it, and to a degree, lived it. And as tragic as it was, it was true."[23]

Another reviewer (signed "Thomas M. Seay") who claims acquaintance with the author also witnesses the genuineness of the account: "For those reviewers who expressed doubts about the authenticity of her story, I can tell you that at least the Welch part of the story rings true to my memory."[24] The fact that these reviewers felt the need to testify to the empirical facts of Walls's memoir through their own firsthand experience speaks, first, to their perception that they owe her the loyalty of friendship, a perception that (I would posit) is produced as much by their interaction with the first-person telling of her autobiography as by their long-ago connection to her hometown.[25] Second, this trend attests to the urgency with which readers of life-writing view the strictures of factuality when evaluating the worth of a text. To observe in action the fact-checking scrutiny that so many readers apply to even the minutiae of a text to determine life-writing's value (and the value of the writing self), one need only peruse these and other discussion boards on Amazon.com. In these forums, readers of Walls's memoir dispute, among other things, whether or not her life story and, implicitly, her textual identity are "true" based on her description of being on a casino floor as a child: some readers argue that it is inconsistent for her to have been there given the gaming regulations at the time.[26]

These comment threads demonstrate how many readers are profoundly uncomfortable with anything potentially nonactual, even in those texts that announce themselves to be openly and intentionally creative, such as in texts of fiction or in the autobiography of a writer, like Walls's. Many readers seem to overlook the fact that, as discussed in chapter 1, all narrative is artifice, which of course includes referential and autobiographical narratives. Attempting to represent the real world in narrative is no less artificial a process for the fact that life-writing seeks to establish a literal connection to the world also inhabited by its reader. This, however, is not an accepted truth for most general readers; it is an idea that many seem actively to avoid and contest. Rather than celebrating the affective reality of the imaginative connections one can experience when reading life-writing, most contemporary readers uncritically approach these texts as if this particular form of literature could offer them the solidity of empirical facts and objective truths—unmediated and thus untainted by context or contingency.[27]

Present reading practices seem to evince a readerly desire to connect intimately with the autobiographer, to learn through her experiences, and to identify emotionally with the teller in order to discover something "true" about the world or about the reader's own self. These desires prevent—or rather, make some readers refuse—the realization that a metaphoric connection of imagination is nonetheless what allows any of the foregoing affective and cognitive processes to take place. What so many of the most outspoken readers of autobiography seem to ignore are the necessarily imaginative processes through which such mental and emotional activities are conducted. I may read *The Glass Castle* to better understand how to come to terms with a challenging childhood and its consequences. Alternately, I could read *Jane Eyre* for the same reasons. But I am no closer to being Jeannette Walls than I am to being Jane Eyre. My identification with Jeannette is equally as imaginary as my identification with Jane. Yet many fans of life-writing do not seem to be aware of the processes of imagination that make them feel that they know, and can know themselves through, Jeannette Walls and other life-writers. To use her and her life as an appropriated model for the self is just as much an act of imaginative mediation as is an identification with Jane Eyre, with the exception that the latter more openly invites the reader to recognize the dynamics of that fictional process. In this way, the perceived guarantee of referentiality that attaches to common readerly expectations of personal life-writing hides the actual processes of metaphoric identification from which the affective value of the work derives.

I am not arguing that readers should not feel emotionally connected to the protagonists of life-writing, nor that the imaginative acts of engagement that life-writing requires are in any way false for being imaginative. Rather, what I am highlighting as problematic is the way in which readerly expectations of referentiality in life-writing often rely on and reinforce an uncritical belief in the objective universality of any narrative truth—whether empirically provable or not. These naïvely empirical assumptions about the nature of truth persist in many parts of our culture today, despite the fact that this view of the world has long been complicated by writers, artists, and philosophers. Even the Victorians knew they could not reconcile strict empirical objectivity with their distinctly subjective experiences of the world, try as they might. To revisit a Victorian preoccupation that has quietly informed this project throughout, we seem to have made surprisingly little progress in learning to recognize and value contingency as a key term in our individual and social experiences of reality. Persistently resisting the notion that all interactions with the world, and with others, are guided by creative mental narratives (to which we are just as much subject as are the people around us) will never allow us to achieve an unmediated access to a Lukácsian "totality." Refusing fictionality does not allow us to escape our postmodern state, in which the intersectional and contextually contingent nature of personal and social meaning(s) is inescapable. Instead, this uncritical approach to reading reality, and especially to the potential of fiction, prevents a more fulsome recognition of the fruitlessness of clinging to the ideal of an absolute inward self-permanence as the basis for a stable external world.

By pathologizing fictional processes as the source of instability rather than embracing them as a potential solution, contemporary subjects only become further alienated from the ability to understand and, perhaps, to affect their own fates through social acts of imagination. Indeed, as Kwame Anthony Appiah suggests in *Cosmopolitanism: Ethics in a World of Strangers*, imaginative networks are one way in which humans from different times, places, and personal circumstances attempt to relate effectively and affectively to one another. Narrative imagination—when consciously recognized and engaged—can become a proactive and prosocial tool for reconceiving the world and one's place in it. In Appiah's writing, the metaphoric work of imaginative identification with another person lays the foundation for the practice of "partial cosmopolitanism," in which "no local loyalty can ever justify forgetting that each human being has responsibilities to every other," and simultaneously in which, as Appiah quotes Cicero, "'we confer the most kindness on those with whom we are most closely associated.'"[28] The cosmopolitan person, he argues, understands that the imaginary bond between peoples is not limited to or dependent upon categorical identities and similarities. Appiah notes that "we can respond to art that is not ours [by national affiliation]. . . . My people—human beings—made the Great Wall of China, the Chrysler Building, the Sistine Chapel: these things were made by creatures like me, through the exercise of skill and imagination. I do not have these skills, and my imagination spins different dreams. Nevertheless the potential is also in me."[29] Appiah recognizes the affective pull of imagined identities such as these, especially those that permit connection without erasing difference, pointing out that "the connection through a local identity is as imaginary as the connection through humanity, . . . but to say this isn't to pronounce either of them unreal. They are among the realest connections we have."[30] These are the types of intersubjective affiliation today's readers are hungry to feel but which they fear to create through the necessarily fictional means.

Finding Fiction
Simultaneous Narration and Fictional Life-Writing

The trend of first-person, present-tense narration in fiction extends, in some ways, the cultural attachment to anything seemingly unmediated. It also reflects the ever-growing investment in and perceived need for up-to-the-minute reporting, whether it is reporting of the self or of the world. With the prevalence of smartphones, the twenty-four-hour news cycle, and constant self-updating on sites such as Facebook, Twitter, and Instagram, we seem to consider ourselves substantially well informed, if also wildly overstimulated. There is so much information at our fingertips constantly being updated that our present relationship to "knowledge" works on a feedback loop: immediate gratification with little effort, thought, or substance begets the desire for easy and instant fulfillment.[31] Richard Lea of *The Guardian* notes the correlation between our "connected" culture and our predilection for present-tense narration: "The internet, mobile phones, Twitter: all gnaw away at our capacity to reflect; all push us to experience life as a series of unconnected moments. As we blog our lives away to the accompaniment of the 24-hour rolling news, can it be any coincidence that novelists are reaching for the present tense?"[32] While I disagree with Lea's implication that we are relinquishing the practice of narrative in our self-conceptions—after all, what does Facebook's timeline format achieve if not a highly curated and sequential record of a life?—I think he does well to prompt readers to perceive the unreflective tendency to immerse ourselves in technologies of illusionary immediacy.

The more immediacy we receive, the less we are able to value the kinds of productive distance that Amanda Anderson highlights as a key to Victorian practices of ethics, knowledge, and representation.[33] That is to say, contemporary subjects may be writing the narratives of themselves in their digital worlds, but they seem to be doing so much less self-consciously than did any of the fictional autobiographers analyzed in the foregoing chapters. Unlike Lucy Snowe, for instance, who "seems always already to have constituted herself as an onlooker of her own existence"[34] in her self-reflective autobiography, many contemporary subjects are both constantly self-fashioning and unable to perceive their actions as distinct acts of identity construction. In the creation of internet identities, the awareness of self-making is often submerged beneath acts of so-called self-expression; instead of perceiving life narratives as consciously created trajectories, the conventional digital self encountered in social media seems unreflectively to rewrite identity based on the emotion of the moment, subsuming these revisions of identity under the rubric of "self-discovery." The Victorian obsession with being in history, in other words, has become the contemporary obsession with being in the here-and-now, characterized only by the most cursory recognition of the relationship between then, now, and someday.

However, in being overtly fictional—like the fictional autobiography—novels that privilege first-person, present-tense tellings might offer certain thoughtful readers the kind of creative revelations of fictionality's value that the fictional autobiography offered the Victorians. After all, unlike the uncritical attachment to naïve empiricism associated with the popular rhetoric surrounding texts of life-writing, readers of an explicit fiction tacitly recognize and engage their imaginative faculties. And although Cohn has proposed that "life tells us that we cannot tell it while we live it or live it while we tell it,"[35] the culture's present obsession with communication apps, blogs, personal YouTube channels, and social-networking sites of all sorts would seem to counter her point with even the most mundane actions of daily experience.[36] Cohn's voicing of the common narratological assumption that we "live now, tell later"[37] no longer feels as self-evident as it might have before the new millennium.

But simply because many people have internalized the presumption of unmediated immediacy that characterizes self-representation on social media does not mean that first-person, present-tense narration has become logically unproblematic. Indeed, Cohn's theory of "simultaneous narration" helps to delineate how this form might encourage a rethinking of the fixation with seemingly essential selves. Cohn proposes that readers understand novels such as Nathalie Sarraute's *Martereau* and Robert M. Pirsig's *Zen and the Art of Motorcycle Maintenance* (or, more recently, Collins's *Hunger Games*), through the category of "simultaneous narration."[38] Simultaneous narration is different from the use of present tense in texts with a heterodiegetic narrator, in which such passages represent a character's "interior monologue" (such as the "Penelope" section of *Ulysses*). It is also different from narration in which present tense is framed by other tenses, what Cohn calls the "historical present," in which past events are cast in the present tense for certain effect (such as in *David Copperfield*'s second chapter, "I Observe").[39] Rather, Cohn argues, simultaneous narration is a curious, because non-mimetic, form of narration; it is an "analytic," planned act of communication—that is, it is a distinctly *narrated* discourse—that readers are nonetheless asked to process as occurring simultaneously with the events, feelings, and states of mind that are being described by that same narration.[40] The narrating protagonist lives and tells at once.

The ability to experience life and to narrate it simultaneously represents an impossibility for Cohn, which accounts for the "non-mimetic" quality of this kind of narration.[41] After all, if "narration" is understood to be (at least on some level) planned, plotted, and constructed with knowledge of what happens before, during, and after any given point in a story, then it should be clear why someone who is living the events she tells cannot "narrate" them in this particular conception of narration. How can one select what and how to tell as one simultaneously experiences the chaos of life? As in fictional autobiography, texts of simultaneous narration have a character-narrator (who is sometimes a narrator-protagonist); the difference in these texts is that "the temporal hiatus between the narrating and the experiencing self . . . is literally reduced to zero: the moment of narration *is* the moment of experience, the narrating self *is* the experiencing self." Because most people presumably cannot plan and write or otherwise record narrated discourse at the same time that they live what they are describing (speaking, running, eating, interacting with others, etc.), this means that in texts of simultaneous narration "the relationship of the narrative language to its source remains vexingly elusive, irretrievable on realistic grounds."[42]

To give an illustration of how simultaneous narration may reconcile some readers to fiction's ubiquity and productive potential, I turn to an example from the first book of Collins's *Hunger Games* series. This series is set in a dystopian totalitarian state in which the immensely wealthy and wasteful "Capitol" taxes and terrorizes the formerly rebellious outlying "districts" with a yearly televised event featuring a fight to the death in which the competitors are children and teens from the oppressed regions. Throughout the novel, the experiencing narrator-protagonist, Katniss Everdeen, speaks, thinks, and hunts (among many other things), all while narrating these same actions. In the beginning pages of the novel, readers discover that Katniss regularly escapes into the forest, past the permissible limits of District Twelve, where she lives, to "poach" some wild animals to keep her family from starving. As she slips past the once-electrified fence, she narrates: "'District Twelve. Where you can starve to death in safety,' I mutter. Then I glance quickly over my shoulder. Even here, even in the middle of nowhere, you worry someone might overhear you."[43] How does Katniss manage to speak, to feel her paranoia, to maintain her watchfulness, to narrate, and to register in her diction the order of her narrated events, all at the same time? Her word choice, after all, suggests that she is aware that she is the narrator of a discourse, not merely a thinker of private thoughts. Note that she writes "*Then* I glance quickly over my shoulder" rather than "Now I glance quickly" or "I glance quickly," suggesting a recognition of the relative order of her statements. "Then" indicates consciousness of a before, after, and yet to come in the order of the discourse, which usually requires retrospection. And in an environment that resembles an early twentieth-century mining town in setting and technological capacity, how can her discourse arrive, intact, in the reader's hands? After all, she has no method for recording her narration. Furthermore and thematically speaking, her narration, much like the spoken mutterings she narrates and fears will be overheard, is highly treasonous and therefore dangerous in the world her words invent and describe. How and why does her narration exist? As Cohn points out, these questions are not answerable in ways that both maintain Katniss and her "I" as the source of the discourse and conform to the epistemological principles of the real world.[44]

The simultaneity of selves—narrating and experiencing—that are collapsed into the "I" of Katniss's simultaneous narration seems both to parallel and to parody interactions with internet media specializing in self-expression and self-production. On one level, first-person, present-tense fiction such as *The Hunger Games* seems to suggest the "natural" and "immediate" quality of a perfectly coherent self, complete with a compelling narrative, in its "seamless continuity" between experience and logically narrated discourse.[45] However, it also parodies a belief in this perfectly "seamless" and spontaneous narrative of self by representing a narrative situation that is impossible in the real world. Instead of simply internalizing this unified model of the self, a careful reader of *The Hunger Games* might rather come to realize the conceptual sleight of hand beneath the impossible "simultaneity" of Katniss's narrating and experiencing "I." How can any narrative of the world, of chaos, prove coherent without first being considered, shaped, selected into that coherent form? How can any identity, then, feel so complete if it is not itself the product of fictional processes? When a reader perceives that these texts present him with a necessarily fictional situation in which the narrator-protagonist can at once experience and reflectively report on the present moment, and somehow translate this to an externally accessible text, the foregoing questions might just follow. Through a close reading of form, fictions in the first person and present tense ask their audience to recognize the artifice of their narrative situation and the requisite fictionality of any seemingly "seamless" self. To put it another way, perhaps books like *The Hunger Games* are not just a symptom of a cultural discomfort with fiction's metaphoric processes; perhaps, with careful reading, these fictions can be part of the contemporary reconciliation with fiction and its possibilities.

And indeed there is an indication in just the last few years that a contemporary form of fictional life-writing may be emerging—and growing in popularity—that could productively complicate readers' persistent preoccupation with essentialist ideals of identity, as did the fictional autobiography for its Victorian audiences. Since 2015 several first-person fictions have topped bestseller lists and received media coverage from outlets such as the *New Yorker* and National Public Radio's *Morning Edition*.[46] While this perhaps suggests only a limited resurgence in popular interest in texts that openly complicate the predominant ideals of identity, truth, and fictionality, it is a trend worth noting nonetheless. In addition to the novels of Kristin Hannah, Fiona Barton, and Paula Hawkins mentioned earlier, all of which incorporate some first-person, present-tense narration, in 2016 Elizabeth Strout published a first-person, past-tense life story entitled *My Name Is Lucy Barton*. Similarly, Petina Gappah's 2015 novel *The Book of Memory*—also a first-person, past-tense book of fictional life-writing—has received substantial attention from the American media. While many of these texts could be categorized as "literary" fiction, on the trade fiction side of things there is Debbie Macomber's dual-narrated first-person, past-tense fictional self-help book *A Girl's Guide to Moving On*.

No two of these recent novels use first-person narration or tense in precisely the same way; some have multiple narrators, and few stick to a single mode of narration in any uncomplicated manner. But together, I propose, they nonetheless may form a pattern. Twenty-first-century first-person stories of a teller's life, whether narrated in present or past tense, seem less aligned with the tropes of classical autobiography (as in Victorian fictional autobiographies) and more in tune with recent trends in the broader genre of personal life-writing. Namely, they seem to focus on the traumatic elements in the stories of their tellers (either by inclusion or pointed omission), a preoccupation that instantly recalls the readerly fixation on Walls's and other life-writers' revelations of the difficult moments through which they have come and emerged triumphant, or at least alive. While an interest in what goes wrong in socially situated individual lives occupies the tales of Jane Eyre, Esther Summerson, David Copperfield, and Lucy Snowe as well, their narratives usually include the obstacles they face without placing primary emphasis on them. Their stories, by contrast with these contemporary stories, evoke such hurdles as a means to manufacture, in self-consciously fictional ways, at least partial resolutions to life's traumas.

But the extreme refusal of resolution at the end of *Villette* seems to have become the rule in contemporary texts of fictional life-writing. Fictional life-writing today shows what happens instead of, or after, the pairings and domestic settlements that dominate (even as they are complicated by) their Victorian predecessors. The forms of these recent works are much more diverse than those found in the Victorian fictional autobiography, in part because, as Sidonie Smith and Julia Watson suggest, personal life-writing in the twentieth and twenty-first centuries is more "heterogeneous" than it used to be.[47] What these and other recent texts do share, and what places them— if loosely—in the category of fictional life-writing, is a preoccupation with trauma and its repercussions for the parallel acts of living and narrating a life. This focus on the intersection of identity and textuality means that works in this category feature first-person narration that links the writing and the written selves of the protagonist to the (fictional) production of at least parts of the text, whether the situation of that production is explicitly addressed or not. On the thematic side, most of these novels seem to promote an ambivalence about the means and possibilities of overcoming obstacles. They gesture at the complications of the "survivor's story," and they illuminate how identity is implicated in these failures of narrative coherence, instead of telling a straightforward tale of individual success founded upon essential inwardness. This could be interpreted as a development on their Victorian inheritance: the preceding chapters demonstrate that even in the nineteenth-century fictional autobiography, there was plenty of hesitancy about how complete such narrative triumphs over circumstance actually were for individuals situated in society and in history.

Though these contemporary first-person texts might fit into a broader category of fictional life-writing instead of fictional autobiography, they could operate phenomenologically to similarly doubled ends. These works still challenge their audiences to engage with referential genre tropes in texts that— at least in the case of first-person, present-tense narration—are even more explicitly fictional because their telling would be impossible in the real world. Fictional life-writing, like the fictional autobiography, may promote in some readers a distinctly doubled understanding of identity in and through these fractured narratives of life and self. In other words, perhaps carefully reading Katniss Everdeen is not the only hope for recuperating some of the productive awareness of fictional selves that characterizes the Victorian fictional auto-biography. Perhaps the new popularity of overtly fictional selves telling their stories in referentially affiliated ways will re-attune today's readers to the possibilities of identities that are self-consciously narrative, imagined, and social.

Transformative Imaginations

Whether it is in Katniss Everdeen's simultaneously narrated account of her life or David Copperfield's reflectively autobiographical narration, close reading of the first-person form can reveal how essential fictional creation is to an understanding of ourselves and to our affective connections with others. The works I have analyzed also suggest, by foregrounding through form and theme the processes of fiction, that one must be aware of fiction's presence and potential in order for that potential to be fully realized. The resonance of my findings, as I have hoped to indicate in this coda, extend beyond a renewed conception of fiction in the Victorian period to indicate the necessity for a similar rethinking of imaginative, social narratives in today's world.

Quite appropriately, it is the potential of reality that fiction creates and illuminates. Of course, not every reader will perceive the curious implications of the fictional autobiography. Not everyone who picks up these novels will become invested in the narrating protagonists. Not all members of the reading public will actively engage the ideas these texts propose about the possibilities and problems of our own selves as fictional constructs. And yet, for those who do read and think in these ways, the fictional autobiography and its contemporary descendants have the potential to generate real emotions, real revelations, and real self-awareness. The potential of fiction lies in the possibility of real moments of transformation that it extends to the careful, caring reader.

Notes

Introduction | Fictional Self-Making in a Changing World

1. Charlotte Brontë, *Jane Eyre: An Autobiography*, 9.

2. Sandra Gilbert and Susan Gubar, *The Madwoman in the Attic: The Woman Writer and the Nineteenth-Century Literary Imagination*, 576; Anna Gibson, "Charlotte Brontë's First Person," 220; Adrienne Rich, "Jane Eyre: The Temptations of a Motherless Woman," 90.

3. Susan Sniader Lanser, *Fictions of Authority: Women Writers and Narrative Voice*, 186.

4. Mark M. Hennelly Jr. maintains in "*Jane Eyre's* Reading Lesson" that the novel's structure makes "selfhood" the central "mystery" of the text and notes in passing that "this mystery of selfhood, of course, is the kind we daily try to 'read' in the plots of our friends and acquaintances" (703, 709).

5. Lanser, *Fictions of Authority*, 186.

6. Carl Goldberg, a psychotherapist, and other scholars have proposed something similar about the dynamic narrative construction of selfhood. Goldberg writes in his article "The Pursuit of the Fictional Self" that "our sense of self is an active process of inventing a unified identity" (217). Philosopher Anthony Paul Kerby in *Narrative and the Self* uses fiction specifically as an analogy for lived identity: "The self is perhaps best construed as a literary character not unlike those we encounter almost every day in novels, plays, and other story media" (1). Kerby's comparison, however, is in service to explaining his broader claim that "the self in fact arises . . . out of our linguistic behavior" (6). The present study examines how the "active," "literary" process of self-making is both enacted and revealed in the Victorian fictional autobiography. My work develops the idea of the fictional self to show that the lived experience of selfhood operates in ways that tend to be structurally identical to the processes through which fictional worlds and characters come to seem "real" to certain readers. And though Goldberg and others place primary emphasis on Friedrich Nietzsche as the philosopher whose work began to undermine essential notions of selfhood in European thinking, I demonstrate that a constructivist understanding of identity is already latent in the fictional autobiographies of the early and mid-Victorian period.

7. The idea of "doubleness" as a revealing property of fiction has been developed by many critics, including Peter J. Rabinowitz in "Truth in Fiction: A Re-examination of Audiences"; Robyn Warhol in "Double Gender, Double Genre in *Jane Eyre* and *Villette*"; and others. Most significant to this study is Dorrit Cohn's work in *The Distinction of Fiction*, which is discussed at length later in this introduction. Cohn argues that the fictional autobiography operates through a "*double* pact" of fictionality and autobiographicality (33, original emphasis).

8. Catherine Gallagher, *Nobody's Story: The Vanishing Acts of Women Writers in the Marketplace, 1670–1820*, xvi.

9. Thomas Hardy, *Tess of the D'Urbervilles: A Pure Woman*, 30.

10. Sally Shuttleworth, *Charlotte Brontë and Victorian Psychology*, 3, 9, 10, 15.

11. See, for example, William Uzgalis's representation of Locke's cultural effect in "The Influence of John Locke's Works." Uzgalis implicitly discounts the impact of Locke's "revolutionary" thinking about identity in the Victorian period, writing that thinkers of the eighteenth and twentieth centuries "debated hotly" Locke's philosophies of identity and "free agency" (n.p.). The omission of the Victorians from this description of Locke's influence may be because they engaged more indirectly (though not less meaningfully) with Lockean philosophies of self.

12. John Locke, *An Essay concerning Human Understanding*, chap. 27, sec. 9.

13. H. Porter Abbott, *The Cambridge Introduction to Narrative*, 13 (original emphasis).

14. David Hume, *A Treatise of Human Nature*, bk. 1, pt. 4, sec. 6, paras. 2, 1, 4, 6.

15. Adam Smith, *The Theory of Moral Sentiments*, pt. 1, sec. 1, chap. 1, pp. 7–9.

16. Rae Greiner, *Sympathetic Realism in Nineteenth-Century British Fiction*, 17, 22, 23.

17. In addition to Émile Benveniste and Judith Butler, several other recent theorists have also influenced my thinking. Paul John Eakin proposes that narrative self-making in specific contexts dictates who we believe ourselves to be, linking such a process to the generic conventions of autobiography and the public expectations thereof (*Living Autobiographically: How We Create Identity in Narrative* [2008], 1–2, 8–17, 21–51; "What Are We Reading When We Read Autobiography?" [2004], 129). Eakin also builds on the findings of neuroscientists Oliver Sacks and Antonio Damasio regarding identity as a cognitive effect instead of as cognition's agent. Anthony Giddens's phenomenological study *Modernity and Self-Identity: Self and Society in the Late Modern Age* (1991) claims that the idea of a fixed "self," and other "natural attitudes" (or "non-conscious" assumptions about what is true in the world), would "wither" if examined "sceptically" (36). Giddens argues that the presumption of "the identity of objects, other persons and . . . the self" is, thus, both "sturdy and fragile" (36, 37). See also Kerby's 1991 *Narrative and the Self* (in which he proposes that "*self-narration*" is "*fundamental to the emergence and reality*" of the human subject [4, original emphasis]) and philosopher Charles Taylor's 1989 *Sources of the Self: The Making of Modern Identity* (which explores how narrative acts of various kinds shape the experience of a continuous self through time). For the psychological and psychoanalytic side of the identity-as-narrative conversation, see Carl Goldberg, "The Pursuit of the Fictional Self" (2004); D. W. Winnicott, "Ego Distortion in Terms of True and False Self," in *The Maturational Process and the Facilitating Environment:*

Studies in the Theory of Emotional Development (1965), and *Playing and Reality* (1971); and Donald Spence, *Narrative Truth and Historical Truth: Meaning and Interpretation in Psychoanalysis* (1982). For recent work in cognitive psychology, which lends further empirical evidence to the claims about the nature of identity that I make in this book, see Maja Djikic, Keith Oatley, Sara Zoeterman, and Jordan B. Peterson, "On Being Moved by Art: How Reading Fiction Transforms the Self" (2009), and Timothy Wilson, *Redirect: The Surprising New Science of Psychological Change* (2011), on how "story-editing" of our "core narratives" can redefine who we think we are. An episode of Alix Spiegel and Lulu Miller's podcast *Invisibilia* entitled "The Personality Myth" (first aired June 24, 2016) also references several scientists whose work pushes back against the persistent cultural idea that one's permanent personality derives from an internal and unchanging "core consistency," as Spiegel phrases it.

18. Émile Benveniste, "Subjectivity in Language," 224; Judith Butler, *Gender Trouble: Feminism and the Subversion of Identity*, 24–25, 27–29.

19. Wolfgang Iser, *The Fictive and the Imaginary: Charting Literary Anthropology*, 3–4, xviii, 3, 11, 12.

20. Mary Brunton, *Discipline: A Novel*, chap. 1.

21. Amelia Ann Blanford Edwards, *Barbara's History: A Novel*, 6.

22. Eliza Lynn Linton, *The Autobiography of Christopher Kirkland*, v, vi.

23. Wolfgang Iser, *The Implied Reader: Patterns of Communication in Prose Fiction from Bunyan to Beckett*, 123–35.

24. Lanser, *Fictions of Authority*, 177.

25. Hsiao-Hung Lee, *Possibilities of Hidden Things: Narrative Transgression in Victorian Fictional Autobiographies*; James Phelan, "Dual Focalization, Retrospective Fictional Autobiography, and the Ethics of *Lolita*" and *Living to Tell about It: A Rhetoric and Ethics of Character Narration*; Rachel Ablow, "Addressing the Reader: The Autobiographical Voice"; Anna Gibson, "Charlotte Brontë's First Person." Lee's *Possibilities of Hidden Things* is the only other full-length study I have encountered that focuses exclusively on Victorian fictional autobiographies. However, Lee's interest is mainly in tracing the deconstructive potential of "narrative transgressions" in three example texts rather than in discussing the fictional autobiography as a distinctive form of literature in the Victorian period.

26. Philippe Lejeune, *On Autobiography*, 11, 12, 20.

27. Dorrit Cohn, *The Distinction of Fiction*, 33–34 (original emphasis). The idea that authors communicate their implied messages to readers "behind the narrator's back" is proposed by Wayne Booth in *The Rhetoric of Fiction* (300), whom Cohn later quotes in her book (125).

28. Alison Case, "Gender and History in Narrative Theory: The Problem of Retrospective Distance in *David Copperfield* and *Bleak House*," 312, 313. Gérard Genette originated the term *paralipsis* to talk about a "lateral ellipsis" of information from the discourse (*Narrative Discourse: An Essay in Method*, 52). James Phelan discusses the "paradoxical nature" of this phenomenon in *Narrative as Rhetoric: Technique, Audience, Ethics, Ideology* (82–83), as well as in *Living to Tell about It* (35n4). Phelan claims that, despite the "paradoxical situation" of telling less than the character-narrator retrospectively knows or feels about a moment in the story, in his example text this discrepancy "would not be noticed" by the audience, since we are—like the

character-self of the teller—experiencing things more or less chronologically (*Narrative as Rhetoric*, 83). Nonetheless, as Case implies and as I further show in chap. 3, Esther's narration in *Bleak House* makes readers pointedly aware of this paradox (Case, "Gender and History," 313–14). However, I maintain that this augments the "mimetic" (Phelan, *Narrative as Rhetoric*, 83) quality of Esther as a fictional autobiographer, while also challenging the reader's assumptions about what makes an identity feel mimetic, or realistic.

29. Case, "Gender and History," 314–17.

30. Charles Dickens, *Bleak House*, 39.

31. Genette uses the term *narrative competence* in *Narrative Discourse* to refer to a different phenomenon: the reader's ability to fill gaps in accordance with the "code" of a particular text or genre (76, 77). Similar to what I am calling narrative competence on the part of the fictional autobiographer is the idea of "aesthetic control," described by Phelan in *Living to Tell about It* as "the narrator's ability to achieve the effects he seeks and to have those effects endorsed by the implied author" (104).

32. *Routledge Encyclopedia of Narrative Theory* (2005), s.v. *autobiography* (emphasis mine).

33. Cohn, *Distinction of Fiction*, 30.

34. Michael Mascuch, *Origins of the Individualist Self: Autobiography and Self-Identity in England, 1591–1791*, 7.

35. Although the real-world authors of these fictional autobiographies very likely wished to make their protagonists feel lifelike through the narrative strategies my analysis highlights, I do not argue that these Victorian writers consciously intended to expose the fictionality of selfhood in their texts.

36. More specifically, readers sometimes interpret their impressions of a text's authenticity as evidence of the "true self" of the real-world author, as if it were somehow encoded and discoverable in the text. Cohn's theory indicates readers' predilection for such assumptions, and I address and complicate this interpretive possibility in chap. 2.

37. Gallagher, *Nobody's Story*, xv.

38. Edwards, *Barbara's History*, 354.

39. Sidonie Smith and Julia Watson, *Reading Autobiography: A Guide for Interpreting Life Narratives*, 115.

40. James Treadwell, *Autobiographical Writing and British Literature, 1783–1834*, 7.

41. Marie-Laure Ryan, "Postmodernism and the Doctrine of Panfictionality," 166.

42. Cohn, *Distinction of Fiction*, 13.

43. Martin Löschnigg, "English Autobiography and Its Fictional Other: A Diachronic View along Narratological Lines," 407.

44. The Victorian autobiography is a genre in which the value of individual subjectivity coexists with, and is often built upon, a commitment to empirical accuracy. Victorian readers, like twenty-first-century ones, were interested in monitoring the quality of the autobiographer's claims and judgments. For instance, the anonymous reviewer of the autobiography of Thomas Somerville, D.D., in *Blackwood's Edinburgh Magazine* lauds the book for containing extensive footnotes, which assist the reader in the task of understanding and contextualizing, commenting that the notes "save the reader from going to his authorities to complete his knowledge of the subject

under discussion" ("Another Minister's Autobiography," *Blackwood's Edinburgh Magazine* 90 [August 1861]: 255). At the same time, however, as Roy Pascal and Linda Peterson have noted, the Victorian autobiography's "centre of interest is the self" (Pascal, *Design and Truth in Autobiography*, 9), and its main "plot" is the writer's processes of textual self-interpretation (Peterson, *Victorian Autobiography: The Tradition of Self-Interpretation*, 2, 17, 19).

45. Löschnigg, "English Autobiography," 404.

46. Cohn, *Distinction of Fiction*, 32. Lanser, in her theorization of "personal voice"— her term for the autodiegetic narration characteristic of fictional autobiography— also remarks that such works are "formally indistinguishable from autobiography" (*Fictions of Authority*, 20); that fictional autobiography and referential autobiography are formally indistinguishable has become a common critical opinion.

47. Cohn, *Distinction of Fiction*, 125.

48. Löschnigg, "English Autobiography," 407, 409.

49. Ablow, "Addressing the Reader," 278.

50. Peterson, *Victorian Autobiography*, 3, 6.

51. Genette, *Narrative Discourse*, 245. To some extent, Genette does not fully separate these types of narration, but sees "autodiegetic" as the "strong degree" of homodiegetic narration.

52. Ibid.

53. Ibid.

54. Case, "Gender and History," 315 (original emphasis).

55. Ian Watt in *The Rise of the Novel: Studies in Defoe, Richardson and Fielding* identifies "formal realism" as the defining methodology of the novel, which builds meaning through sustained attention to "particular people in particular circumstances" (15). George Levine in *The Realistic Imagination: English Fiction from Frankenstein to Lady Chatterley* identifies the novel's investment in particularity as one mode of recapturing an "alternative transcendence" in a secularizing and skeptical age (11). In *Narrating Reality: Austen, Scott, Eliot,* Harry Shaw emphasizes that "that which makes reality real is immanent in the mundane itself," arguing that novelistic specifics of the quotidian world function metonymically (99, 100, 103). In *The Rhetoric of Fictionality: Narrative Theory and the Idea of Fiction*, Richard Walsh's formulation of how realist fictional narratives function underscores the processes of cognition that fiction engenders: he maintains that "with fiction, the relation of particular to general is the dialectical relation of imaginary data to narrative understanding, the former largely for the sake of the latter" (51).

56. Genette, *Narrative Discourse*, 228–29, 244–45.

57. Ibid., 245.

58. Brontë, *Jane Eyre*, 102, 129.

59. George Eliot, *The Mill on the Floss*, 21, 42.

60. Brontë, *Jane Eyre*, 129.

61. Eliot, *Mill on the Floss*, 287.

62. Brontë, *Jane Eyre*, 99.

63. Jane's and Brontë's rhetorical choice here recalls those of Jean-Jacques Rousseau, whose *Confessions* would have been well known to Victorian readers. In bk. 5, as he defends the honor of Mme. de Warens, he declares that "anyone is at liberty to

argue the matter as he will, and prove learnedly that I am wrong [about her nature]. My function is to tell the truth, not to make people believe it" (192). Rousseau's occasional antagonism to the reader echoes throughout *Jane Eyre*, but in more prosocial and nuanced ways.

64. Iser, *The Fictive and the Imaginary*, 13.

65. Consider, for instance, Iser's phenomenological claim that "the reality in the text is not meant to represent reality; it is a pointer to something that it is not, although its function is to make that something conceivable" (ibid.). In other words, the "use" of fictional texts is to introduce separation between "the world and our natural attitudes," or our assumptions about reality, and thus to make some truth about reality (the "something") comprehensible, often in new ways, revising the natural attitudes of readers (ibid.).

66. Gibson, "Charlotte Brontë's First Person," 205, 203.

67. Jerome H. Buckley, *The Triumph of Time: A Study of the Victorian Concepts of Time, History, Progress, and Decadence*, 9.

68. Buckley signals this ambivalence about progress: "Though often opposed to particular innovations, many Victorians accepted the idea [of progress] almost as an article of faith" (ibid., 9, 10). Some of these problematic innovations included the theories of Charles Darwin about natural selection and of Lord Kelvin, who, extrapolating from the second law of thermodynamics, asserted that the sun would burn out within a few "millions of years" (Robin Gilmour, *The Victorian Period: The Intellectual and Cultural Context of English Literature, 1830–1890*, 136).

69. Gilmour, *The Victorian Period*, 3, 19.

70. John N. Morris declared in *Versions of the Self* in 1966 that "'self' became the modern word for 'soul'" (6).

71. Nicholas Paige expresses the paradoxical tension inherent in modern ideals of inward selfhood in his study *Being Interior: Autobiography and the Contradiction of Modernity in Seventeenth-Century France*, declaring that "the space of our authenticity is also the evidence of our alienation" (4).

72. Lanser, *Fictions of Authority*, 177.

73. According to Walter Jerrold, this narrative was originally published serially in *Fraser's Magazine* under the title *The Luck of Barry Lyndon, Esq., A Romance of the Last Century*. Thackeray later published it in his *Miscellanies* with the title *Memoirs of Barry Lyndon, Esq., Written by Himself*. As the editor of the collection *The Prose Works of William Makepeace Thackeray*, Jerrold calls it *Barry Lyndon*. See Jerrold's "Bibliographical Note" to the collection remarking on the work's titles and history at http://www.gutenberg.org/files/4558/4558-h/4558-h.htm.

74. The omission of *Great Expectations* from my primary example texts might strike some readers as unusual. However, *Great Expectations* is a partial exception to the phenomenological claims I make about the interpretive possibilities of the best examples of the subgenre. Though Pip tells his own retrospective tale of development, he resists identification of his character-self with his narrator-self. His evident shame at his past choices shows not just the requisite "maturity" of the Victorian autobiographer nor even just the fracturing of his desired self as he plays "other parts in other stories" (as Patricia McKee interprets it in *Reading Constellations: Urban*

Modernity in Victorian Fiction, 38, 50). In resisting identification with his past self, narrator-Pip internalizes the anxiety of modernity's break with the social structures of the past, making the effect of his narration more similar to that of a heterodiegetic narrator. His ironic distance from his younger self is so complete that it is difficult to consciously interpret Pip as a fictional autobiographer, making readers less likely to associate his fragmented selfhood with their own. His discourse also lacks most of the explicit signs of self-awareness in an autobiography: mentions of his writing choices are rarer than in the fictional autobiographies herein discussed. In this way, the doubled reading stance that the fictional autobiography at its most interpretively potent can solicit is, to my mind, less likely to occur for readers of *Great Expectations*. See my discussion of Thackeray's historical fictional autobiography *The History of Henry Esmond* in the section "Being Real and Structuring Selves in Victorian Literature" in chap. 1 for a similar (though not identical) example of such a case of alienation between the written and the writing selves.

Chapter One | The Victorian Fictional Autobiography in Context: Fiction, Reference, and Reader Expectations

1. William Makepeace Thackeray, *Barry Lyndon*, in *The Prose Works of William Makepeace Thackeray* (London: J. M. Dent, 1902; Project Gutenberg, 2016), chap. 1. http://www.gutenberg.org/files/4558/4558-h/4558-h.htm.

2. Cohn, *Distinction of Fiction*, 30. Cohn identifies this as a common position shared by herself, Michál Glowínski ("On the First-Person Novel"), Philippe Lejeune (*On Autobiography*), and Elizabeth Bruss (*Autobiographical Acts: The Changing Situation of a Literary Genre*).

3. Cohn, *Distinction of Fiction*, 30.

4. Nicholas Paige, *Before Fiction: The Ancien Régime of the Novel*, 13.

5. As mentioned in the introduction, this difference between twentieth- and twenty-first-century scholarly understandings of the fictional autobiography and Victorian approaches to this subgenre is reinforced by the example texts most often used to illustrate it. Cohn and others (e.g., James Phelan with *Lolita*'s Humbert Humbert [in "Dual Focalization"] and Alison Case with her against-the-grain reading of *Bleak House*'s Esther [in "Gender and History"]) most often discuss texts that encourage readers to view the fictional tellers as markedly unreliable in some fashion. This is not unheard of in Victorian fictional autobiographies (Thackeray's *Barry Lyndon*, for instance), but it is certainly a less common trait in Victorian instances of the genre. In nineteenth-century fictional autobiographies, even the complicated character-narrators (such as Esther Summerson or Lucy Snowe) are far from inviting the reader to judge them entirely unreliable or ideologically alien to their writer's sensibilities (thus distancing readers from desirable intimacy with those fictional beings). In other words, Victorian fictional autobiographies very rarely encourage their audiences to "read around" the narrating character in order to mind-read the flesh-and-blood author (the latter interpretive stance being the result of the fictional autobiography's doubleness, in Cohn's account). See the introduction, especially the section "Definitions, Doubleness, and Contextualized Analysis," for more in-depth discussion of this issue.

6. Unsigned review of *Washington Grange: An Autobiography*, by William Pickersgill, *Literary Gazette* 48 (May 28, 1859): 636.

7. The previously quoted reviewer of Pickersgill's *Washington Grange*, for instance, begins the review by declaring that fictions that "are autobiographical" have "the advantage, when well employed, of giving a great air of truth to the creations of the fancy, and of adding the liveliness of an apparent personal feeling to the tale" (ibid., 635).

8. Unsigned review of *Cometh Up as a Flower: An Autobiography*, by Rhoda Broughton, *Times* (London), June 6, 1867, 9, from *The Times Digital Archive*. See the section "The Fictional Autobiography vs. the Non-autobiographical First-Person Novel" in the introduction to this book for the definition of *autodiegetic*.

9. This may be a misprint for *caitiff*.

10. Unsigned review of *Cometh Up as a Flower*, 9.

11. Ibid.

12. Elizabeth Rigby, "1. *Vanity Fair; A Novel without a Hero*; 2. *Jane Eyre: An Autobiography*; 3. Governesses' Benevolence Institution—Report for 1847," review of *Vanity Fair*, by William Thackeray, and *Jane Eyre*, by Charlotte Brontë, 504, 505, 503.

13. Justin Sider, "'Modern-Antiques,' Ballad Imitation, and the Aesthetics of Anachronism," 463–64.

14. Michael McKeon, *The Origins of the English Novel, 1600–1740*, 266.

15. Pascal, *Design and Truth*, 33.

16. Watt, *Rise of the Novel*, 14.

17. Catherine Gallagher, "The Rise of Fictionality," 338, 340.

18. Watt, *Rise of the Novel*, 11, 14, 77; McKeon, *Origins of the English Novel*, 21, 44.

19. Watt, *Rise of the Novel*, 13.

20. Peterson, *Victorian Autobiography*, 6, 15.

21. Mascuch, *Origins of the Individualist Self*, 20; Martin Danahay, *A Community of One: Masculine Autobiography and Autonomy in Nineteenth-Century Britain*, 12; Treadwell, *Autobiographical Writing*, 7. Treadwell analyzes William Taylor's "hesitant" early use of the term *autobiography*, noting the writer's skepticism about the neologism he coins to replace the Anglo-Greek hybrid term *self-biography* (7; the citation given by Treadwell for Taylor's 1797 review is *Monthly Review*, NS iixv, 375). Robert Folkenflik, in the introduction to his edited collection *The Culture of Autobiography: Construction of Self-Representation* (Stanford: Stanford University Press, 1993), gives additional historical background for the creation and early appearances of the term *autobiography* in English and German (1–5). Folkenflik notes an adjectival use of the word ("autobiographical") in the preface to Ann Yearsley's *Poems* as early as 1786 (1).

22. Löschnigg, "English Autobiography," 405.

23. Treadwell, *Autobiographical Writing*, 5, 14.

24. Ibid., 14.

25. Pascal, *Design and Truth*, 8.

26. Georg Lukács, *The Theory of the Novel*, 78.

27. Ibid., 32 (original emphasis), 29, 77, 56.

28. Pascal, *Design and Truth*, 8.

29. Mascuch, *Origins of the Individualist Self*, 20.

30. Lukács, *Theory of the Novel*, 77.

31. The possible worlds theory of fictional existence holds that the story worlds produced in fictional texts are ontologically different from the "real world" and that they are both created and represented by the semiotic processes that constitute them. The language of the text performs the fictional world into being (in the sense defined by J. L. Austin), while also "referring" to a fictional world distinct from our own. See Ryan, "Postmodernism," and Lubomír Dolezel, *Heterocosmica*, for more on possible worlds theory.

32. Paige, *Before Fiction*, x, 11 (quoting Foley's *Telling the Truth: Theory and Practice of Documentary Fiction* [Ithaca: Cornell University Press, 1986]), 9–10.

33. Ibid., 13. Paige's formulation also handily expresses the commitment of realist fictions more specifically. Paige, however, unlike Gallagher and others, does not believe that fictionality was wholly new to the eighteenth century or to modern Western cultures (see his introduction to *Before Fiction*). Nonetheless, its existence in Paige's account as the dominant mode of invented literary creation coincides with the end of the eighteenth century, which is the key point for the present analysis.

34. The ancient Roman work *The Golden Ass*, by Apuleius, though more picaresque than autobiographical in its plot and characters, is at least one example of an invented autodiegetic tale that long predates the modern period.

35. Charles Haskell Hinnant, "*Moll Flanders*, *Roxana*, and the French Tradition of the Pseudo-Memoir," 206.

36. Donna Kuizenga, introduction to *Memoirs of the Life of Henriette-Sylvie de Molière*, by Madame de Villedieu, 9.

37. Hinnant, "*Moll Flanders*," 206.

38. Kuizenga, introduction to *Memoirs of the Life*, 9–10.

39. Ian Bell argues that *Robinson Crusoe* is even less interested in the narrator's personal identity than Defoe's other protofictional autobiography, *Moll Flanders*, noting that "whereas Crusoe's narration was simply the conventional procedure of the chronicle, serving no other end than getting the story told, Moll's way of presenting her tale is made central to any reading of it" (Ian Bell, "Narrators and Narrative in Defoe," *Novel—A Forum* 18 [1985]: 154–72 [quotation on p. 158], quoted in Hinnant, "*Moll Flanders*," 225n3). Though interiority in the modern sense is still lacking for the most part in *Moll Flanders*, Bell proposes that how Moll narrates matters to who readers think she is. This latter attribute developed into a key feature of Victorian fictional autobiography.

40. Blakey Vermeule, *Why Do We Care about Literary Characters?*, 14.

41. Gallagher, *Nobody's Story*, xvi.

42. Gallagher, "Rise of Fictionality," 350, 351.

43. Catherine Gallagher, "Gender, Property, and the Rise of the Novel," 272.

44. Ibid. Gallagher is adapting Edmund Burke's phrase "inquisitive without impertinence," from "A Philosophical Inquiry into Our Ideas of the Sublime and the Beautiful," available in *The Works of Edmund Burke* (Boston: Little and Brown, 1839), 1:95.

45. See the section "The Fictional Autobiography vs. the 'Omniscient' Realist Novel" in the introduction for a more in-depth discussion of the fictional autobiography

184 / Notes to Pages 52–56

and literary realism. In realism, the content is explicitly invented, but the structures that content reveals and the mode of telling can be indicative of systems that characterize the real world.

46. Gallagher, "Rise of Fictionality," 348, 349. Lisa Zunshine's *Why We Read Fiction: Theory of Mind and the Novel* similarly proposes that "our enjoyment of fiction is predicated—at least in part—upon our *awareness* of our 'trying on' mental states *potentially available* to us but at a given moment *different* from our own" (17, original emphasis).

47. In *The Theory of the Novel*, Lukács asserts that "art, the visionary reality of the world made to our measure, has thus become independent: it is no longer a copy, for all the models have gone; it is created totality" (37).

48. In *Design and Truth in Autobiography*, Pascal writes that it is the promise of "intimate communion" with another's subjectivity that "wins over" the reader of a classical autobiography. More specifically, it is being invited by the autobiographer himself to share his "hero's" story—"as in a novel," Pascal remarks—that makes this intimacy so appealing (1).

49. Walsh, *Rhetoric of Fictionality*, 14.

50. Elizabeth Bruss, *Autobiographical Acts: The Changing Situation of a Literary Genre*, 11, quoted in Cohn, *Distinction of Fiction*, 31 (Cohn's emphasis).

51. Cohn, *Distinction of Fiction*, 31.

52. Lukács, *Theory of the Novel*, 37.

53. Walsh, *Rhetoric of Fictionality*, 32, 43.

54. Ibid., 18–20.

55. Ibid., 50–51.

56. Ibid., 51.

57. Ibid.

58. Tillman Köppe and Julia Langkau, in their article "Fiction, Self-Knowledge and Knowledge of the Self," provide a philosophically rigorous argument for fiction's capacity to reveal to readers something about their own conscious attitudes and sensations ("self-knowledge"), and also, more significantly, about their less self-evident dispositions, what the authors refer to as the "core" or "essence" of "self" ("knowledge of the self") (51–52). Theirs is a variation on the hermeneutic view of fiction's value, informed by a concept of selfhood that takes core identity to be something inward (cognitive and affective) and discoverable, if complex.

59. For a recent neuroscientific study on the brain's activity while reading imagined narratives, see Nicole K. Speer, Jeremy R. Reynolds, Khena M. Swallow, and Jeffrey M. Zacks, "Reading Stories Activates Neural Representations of Visual and Motor Experiences." In this fMRI study, the researchers found evidence that readers' brains, when processing narratives, activate those regions required to perform the actions about which they are reading and that this activity is "dynamically updated" when the conditions within the narrative change (996). This suggests a neurological as well as an imaginative and perceptual link between fictional worlds and a reader's lived experience. Although Speer et al. choose to call this cognitive-neurological experience a "simulation," it is because readers do not physically complete the actions their brains are processing. That is, readers generally do not reach out their hand when reading about someone trying to flip a light switch, even though their brains

are activated in the same way as if they were. The mind work, as it were, appears to be the same. See also the three articles by Maja Djikic, Keith Oatley, and their colleagues in the bibliography; they have performed several experiments and written several review articles on the psychological, personality, and social effects of reading literary fiction more specifically.

60. George Brimley, "Thackeray's *Esmond*," review of *The History of Henry Esmond*, by William Makepeace Thackeray, *Spectator* 25 (November 6, 1852), in Geoffrey Tillotson and Donald Hawes, eds., *Thackeray: The Critical Heritage*, 139.

61. John Forster, "Thackeray, *Henry Esmond*," review of *The History of Henry Esmond*, by William Makepeace Thackeray, *Examiner* (November 13, 1852), in Tillotson and Hawes, *Thackeray*, 146–47.

62. Anthony Trollope, *An Autobiography*, 183.

63. John Stuart Mill, *On Liberty*, 108–10.

64. George Brimley, "Dickens' *Bleak House*," review of *Bleak House*, by Charles Dickens, *Spectator* 26 (September 24, 1853), in Philip Collins, ed., *Dickens: The Critical Heritage*, 283, 284.

65. For a more recent discussion of self-consistency, see Paul John Eakin's overview of Ulrich Neisser's concept of the "extended self" in *Living Autobiographically* (xii–xiv).

66. Brimley, "Dickens' *Bleak House*," in Collins, *Dickens*, 285.

67. Shlomith Rimmon-Kenan, *Narrative Fiction: Contemporary Poetics*, 32.

68. The principle of minimal departure, defined by Marie-Laure Ryan in her book *Possible Worlds, Artificial Intelligence, and Narrative Theory*, holds that the fictional world varies as little as possible from the extratextual world, unless otherwise explicitly stated in the text. Ryan introduces the concept of minimal departure as an attempt to reconcile possible worlds theory's insistence on the "necessarily complete" nature of fictional worlds with the literary fact that all texts are composed of gaps, both major and minor. The idea of minimal departure also helps her to articulate how one can make truth-value judgments about nonfactual (or "counterfactual") statements, specifically in the case of literary fictions, and how these counterfactuals can then be used to generate knowledge about the real world (48–51).

69. Walsh, *Rhetoric of Fictionality*, 11.

70. Ibid.

71. Lubomír Dolezel, "Truth and Authenticity in Narrative," 18.

72. Brontë, *Jane Eyre*, 13.

73. Gilbert and Gubar's classic chapter "A Dialogue of Self and Soul: *Jane Eyre*," in their book *The Madwoman in the Attic*, traces the influence of Bunyan's *Pilgrim's Progress* on Jane's protofeminist narrative and is one example of critical attention to Jane's bibliophilia.

74. Jane's achievement of intellectual and eventually physical and emotional freedom through literacy is cited by Julia Sun-Joo Lee in *The American Slave Narrative and the Victorian Novel* as an example of how this text, like many other Victorian novels, was inspired by tropes from American slave narratives and autobiographies written by formerly enslaved African Americans (9, 30).

75. Trollope, *Autobiography*, 25–26.

76. Sarah Gilead, "Trollope's *Autobiography*: The Strategies of Self-Production," 276.

77. Löschnigg, "English Autobiography," 404.

78. In other words, recognizing fiction's self-constituting reality allows readers to rank as less relevant (recalling Walsh) the stricter standards of empirical epistemology that are often applied to nonfictional autobiographies. In fiction it is pointless to question every piece of information offered by a narrator because there is no other way to experience his world than by what he tells. As Walsh in *The Rhetoric of Fictionality* points out, readers rarely expend mental energy on forming assumptions with no relevance or possible interpretive payoff (18).

Chapter Two | The Author and the Reader: The Individual and/as Narrative Community

1. Dickens, *David Copperfield* (hereafter cited in text as *DC*), xxvii.

2. In the 1869 preface to the Charles Dickens Edition of *David Copperfield*, Dickens reiterates his sentiments from the 1850 preface and further confides, "I have in my heart of hearts a favourite child. And his name is DAVID COPPERFIELD." Available on Project Gutenberg, http://www.gutenberg.org/files/766/766-0.txt.

3. Ibid.

4. Ibid.

5. Lukács, *Theory of the Novel*, 56.

6. Bo Jeffares in *The Artist in Nineteenth-Century English Fiction* notes that the figure of the Victorian artist as a "unique, imaginative creator" occupied a special place in the Victorian imagination: he was highly individual ("original") by definition, and, simultaneously, "his work seemed to show the workings of a divine inspiration" (18).

7. Thomas Carlyle, *Past and Present*, 391 (original emphasis).

8. George Levine notes that the Victorian realists learned "how to give to the particular and ordinary the resonances traditionally to be found in the universals of an earlier philosophy and literature" (*The Realistic Imagination*, 13). In my analysis of Carlyle's rhetoric, I am building on this observation of the transformation of the (fictional) particular into the (referential) universal, with the "unique individual" as the bridge between such seemingly opposite conditions and urges.

9. Thomas Carlyle, "Lecture V. The Hero as Man of Letters: Johnson, Burns, Rousseau," 155–56 (original emphasis).

10. Writing about *Sartor Resartus*, Carlyle's novel exploring autobiographical authorship (among other things), Greg Sieminski comments that the novel's protagonist, Diogenes Teufelsdrockh, "becomes a hero in the Carlylean sense, for his God-appointed calling as a writer has social significance. . . . There is urgency in his message because of the potential for imminent social upheaval" ("Suited for Satire: Butler's Retailoring of *Sartor Resartus* in *The Way of All Flesh*," 32). Sieminski's description highlights the suturing together of inner and outer—and the real-world implications of that imagined connection—that the figure of the author did so well for the Victorian imagination.

11. Carlyle, "Hero as Man of Letters," 155.

12. Clinton Machann, *The Genre of Autobiography in Victorian Literature*, 160–61.

13. I adapt this use of the word *parable* from Garrett Stewart's *Dear Reader: The Conscripted Audience in Nineteenth-Century British Fiction*, in which it means any scene of interpretation that evokes the act of reading (60). For Stewart, parables of reading signal the "deferred contact" between fictional world and actual reader by gesturing to the layers of invention and interpretation required to make that connection. Parables of self-making in fictional autobiography highlight the "logic of absenteeism" (60)—meaning, in the present study, the founding lack of essence—upon which the fictions of personal identity are built, and through which readers come to construct the selves that feel so real.

14. Chris R. Vanden Bossche, "Cookery, not Rookery: Family and Class in *David Copperfield*," 89.

15. Matthew Titolo, "The Clerk's Tale: Liberalism, Accountability, and Mimesis in *David Copperfield*," 173.

16. As the word *influence* and the mention of "anxieties" earlier in the paragraph might suggest, in its general shape my argument about *Copperfield* is itself informed by Harold Bloom's canonical theory on the Romantic poets, as outlined in *The Anxiety of Influence: A Theory of Poetry*. The idea that the poet (or in this case, the "true" author) must distinguish himself from other figures of authority through textual means serves as a useful if implicit jumping-off point for my analysis of David's discursive relationship to the notion of authorship, the other authorial figures within his text, and even the readers who take part in his self-creation.

17. Smith and Watson, *Reading Autobiography*, 114–15.

18. Alexander Welsh, *From Copyright to Copperfield: The Identity of Dickens*, 160–66. Dickens's "autobiographical fragment" and the personal hardships it describes—including his time working in Warren's blacking factory as a young boy—were not made public until 1876. The fragment of Dickens's autobiography was finally published in John Forster's biography of Dickens, which came out after the author's death. Not even Dickens's children had previously known about their father's childhood difficulties.

19. "Charles Dickens and *David Copperfield*," unsigned review of *David Copperfield*, by Charles Dickens, *Fraser's Magazine* 42 (December 1850), in Collins, *Dickens*, 246.

20. Welsh, *From Copyright to Copperfield*, 166.

21. Ibid., 169.

22. Jennifer Ruth, *Novel Professions: Interested Disinterest and the Making of the Professional in the Victorian Novel*, 74–75.

23. Michael Slater, *Charles Dickens: A Life Defined by Writing*, 204.

24. Ruth, *Novel Professions*, 75.

25. Ibid., 74.

26. Carlyle, "Hero as Man of Letters," 166.

27. For instance, in Murdstone and Grinby he stands out from the other boys, as he also does at Salem House, and again later at Dr. Strong's school. As Ruth points out in *Novel Professions*, David's "distinction emerges seamlessly from his power of invention" (66), explicitly linking originality, difference, and authorship.

28. As Jerome Buckley writes in *The Triumph of Time*, "However seductive it may have appeared in retrospect, the past, whether private or public, receded more and more rapidly as the tempo of nineteenth-century change and innovation accelerated. . . . The past persisted, if at all, in mere fragments; its wholeness and even its reality became a subjective illusion to be experienced, briefly and precariously, through the exercise of the disciplined imagination" (116). Frederic Jameson in "Marxism and Historicism" makes a similar claim that all interaction with history is governed by imaginative, and often ideological, structures of interpretation (152).

29. Heather Henderson, who also reads *David Copperfield* and *Jane Eyre* as "the fictional autobiographies of David Copperfield and Jane Eyre—not of Charles Dickens and Charlotte Brontë," writes of the implications of the David/Uriah doubling in *The Victorian Self: Autobiography and Biblical Narrative*: "The point is that David/Dickens is engaged in looking in the mirror through the act of writing autobiography. And Uriah mirrors only too well the suppressed aggression of their hunger to be middle class and successful. Dickens displaces the ugly side of ambition—the egotism and ruthlessness required to climb out of the 'heep' at all costs—onto Uriah" (162n1, 172–73). In "The Mirror in *The Mill on the Floss*: Towards a Reading of Autobiography as Discourse," Janice Carlisle notes, "It is not simply that David Copperfield's urges are reflected in those of Uriah Heep: they could not be perceived by David at all if they were only his own. Without the mirror that Uriah provides, David could not acknowledge, even covertly, his feelings for Agnes. His identity is never single, independent, whole; because it is defined by its autobiographical context, it is necessarily fragmented, dependent, and dispersed" (181).

30. The idea that David "forms" the lives, characters, and stories of others will be developed further in chap. 4.

31. Welsh, *From Copyright to Copperfield*, 159.

32. Robert Altick, *The English Common Reader: A Social History of the Mass Reading Public, 1800–1900*, 5.

33. Greiner, *Sympathetic Realism*, 22.

34. Writers often evoke this image, from Dickens's famous appellation for the angry crowd in *The Pickwick Papers*, as an apt (if not so complimentary) term for the perceived mob-like qualities of the ever-increasing reading audiences of the Victorian period.

35. Bradley Deane, *The Making of the Victorian Novelist: Anxieties of Authorship in the Mass Market*, x.

36. Ibid., 60.

37. These are, obviously, false binaries, and through them I wish to characterize not the reality but the imagined options of the Victorian career writer. These extreme images of the Victorian writer, if not fully accurate in themselves, were nonetheless prominent stereotypes of authorship in the Victorian period.

38. Charles Dickens to Henry Austin, May 1, 1842, *The Letters of Charles Dickens from 1833 to 1870*, 67.

39. George Eliot to Charles Bray, September 26, 1859, *The George Eliot Letters*, 3:164.

40. Deane, *Making of the Victorian Novelist*, xi, xiv, 28–29.

41. Stewart, *Dear Reader*, 4 (original emphasis). Regarding the role of the reader in fiction (both as a represented figure and as an agent engaged in determining its meanings), Roger Chartier argues in *The Order of Books* that meaning is generated through "the complex, subtle, shifting relationships" between specific literary forms and "the various publics for those works" (xi). Wolfgang Iser also notes, in *The Act of Reading: A Theory of Aesthetic Response*, that all "acts of reading" emerge from the "dynamic interaction *between* text and reader" (107, original emphasis).

42. Stewart, *Dear Reader*, 6.

43. Cora Kaplan, "Girl Talk: *Jane Eyre* and the Romance of Women's Narration," 16.

44. Stewart, *Dear Reader*, 8.

45. Ibid., 12.

46. Regenia Gagnier, in *Subjectivities: A History of Self-Representation in Britain, 1832–1920*, has noted intersubjective patterns of identity construction in texts by working-class life-writers (11). Such a practice complements the fictional autobiography's construction of identity as imaginative and social, suggesting that both types of text participate in a more widespread cultural trend in the period.

47. Stewart, *Dear Reader*, 30, 31.

48. Numerous critics have commented on the importance of textuality and reading in *Jane Eyre*. Carol Bock, in *Charlotte Brontë and the Storyteller's Audience*, notes the significance of the shifting roles of teller, text, and reader among characters in *Jane Eyre*, particularly in the relationship of Jane and Rochester (71–72).

49. Brontë, *Jane Eyre* (hereafter cited in text as *JE*), 20.

50. Vicky Simpson, "'The Eagerness of a Listener Quickens the Tongue of a Narrator': Storytelling and Autobiography in *Jane Eyre*," n.p.

51. Kaplan, "Girl Talk," 24 (original emphasis).

52. Kaplan argues in "Girl Talk" that it is a misreading to imagine ourselves—the readers—as the "ideal listener[s]" to fulfill Jane's narrative search for reciprocity. Instead, she proposes, we should recognize the impossibility of true reciprocity for Jane, given the limiting "social organizations" of her time and place (8, 23, 25–26). However, Jane's "unfulfilled" search for true mutuality contributes to the appeal of Jane as an identity that many readers wish to "complete" in that this very lack of completion illuminates yet another point of contact between Jane's fictional self and the lived experience of identity.

53. Bock, *Storyteller's Audience*, 81.

54. Stewart, *Dear Reader*, 303, 8.

55. Stewart, *Dear Reader*, 244–47; Kaplan, "Girl Talk," 16.

56. Deane, *Making of the Victorian Novelist*, 28–29.

57. Stewart, *Dear Reader*, 243–44.

58. The second instance in the book in which Jane conflates story and discourse time in an address to the reader is in chap. 17. Narrator-Jane describes character-Jane's impressions of Blanche Ingram, recounting her younger self's musings on whether Mr. Rochester was likely to choose Blanche as a wife despite her lack of "good nature." Narrator-Jane then admonishes, "You are not to suppose, reader, that Adèle has all this time been sitting motionless at my feet" (*JE*, 200–203). This

change of subject away from the then-painful thought of Mr. Rochester's choosing another woman conflates character-Jane's time of observation and her emotions in the past moment with narrator-Jane's present moment and process of writing.

59. Stewart, *Dear Reader*, 244.

Chapter Three | Domestic Interiors and the Fictionality of the Domestic: Esther Summerson Writes Home

1. John Forster, unsigned review of *Bleak House*, by Charles Dickens, *Examiner* (October 8, 1853), in Collins, *Dickens*, 291–92.

2. Ibid.

3. Nancy Armstrong, *Desire and Domestic Fiction: A Political History of the Novel*, 37, 3–8. See also Armstrong's introduction and chap. 4.

4. Audrey Jaffe, *Scenes of Sympathy: Identity and Representation in Victorian Fiction*, 14.

5. Leila Silvana May builds on the work of Armstrong and others in "The Strong-Arming of Desire: A Reconsideration of Nancy Armstrong's *Desire and Domestic Fiction*." May identifies the Victorian domestic woman as "*the* modern individual" (268, original emphasis) through the middle-class valuation of that which is private, sacred, and sentimental—in other words, through that which is coded as "feminine." In this way, the homemaker's cultural and discursive identity shows its similarity to the paradigmatically individual—because inwardly original—figure of the author.

6. Susan Johnston, *Women and Domestic Experience in Victorian Political Fiction*, 85.

7. George Brimley, "Dickens' *Bleak House*," review of *Bleak House*, by Charles Dickens, *Spectator* (September 24, 1853), in Collins, *Dickens*, 285.

8. Unsigned review of *Bleak House*, by Charles Dickens, *Bentley's Miscellany* 34 (October 1853), in Collins, *Dickens*, 288–89.

9. Robert Newsom, "*Villette* and *Bleak House*: Authorizing Women," 70.

10. Case, "Gender and History," 320 (original emphasis). Though I challenge aspects of her reading, I nonetheless take Case's point seriously; her interpretation of Esther's narration as evidence of Dickens's own assumptions about the "natural" proclivities of each gender may indeed indicate the reason that Esther is written as she is. However, I am proposing an alternative way to read Esther that is less concerned with the extratextual provenance of her narration than with its potential effects. Indeed, our interpretations are not mutually exclusive.

11. Alex Zwerdling, "Esther Summerson Rehabilitated," 430.

12. Rachel Ablow, *The Marriage of Minds: Reading Sympathy in the Victorian Marriage Plot*, 8.

13. Greiner, *Sympathetic Realism*, 1–3, 10.

14. Ibid., 4, 22–23.

15. Charles Dickens, *Bleak House* (hereafter cited in text as *BH*), 28.

16. Rebecca Mitchell, *Victorian Lessons in Empathy and Difference*, 2, 12. Mitchell proposes that recognizing difference is an ethical gesture (in the tradition of Emmanuel Levinas) and that Victorian novels "demonstrate that moving into the recognition of alterity is a process through which one comes to realize one's limits" (2).

Esther seems almost uncannily to align with Mitchell's conception of the ethical realization of difference as a foundation for meaningful interactions among people.

17. Chap. 67 opens with Esther anticipating the cessation of her narrative, which has been requested by the "unknown friend to whom I write"; characteristically, she promises "much dear remembrance on my side" (*BH*, 965).

18. The vacillation between the anonymous, present-tense narrator and Esther may reflect Dickens's awareness that his biting portrayal of Victorian society and institutions required a more emotionally engaging counterpoint. It may be for this reason that he chose not only a first-person, autobiographical narrator—a form that particularly foregrounds the sympathetic nature of fiction reading—but also a domestic woman to be the voice of the personally meaningful in *Bleak House*.

19. In his psychological reading of Esther, Zwerdling similarly suggests that she believes love must first be won through hard work ("Esther Summerson Rehabilitated," 430).

20. Monica Feinberg, "Family Plot: The Bleak House of Victorian Romance," 5, 6, 7. Feinberg does note, however, that Esther's narration of the space of Bleak House "relies on either the reader's or the character's imaginative contribution" to animate her own discourse (7), though she takes this to be a mystification of the psychological turmoil (Esther's and Dickens's) underlying the narrative.

21. See, for instance, John O. Jordan's gloss of this part of the novel in *Supposing "Bleak House"*: "Her readiness to accept these derogatory nicknames and to allow her own name to be lost among them signals the instability of her identity and her complicity with the well-intentioned but demeaning constructions of her friends" (11). Jordan seems to assume that an invented identity is tantamount to an inauthentic one, and that a stable identity is not only possible and natural but also desirable. For those reasons, he here overlooks the advantages Esther derives from these reappropriated names.

22. Esther states her philosophy several times, the first occasion being when she tells Mr. Jarndyce of her concern for the Jellybys, brought on by their mother's "telescopic philanthropy" mission for Borioboola-Gha, which leaves her family wholly without care, attention, or support (*BH*, 83). While Esther's assertions are tentative, her opinion on the flexible conditions of reciprocity never varies, and since this opinion is expressed several times in her discourse, it would be difficult to persist in a reading that deauthorizes Esther's sentiments.

23. Newsom, "*Villette* and *Bleak House*," 65.

24. Amanda Anderson, *The Powers of Distance: Cosmopolitanism and the Cultivation of Detachment*, 41.

25. As defined by Genette in *Narrative Discourse*, an anachrony is a "discordance" between the chronological order in which the story events occur in the diegetic world and the order in which these events are related in the discourse (35–36).

26. Meir Sternberg, *The Poetics of Biblical Narrative: Ideological Literature and the Drama of Reading*, 237.

27. See *BH*, 59, 85, 89, and 265, for just a small sampling of this trend.

28. Iser, *Implied Reader*, 168.

29. In "Alluring Vacancies in the Victorian Character," Nina Auerbach suggests that Esther's inconsistencies—here meaning not gaps, but rather the disjuncture between how Esther describes herself and how she behaves and narrates—"'seduce' us into reading her" by making us think that Esther has "a hidden reality" (37).

30. See Meir Sternberg's explanation of how gaps produce these effects, along with suspense, in "How Narrativity Makes a Difference," 116–17.

Chapter Four | "No True Home": Difficult Domesticity and Controlling Collaboration in *David Copperfield* and *Villette*

1. Charlotte Brontë, *Villette* (hereafter cited in text as *V*), 421. In chap. 31, when M. Paul asks Lucy if she is "home-sick," she replies, "To be home-sick, one must have a home." It is in response to this that M. Paul describes her need for a "careful friend" who will "watch" and "watch over" her, as he himself does (421). This is one of many instances in which M. Paul is figured as Lucy's ideal reader—one who sees her "faults," namely, her inner fire and passion, and who, because of these very qualities, seeks to shape (and allows himself to be shaped by) her.

2. Alexander Welsh and Garrett Stewart both identify Micawber as a potential rival of David's authority. Welsh quotes Stewart from *Dickens and the Trials of Imagination*: "Micawber is the great rival author in *David Copperfield*, a commanding stylist against whose prose David must define his own expressive tendencies. . . . Over the long course of the novel, however, Dickens carefully works free of Micawber as a possible father figure" (Stewart, 138–39), finally exiling the happy emigrant to Australia, where he begins a new life as a magistrate. In this way, according to Welsh, Micawber is made to live out Dickens's own adolescent career goals (Welsh, *From Copyright to Copperfield*, 154, 155). The great distance to which David (and Dickens) goes (literally and figuratively) to extricate himself from Micawber's literary and paternal influences speaks once more to the problematic role of social relationships in the process of artistic self-creation for David.

3. John Picker, "The Soundproof Study: Victorian Professionals, Workspace, and Urban Noise," 428.

4. Throughout *David Copperfield*, domesticity that fails in some respect (whether in mismanagement or in not conforming to social norms) appears to be beneficial to the male professional. From David himself, to Thomas and Sophy Traddles (working and secretly dwelling in Thomas's cramped law office), eventual success is often predicated on experiences combining the domestic and the professional. In the world of *David Copperfield*, the "curious status as [a] housebound professional" benefits, rather than damages, the affirmation of his "vocational status" (Picker, "Soundproof Study," 428).

5. Carlyle, "Hero as Man of Letters," 137.

6. Mary Poovey, *Uneven Developments: The Ideological Work of Gender in Mid-Victorian England*, 100–101.

7. The impression David gives of likeness through difference with his audience is potentially activated earlier in the novel as well, when David tells about his secret courtship of Dora. His illicit love notes to her and their private meetings secured through the complicity of her friend Julia Mills structurally parallel another secret

affair happening nearly simultaneously: that of Steerforth and Emily. While David's intentions toward Dora are "honorable," and Steerforth ultimately seduces and "ruins" Emily, the two men use identical tactics to secure the affections of their objects. Indeed, the revelation of the secret courtship between David and Dora is very strongly implied—by narrator-David himself—to be a contributing factor in Dora's father's, Mr. Spenlow's, sudden death. Though most of David's confessed indiscretions are indeed youthful errors that prove relatively easy to reconcile with his "good" character, his early courtship of Dora (its risks to Dora and her family through its parallels to a seduction), his Murdstonean treatment of Dora during their early marriage, and his physical aggression toward Uriah Heep are much more complicated instances of confession that may force the reader to construct for David a less shining, if also markedly more individualized, character.

8. Alexander Welsh, "Writing and Copying in the Age of Steam," 30.

9. Poovey, *Uneven Developments*, 100.

10. Ibid., 101.

11. Ibid., 100–101.

12. Ibid., 98.

13. See *On Liberty*, chap. 3, "Of Individuality as One of the Elements of Well-Being," in which Mill critiques the "despotism of custom" and its deadening effect on "progress or improvement" (132). He argues that "individuality" and the "unlikeness of one person to another" is what motivates our perception of either "imperfection" or "superiority" in human character, and thus allows us to "produc[e] something better than either" (134). He appeals to "the East" and China in particular as "a warning example" of what occurs when a society does not value his brand of individuality. Despite having a "nation of much talent," "[the Chinese] have become stationary— have remained so for thousands of years; and if they are ever to be farther improved, it must be by foreigners" (135–36). At once justifying British imperialism and promoting his particular doctrine of individuality as the *development* of innate traits, Mill also menaces his Victorian readers with the threat that if they become stagnant or static, their society too may become a legitimate target for "foreign" improvement (136). David's individual anxiety about illegitimate external influence resonates with Mill's writing on a grand and globally minded scale.

14. For a comparative examination of the dynamics of "Gothic homelessness" and identity performance in Jamaica Kincaid's *Lucy* and *Villette*, see Evie Shockley, "The Horrors of Homelessness: Gothic Doubling in Kincaid's *Lucy* and Brontë's *Villette*," particularly pp. 49–50.

15. More than once Lucy remarks on her "curious" legibility to others, especially "inn-servants and ship-stewardesses," who can always tell that she is "an individual of no social significance" and who treat this well-spoken yet solitary and unconnected female traveler like the uncomfortable social anomaly that she is (*V*, 66, 50, 52, 53). Of course, as in the cases of M. de Bassompierre and, more painfully, John Graham Bretton, most "readings" of Lucy by others—as she does not hesitate to demonstrate to her audience—are not acceptable because, she forcefully implies, they are inaccurate and fail to perceive the well-hidden inner self that in fact takes shape through Lucy's resistant discourse (*V*, 348–49, 366–67).

16. Anna Gibson in "Charlotte Brontë's First Person" argues that *Villette*, more so than Brontë's other first-person novels, enacts a movement away from thinking of the self as a unified essence that preexists its enunciation, connecting Brontë's last novel to psychological and phrenological discourses in the Victorian period (208). Gibson's argument, though it concerns the materialist aspects of selfhood and embodiment more than the present study does, proposes that *Villette*'s narration encourages an understanding of personal identity as "processual" and thus complements the interpretation I develop (204, 208).

17. One notable exception to this critical paradigm is Gibson, who insists that calling Lucy "controlling" means that one is treating Lucy as a "person" who preexists the discourse that creates her (ibid., 204). If one reads Lucy as a fictional autobiographer, however, one maintains an active sense of Lucy's fictionality, her fundamental lack of essence and pre-discursive "personhood," even while recognizing how the discourse itself produces the *effect* of individual essence. The reading I propose illuminates how the telling makes Lucy feel very much like a "person," exposing the processes that make any self seem unified and stable. When I call Lucy "controlling" it is not to insist on her basis in extratextual essence but rather to highlight how her narration produces a lifelike character whose mode of self-making simultaneously demonstrates the absence of essence in personhood beyond the text.

18. Garrett Stewart in *Dear Reader* comments on how Lucy's explicit challenges and overt gaps construct reader engagement. But Stewart focuses most intently on the purpose of these moments for the author and her sisters, commenting that "the Brontës write to quell (without quite dispelling) the otherness of death and loss" (273).

19. Robyn Warhol, for instance, talks about that which Lucy holds back, explaining it in terms of verisimilitude ("Double Gender," 863). But Warhol's assertion that Lucy's overt distinction between her knowledge as narrator and her knowledge as character "[implies] a commitment to realism, to representing 'how it really was,' for the heroine" (863) does not account fully for the simultaneous suppression of information that occurs on both the discourse and the story level. In "'I Seemed to Hold Two Lives': Disclosing Circumnarration in *Villette* and *The Picture of Dorian Gray*," Helen H. Davis calls these omissions and roundabout recountings "circumnarration." She sees Lucy's circumnarration as a way to narrate indirectly a less-than-acceptable female destiny (personal ambition and independent success), thus making it part of the tradition of what narratologists call the "unnarratable" (199–204). But this reading of her resistant narration overlooks the more personal (domestic, romantic) urges that readers are asked to associate with Lucy's omissions from her autobiography.

20. Stewart, *Dear Reader*, 253, 404.

21. See the discussion of the work of Lubomír Dolezel in the section "Making Selves with Less and More: Gaps and Details in Fiction and Autobiography" in chap. 1 for an explanation of the idea of "fictional facts."

22. An especially significant moment that signals Lucy's desire for mutual and unconditional love happens in chap. 15, when she struggles to relate a nightmare that is both a symptom and a cause of the illness she suffers during the isolation of the "long vacation": "Methought the well-loved dead, who had loved *me* well in life, met me elsewhere, alienated" (*V*, 183, original emphasis). The potential of eternal separation

from beloved others, then, is the nearly unspeakable specter that haunts Lucy's life. This is one of the clearest mentions of the family life she has lost and cannot regain, though the mention is brief and (significantly) is buried in a paragraph emphasizing the "nameless" and "unutterable" nature of her experience (*V*, 182–83). The reciprocity of this lost ideal—once Lucy's reality—in which those she loved loved her in return, models for the reader what Lucy desires, and what the sympathizing reader alone can (in some sense, at least) supply.

23. Karen Chase, *Eros and Psyche: The Representation of Personality in Charlotte Brontë, Charles Dickens, and George Eliot*, 67.

24. Janice Carlisle, "The Face in the Mirror: *Villette* and the Conventions of Autobiography," 286.

25. From the third chapter of the novel, Lucy's narration shows Graham and Paulina modeling the kind of adoringly reciprocal self-making that Lucy herself both desires and resists. Paulina's "character" is only expressed to its fullest extent when she is engaged with Graham (*V*, 24, 26), and Graham's personality is most legible to and most fully understood by little Polly (*V*, 28–29). Later, their potential for mutual self-making is brought to fruition, though Lucy reports it in the language of natural affinities: each partner ripens what Lucy sees as the best features of the other (*V*, 491–92). Lucy's own potential to "advance" (*V*, 420), however, she fears is limited to an isolated professional destiny: "Is there nothing more for me in life—no true home—nothing to be dearer to me than myself, and by its paramount preciousness to draw from me better things than I care to culture for myself only?" (*V*, 419). At the story level, M. Paul comes to serve this "paramount" purpose for character-Lucy (if only temporarily) so that at the discourse level, narrator-Lucy can cultivate "better things for [her self]" through her readers' interpretations of that self as (paradoxically) both essential and progressive.

26. Carlisle, "The Face in the Mirror," 272.

27. Warhol, "Double Gender," 863.

28. Lucy's tendency toward allegory and metaphor is a form of reader provocation that draws as much attention to the mode of telling as to the fictional facts being figured by her creative narration. She frequently frames such passages by distancing herself from the narrative methods she employs. "I, Lucy Snowe, plead guiltless of that curse, an overheated and discursive imagination," she writes, before proceeding to describe how little Paulina's grief (a vicarious version of Lucy's own heartache) haunts the house at Bretton (*V*, 11). "Of an artistic temperament, I deny that I am," she declares a few chapters later, though she admits to sharing "the artist's faculty of making the most of present pleasure" as her "fancy budded fresh" on the journey to Villette (*V*, 67). Indeed, in disowning a "discursive imagination" and an "artistic temperament" Lucy gives overwhelming evidence of such capacities and provokes the reader to imagine for her the same traits she explicitly denies.

29. Gibson remarks that "Lucy's narrative silences mirror her character's silence" ("Charlotte Brontë's First Person," 217). She argues that the gap about Dr. John's identity is evidence that "Lucy" comes into existence through the narration itself.

30. Ivan Kreilkamp, "Unuttered: Withheld Speech and Female Authorship in *Jane Eyre* and *Villette*," 331, 338, 341.

31. Chase, *Eros and Psyche*, 83.

32. In the introduction to *Villette*, Ignes Sodré proposes that "the imagery that belongs to the" more recent loss of M. Paul in a shipwreck is actually "cast backwards" by Lucy-as-narrator to "convey symbolically" the loss of her family in chap. 4 (xviii).

33. Cohn, *Distinction of Fiction*, 169.

34. Even Esther conflates the present moment of the telling with the time of the recounted events on occasion. In her conversation with Mrs. Jellyby about the climate of Borrioboola-Gha, Esther represents Mrs. Jellyby's interruption of her character-self as an interruption of her narration, in which she was focalizing, through indirect discourse, the sentiments of her past self. On being asked why she never turned her attentions to Africa, Esther-as-narrator tells the reader,

> I was quite at a loss how to receive it. I hinted that the climate—
> "The finest climate in the world!" said Mrs Jellyby.
> "Indeed, ma'am?"
> "Certainly, with precaution." (*BH*, 54)

35. Robert Newsom in "*Villette* and *Bleak House*" dismisses any notion of ambiguity of M. Paul's fate: "Some readers assert that the ending of *Villette* is ambiguous, and indeed Brontë is said to have softened the ending somewhat, ironically at her father's request. . . . Readers of any discernment at all will not fail to recognize that M. Paul perishes" (58n4). However, what readers of any discernment will also not fail to recognize is that neither Lucy nor Brontë explicitly narrates or writes M. Paul's fate. Given the fictionality of the account, his end (or not) is perhaps not ambiguous but is certainly unspecified. And implication, after all, requires the reader to fill in the gap, to create the story, even as that interpretive process can tend to obscure for some readers their constitutive role in the fictional world. Gibson describes this conclusion as "ending without an ending," claiming that it demonstrates a view of the self as "an always-developing entity"; the novel thus "offers the potential for continuance" ("Charlotte Brontë's First Person," 221).

36. Stewart, *Dear Reader*, 252.

Coda | Fiction and Selfhood in the Twenty-First Century

1. Alix Spiegel and Lulu Miller, "The Personality Myth," 57:28.

2. See Jay Clayton, *Charles Dickens in Cyberspace: The Afterlife of the Nineteenth Century in Postmodern Culture*; Richard Menke, *Telegraphic Realism: Victorian Fiction and Other Information Systems*; and Simon Joyce, *The Victorians in the Rearview Mirror*, as just three pertinent examples of a trend in which twenty-first-century writers seek to understand parts of postmodernity by means of Victorian texts and ideas.

3. Eric Hobsbawm, *Industry and Empire: From 1750 to the Present Day*, 88. Buckley notes that standardized daily time was paralleled by the utter newness of historical time-consciousness in the Victorian era: "Nineteenth-century absorption in the troublous time-element differed both in kind and degree [from earlier generations]. The notion of public time, or history, as the medium of organic growth and fundamental change, rather than simply additive succession, was essentially new" (*Triumph*

of Time, 5). Our newly digital age might mark another, different but similarly substantial, transformation in the consciousness of time.

4. Hobsbawm, *Industry and Empire*, 88.

5. Gilmour notes in *The Victorian Period*, "A subscriber to the *Edinburgh Review* or the *Quarterly* was accustomed to move from, say, a review of Tennyson's poems to a discussion of the latest work in geology, from an article on contemporary astronomy to one on the Oxford Movement, without feeling that science, literature, and theology belonged in separate intellectual compartments" (7).

6. Sally Mitchell, *Daily Life in Victorian England*, xiii.

7. Following Sidonie Smith and Julia Watson in *Reading Autobiography*, I define life-writing as "writing that takes a life . . . as its subject" (4), adding "personal" to indicate that I am referring to self-referential practices. This includes classical autobiography, memoir, and other forms of written self-representation.

8. Periodic exploration of the Amazon.com, *Publisher's Weekly*, and *New York Times* nonfiction bestseller lists in 2016 and 2017 revealed in the top ten life-writing works including *When Breath Becomes Air*, by Paul Kalanithi (the posthumously published memoir of a young neurosurgeon dying of cancer); *Between the World and Me*, by Ta-Nehisi Coates (essays addressed to the author's son that combine history, cultural analysis, and personal narrative to explore race in America); and *Yes Please*, by Amy Poehler (a memoir of the comedian and actor's experiences; often compared to Tina Fey's similarly popular *Bossypants*, from 2013); as well as autobiographies of political figures, celebrities, and what I call "extraordinary subjects" (think: a military sniper, or a survivor of international war).

9. See Amazon's listing for Eggers's novel (http://www.amazon.com/What-Dave -Eggers/dp/0307385906) and the way it presents Deng's life as both unique and representative of many others—the implicit emphasis, here, being on the *otherness* of these others to the presumed American reader. The description crows, "*What Is the What* is an astonishing novel that illuminates the lives of millions through one extraordinary man." This commodification of otherness as part of the appeal of contemporary life-writing texts can prove ethically problematic. For instance, through her various life-writing texts (her blog and particularly her memoir), Malala Yousafzai "has become a symbol for the West," and she seems to represent for Western readers "an individual subject contesting subjugation," as Wendy Hesford describes it in "The Malala Effect" (*Journal of Advanced Composition* 34.1–2 [2014]: 139–64). As Hesford puts it, linguistic and rhetorical "identifications that purportedly give voice to the 'other,' especially when uttered by"—and, I would include, when read and personally naturalized by—"those who occupy spaces of structural privilege and relative safety, often function as rhetorical acts of self-creation to the extent that the enunciator incorporates the identity of the 'other' into her own identity" (152), resulting in appropriation that can overlook difference in favor of reinforcing readers' preexisting natural attitudes.

10. Posnock's comment in "A Great Memoir! At Last!" echoes Thomas Carlyle's narrator in *Sartor Resartus*, who mentions "these Autobiographical times of ours" in chap. 2.

11. McKeon, *Origins of the English Novel*, 21, 44, 48.

12. Joseph O'Brien, "Riffing on *The Hunger Games*: Class Warfare, First-Person Present-Tense Narration, and the Murderous Game Show Genre," n.p.

13. Vicky Smith, "Getting a Little Tense," n.p.

14. Nicola Morgan, "Nicola Morgan's Top 10 Present Tense Books," n.p.

15. Paige, *Before Fiction*, 9–11.

16. Lee Child, "Uninvent This: Telling Tales," n.p.

17. McKeon, *Origins of the English Novel*, 26–27.

18. Dorrit Cohn in *The Distinction of Fiction* lists several famous examples preceding the current "boom," including J. M. Coetzee's *Waiting for the Barbarians* and Margaret Atwood's *Handmaid's Tale* (97). Chuck Palahniuk's *Fight Club* is another example that predates the more recent increased interest in the form.

19. Numerous online writers' discussion boards support such a theory. As one example out of many, see the forums on Absolute Write, especially the one listed under the thread "Why do you hate the first person present tense?" (http://absolutewrite.com/forums/showthread.php?273439-Why-do-you-hate-the-first-person-present-tense). The writers who love this form cite immediacy and "identification" with the narrator as its strengths, as well as the way the limited knowledge of the character allows the writer to create other narrative effects. But the writers who hate it are against it precisely because it reminds them of the artifice of the form, and they implicitly seek a form that mimics real-world epistemological possibilities. See Voirey Linger's entry from July 9, 2013, as an example of the latter.

20. This may seem like a particularly American take on autobiography, and generally it is. But the possibility to be "uplifted" by a "true story" is latent in the reactions of British readers, too, at least in the anecdotal evidence of the comments on Amazon.co.uk. See the discussion of Jeanette Walls's autobiography later in the coda.

21. Zunshine, *Why We Read Fiction*, 6.

22. JohnBrassey, "A Misery Memoir with a Difference," review of *The Glass Castle*, March 16, 2012, https://www.amazon.co.uk/product-reviews/B0032TYQRO/ref=cm_cr_getr_d_paging_btm_3?ie+=UTF8&showViewpoints=1&filterBy-Star=positive&pageNumber=3. His review is not the only one on the UK site to value this aspect of Walls's autobiography. One of the commentators, by the name of "Ms A. Breen" ("An Amazing Story," review of *The Glass Castle*, November 21, 2011), from Coventry, UK, similarly remarks that "the courage and determination of Jeanette and her siblings in escaping their situation is astonishing—a wonderful example of how collaboration is better than competition." While her focus on the reciprocal and social aspects of success are uncommon in the comments on the American Amazon site, her belief that the story can tell us something directly about "true life" (namely, that it "is never black and white") echoes the gist of the comments of the more individual-focused American readers.

23. Beckybramer, "True to Life Account," review of *The Glass Castle*, November 13, 2005, http://www.amazon.com/review/R7XM29C2Y7MMZ/ref=cm_cr_dp_title/184-7722217-9136935?ie=UTF8&ASIN=074324754X&channel=detail-glance&nodeID=283155&store=books.

24. Thomas M. Seay, "Inferno to Paradiso … (Or Close Enough)," review of *The Glass Castle*, December 14, 2005, https://www.amazon.com/gp/customer-reviews/R3PNEFJWDHI23Y/ref=cm_cr_getr_d_rvw_ttl?ie=UTF8&ASIN=074324754X.

25. This perception of a bond of friendship between writer and reader is not unique to the autobiography. In fact, as Bradley Deane writes in *The Making of the Victorian Novelist*, "Sympathetic friendship . . . came to serve as the dominant metaphor of the relationship between novelists and their readers" (28). Unlike the Victorian novelists, however, Walls does not actively represent herself as an intimate friend of the reader; rather, the intimacy implied by the first-person telling of her life story—much as in the fictional autobiography—forges the sense of a relationship between author and reader.

26. See http://www.amazon.com/Questionable-Facts/forum/Fx3AXTSQXAI0 RP3/ Tx34MS9SZ8OP0V6/1/ref =cm_cd_ef_rt_tft_tp?_encoding =UTF8&asin =074324754X.

27. Although I critique the readerly perception that factuality is the sole indicator of personal value in texts of life-writing, it is important for me to state that different genres of writing and language—for instance, legislation, journalism, even some political speech—require different and perhaps less flexible, if equally critical, approaches to the cultural knowledge category we call "facts." This is mainly because texts in those other genres structure the lived realities of both individuals and large groups of people in ways that are much more far-reaching and concrete than do most texts of personal life-writing.

28. Kwame Anthony Appiah, *Cosmopolitanism: Ethics in a World of Strangers*, xvi, xvii, xviii. The beliefs underlying this practice of partial cosmopolitanism curiously echo Esther Summerson's domestic formula for productive intersubjective interaction in and beyond the self and home, examined in chap. 3.

29. Ibid., 135. Here Appiah makes explicit one of the guiding principles that also informs the Victorian preoccupation with the touchstone figures of the author and the homemaker. The potential that defines the paradigmatic individual, through the connection of shared humanity, is also the reader's potential. And, as the fictional autobiography suggests, the potential of the author, the homemaker, the modern individual, is no more and no less than the potential of fictionality itself. Fictional engagements with the reader bring them to life and give them cultural currency.

30. Ibid.

31. Digital technologies' perceived effect of providing instant gratification in the realm of "knowledge," one might even argue, plays an integral role in the recent proliferation and success of false news reports designed to deceive readers. While readers seem willing to cross-check the facts of autobiographers' lives to assess the credibility of their identities, the willingness to vet news sources and political assertions through broad and contemplative reading practices seems to be waning (if it ever existed). Perhaps this is because "debunking" the intimate details of a single person's life story proves less threatening to readers' unified world pictures (their "natural attitudes") than would verifying news reports through competing sources and in-depth research. But this is a topic for another study.

32. Richard Lea, "Very Now: Has Present-Tense Narration Really Taken Over Fiction?," n.p.

33. Anderson, *Powers of Distance*, 3–5.

34. Ibid., 53.

35. Cohn, *Distinction of Fiction*, 96.

36. These forms of media, when replicated by present-tense narration in a fictional text, may operate for contemporary readers more like those older technologies, the diary and the letter, in which shorter increments of time are recounted serially at very short distances of retrospect. Indeed, the present-progressive tense of the omnipresent phrase "I'm Facebooking this!" indicates not only the actions of the speaker in the moment of "narration" but also the widespread conception that internet media are up-to-the-second representations of lived experience. Tellingly, immediacy was also the effect of reading the epistolary novel in the eighteenth century: the narrative gained value because it encouraged the perception that it communicated immediate, personal experience. Ian Watt in *The Rise of the Novel* makes this claim about *Pamela* (191).

37. Cohn, *Distinction of Fiction*, 96.

38. Ibid., 99, 100.

39. Ibid., 100, 102.

40. Ibid., 103, 105.

41. Recent scholarship in the field of unnatural narratology might contest Cohn's insistence on the paradoxical nature of this narration as its key defining feature. In unnatural narratology, the focus shifts away from what theorists see as a limiting distinction between "natural" and "unnatural" speech acts, considering instead effects and implications that accompany so-called unnatural narrative situations. See Aarhus University's Unnatural Narratology project, through their Narrative Research Lab, for more specifics: http://projects.au.dk/narrativeresearchlab/unnatural/.

42. Cohn, *Distinction of Fiction*, 107 (original emphasis), 105.

43. Suzanne Collins, *The Hunger Games*, 4.

44. Cohn insists that "simultaneous narration does imply a narrative situation"— that is, simultaneous narration implies there must be an environment in which such a telling takes place, and a means by which such a telling exists; but the implied "narrative situation" is "one that defies all manners of picturing it on verisimilar lines" (*Distinction of Fiction*, 105). For Cohn, there are no circumstances under which such a narrated utterance as Katniss's could be made to fit "the dictates of formal mimetics" that usually govern realist narration (104).

45. Cohn, *Distinction of Fiction*, 107.

46. I am referring specifically to Amazon.com's and *Publisher's Weekly*'s hardcover-fiction bestseller lists. This means that the trends I note are operating in a sector of the market in which readers have both the means and the motivation to purchase new hardcover fiction. Thus, this pattern should be considered in that context.

47. Smith and Watson, *Reading Autobiography*, 4.

Bibliography

Abbott, H. Porter. *The Cambridge Introduction to Narrative*. New York: Cambridge University Press, 2008.

Ablow, Rachel. "Addressing the Reader: The Autobiographical Voice." In *The Oxford History of the Novel in English*, vol. 3, ed. John Kucich and Jenny Bourne, 274–78. Oxford: Oxford University Press, 2012.

———. Introduction to *The Feeling of Reading: Affective Experience and Victorian Literature*, ed. Rachel Ablow, 1–10. Ann Arbor: University of Michigan Press, 2010.

———. *The Marriage of Minds: Reading Sympathy in the Victorian Marriage Plot*. Stanford, CA: Stanford University Press, 2007.

———. "Reading and Re-Reading: Wilde, Newman, and the Fiction of Belief." In *The Feeling of Reading: Affective Experience and Victorian Literature*, ed. Rachel Ablow, 157–78. Ann Arbor: University of Michigan Press, 2010.

Abrams, M. H. *Natural Supernaturalism: Tradition and Revolution in Romantic Literature*. New York: W. W. Norton, 1971.

Allen, Peter. "Trollope to His Readers: The Unreliable Narrator of *An Autobiography*." *Biography* 19.1 (1996): 1–18.

Allott, Miriam, ed. *The Brontës: The Critical Heritage*. Boston: Routledge and Kegan Paul, 1974.

Altick, Robert. *The English Common Reader: A Social History of the Mass Reading Public, 1800–1900*. 2nd ed. Chicago: University of Chicago Press, 1998.

Anderson, Amanda. *The Powers of Distance: Cosmopolitanism and the Cultivation of Detachment*. Princeton, NJ: Princeton University Press, 2001.

Anderson, Benedict. *Imagined Communities: Reflections on the Origin and Spread of Nationalism*. New York: Verso, 1991.

Appiah, Kwame Anthony. *Cosmopolitanism: Ethics in a World of Strangers*. New York: W. W. Norton, 2006.

Armstrong, Isobel. *Victorian Poetry: Poetry, Poetics, Politics*. New York: Routledge, 1993.

Armstrong, Nancy. *Desire and Domestic Fiction: A Political History of the Novel*. Oxford: Oxford University Press, 1987.

Auerbach, Nina. "Alluring Vacancies in the Victorian Character." *Kenyon Review* 8.3 (1986): 36–48.

Austin, J. L. *How to Do Things with Words*. Ed. J. O. Urmson and Marina Sbisà. Cambridge: Harvard University Press, 1975.

Bell, Michael. *Sentimentalism, Ethics, and the Culture of Feeling*. New York: Palgrave, 2000.

Benveniste, Émile. "Subjectivity in Language." In *Problems in General Linguistics*, trans. Mary Elizabeth Meeks, 223–30. Coral Gables, FL: University of Miami Press, 1971.

Blake, Andrew. *Reading Victorian Fiction: The Cultural Context and Ideological Content of the Nineteenth-Century Novel*. New York: St. Martin's Press, 1999.

Bloom, Harold. *The Anxiety of Influence: A Theory of Poetry*. 2nd ed. New York: Oxford University Press, 1997.

Bock, Carol. *Charlotte Brontë and the Storyteller's Audience*. Iowa City: University of Iowa Press, 1992.

Bodenheimer, Rosemarie. *The Real Life of Mary Ann Evans*. Ithaca, NY: Cornell University Press, 1994.

Booth, Wayne. *The Rhetoric of Fiction*. 2nd ed. Chicago: University of Chicago Press, 1983.

Brontë, Charlotte. *Jane Eyre: An Autobiography*. Ed. Stevie Davies. New York: Penguin Classics, 2006.

———. *Villette*. Introduction by Ignes Sodré and A. S. Byatt. Notes by Deborah Lutz. New York: Random House, 2001.

Bruner, Jerome. "Self-Making and World-Making." In *Narrative and Identity: Studies in Autobiography, Self and Culture*, ed. Jens Brockmeier and Donal A. Carbaugh, 25–38. Philadelphia: John Benjamins, 2001.

Brunton, Mary. *Discipline: A Novel*. London: Richard Bentley, 1849. Hathi Trust, https://babel.hathitrust.org/cgi/pt?id=njp.32101031716986;view=1u p;seq=13.

Bruss, Elizabeth. *Autobiographical Acts: The Changing Situation of a Literary Genre*. Baltimore: Johns Hopkins University Press, 1976.

Buckley, Jerome H. "Autobiography in the English *Bildungsroman*." In *The Interpretation of Narrative: Theory and Practice*, ed. Morton Bloomfield, 93–104. Cambridge: Harvard University Press, 1970.

———. *The Triumph of Time: A Study of the Victorian Concepts of Time, History, Progress, and Decadence*. Cambridge: Harvard University Press, 1966.

Buckton, Oliver S. *Secret Selves: Confession and Same-Sex Desire in Victorian Autobiography*. Chapel Hill: University of North Carolina Press, 1998.

Butler, Judith. *Gender Trouble: Feminism and the Subversion of Identity*. New York: Routledge, 1999.

Carlisle, Janice. "The Face in the Mirror: *Villette* and the Conventions of Autobiography." *ELH* 46 (1979): 262–89.

———. "The Mirror in *The Mill on the Floss*: Towards a Reading of Autobiography as Discourse." *Studies in the Literary Imagination* 23.2 (1990): 177–97.

———. *The Sense of an Audience: Dickens, Thackeray, and Eliot at Mid-Century*. Athens: University of Georgia Press, 1981.

Carlyle, Thomas. "Essay on Biography." In *Essay on Biography: Selected Biographical and Historical Sketches and Other Writing*, ed. Bliss Perry. New York: Doubleday and McClure, 1902.

———. "Lecture V. The Hero as Man of Letters: Johnson, Burns, Rousseau." In *On Heroes, Hero-Worship, and the Heroic in History*, ed. Carl Niemeyer, 188–95. Lincoln: University of Nebraska Press, 1966.

———. *Past and Present*. 2nd ed. London: Chapman and Hall, 1845. Google Books, http://books.google.com/books?id=ugB4KjHmLLAC&printsec=frontcover#v=onepage&q&f=false.

———. *Sartor Resartus: The Life and Opinions of Herr Teufelsdröckh*. London, 1838. Project Gutenberg, http://www.gutenberg.org/files/1051/1051-h/1051-h.htm.

Case, Alison. "Gender and History in Narrative Theory: The Problem of Retrospective Distance in *David Copperfield* and *Bleak House*." In *A Companion to Narrative Theory*, ed. James Phelan and Peter Rabinowitz, 312–21. Malden, MA: Blackwell, 2005.

Chartier, Roger. *The Order of Books*. Stanford, CA: Stanford University Press, 1992.

Chase, Karen. *Eros and Psyche: The Representation of Personality in Charlotte Brontë, Charles Dickens, and George Eliot*. New York: Methuen, 1984.

Child, Lee. "Uninvent This: Telling Tales." *New Yorker*, May 16, 2016. http://www.newyorker.com/magazine/2016/05/16/the-frightening-power-of-fiction.

Clayton, Jay. *Charles Dickens in Cyberspace: The Afterlife of the Nineteenth Century in Postmodern Culture*. New York: Oxford University Press, 2003.

Clough, Patricia Ticineto. Introduction to *The Affective Turn*, ed. Patricia Clough and Jean Halley, 1–33. Durham, NC: Duke University Press, 2007.

Cohen, Monica. *Professional Domesticity in the Victorian Novel: Women, Work, and Home*. London: Cambridge University Press, 1998.

Cohn, Dorrit. *The Distinction of Fiction*. Baltimore: Johns Hopkins University Press, 1999.

Collins, K. K. *Identifying the Remains: George Eliot's Death in the London Religious Press*. Victoria, Canada: ELS Editions, 2006.

Collins, Philip, ed. *Dickens: The Critical Heritage*. New York: Barnes and Noble, 1971.

Collins, Suzanne. *The Hunger Games*. New York: Scholastic, 2008.

Culler, Jonathan. "Omniscience." *Narrative* 12.1 (2004): 22–34.

Danahay, Martin. *A Community of One: Masculine Autobiography and Autonomy in Nineteenth-Century Britain*. Albany: State University of New York Press, 1993.

Darwin, Charles. *Autobiographies*. Ed. Michael Neve and Sharon Messenger. New York: Penguin Books, 2002.

Davies, Stevie. Introduction to *Jane Eyre*, by Charlotte Brontë. New York: Penguin Classics, 2006.

Davis, Helen H. "'I Seemed to Hold Two Lives': Disclosing Circumnarration in *Villette* and *The Picture of Dorian Gray*." *Narrative* 21.2 (2013): 198–220.

Deane, Bradley. *The Making of the Victorian Novelist: Anxieties of Authorship in the Mass Market*. New York: Routledge, 2003.

De Man, Paul. "Autobiography as De-Facement." *MLN* 94.5 (1979): 919–30.

Dickens, Charles. *Bleak House*. Ed. Nicola Bradbury. New York: Penguin Classics, 2003.

———. *David Copperfield*. Oxford: Oxford University Press, 2008.

———. *The Letters of Charles Dickens from 1833 to 1870*. Ed. Georgina Hogarth and Mamie Dickens. Whitefish, MT: Kessinger, 2004.

Dixon, Thomas. *The Invention of Altruism: Making Moral Meanings in Victorian Britain*. Oxford: Oxford University Press, 2008.

Djikic, Maja, and Keith Oatley. "The Art in Fiction: From Indirect Communication to Changes in the Self." *Psychology of Aesthetics, Creativity, and the Arts* 8.4 (2014): 498–505.

Djikic, Maja, Keith Oatley, and M. C. Moldoveanu. "Opening the Closed Mind: The Effect of Exposure to Literature on the Need for Closure." *Creativity Research Journal* 25.2 (2013): 149–54.

Djikic, Maja, Keith Oatley, Sara Zoeterman, and Jordan B. Peterson. "On Being Moved by Art: How Reading Fiction Transforms the Self." *Creativity Research Journal* 21.1 (2009): 24–29.

Dolezel, Lubomír. *Heterocosmica: Fiction and Possible Worlds*. Baltimore: Johns Hopkins University Press, 2000.

———. "Truth and Authenticity in Narrative." *Poetics Today* 3.1 (1980): 7–25.

Duncan, Ian. *Modern Romance and Transformations of the Novel: The Gothic, Scott, and Dickens*. New York: Cambridge University Press, 1992.

Eakin, Paul John. *Fictions in Autobiography: Studies in the Art of Self-Invention*. Princeton, NJ: Princeton University Press, 1988.

———. *Living Autobiographically: How We Create Identity in Narrative*. Ithaca, NY: Cornell University Press, 2008.

———. *Touching the World: Reference in Autobiography*. Princeton, NJ: Princeton University Press, 1992.

———. "What Are We Reading When We Read Autobiography?" *Narrative* 12.2 (2004): 121–32.

Edwards, Amelia Ann Blanford. *Barbara's History: A Novel.* New York: Harper and Brothers, 1864. Printed by BiblioLife, 2016.

Eliot, George. *The George Eliot Letters.* Vol. 3. Ed. Gordon S. Haight. New Haven, CT: Yale University Press, 1954.

———. *The Lifted Veil.* In *"The Lifted Veil" and "Brother Jacob."* Oxford: Oxford World's Classics, 1999.

———. *The Mill on the Floss.* Ed. and notes by A. S. Byatt. New York: Penguin Classics, 2003.

———. "The Natural History of German Life." In *The Essays of 'George Eliot,'* ed. Nathan Sheppard, 141–77. New York: Funk & Wagnalls, 1883.

Esterhammer, Angela. "1824: Improvisation, Speculation, and Identity-Construction." *BRANCH: Britain, Representation and Nineteenth-Century History.* Ed. Dino Franco Felluga. Extension of *Romanticism and Victorianism on the Net.* http://www.branchcollective.org/?ps_articles=angela-esterhammer -1824-improvisation-speculation-and-identity-construction.

Feinberg, Monica. "Family Plot: The Bleak House of Victorian Romance." *Victorian Newsletter* 76 (1989): 5–17.

Fisher, Judith. *Thackeray's Skeptical Narrative and the 'Perilous Trade' of Authorship.* Burlington, VT: Ashgate, 2002.

Flint, Kate. *The Woman Reader, 1837–1914.* New York: Oxford University Press, 1993.

Folkenflik, Robert. Introduction to *The Culture of Autobiography: Constructions of Self-Representation,* 1–20. Stanford, CA: Stanford University Press, 1993.

Franklin, J. Jeffrey. *Serious Play: The Cultural Form of the Nineteenth-Century Realist Novel.* Philadelphia: University of Pennsylvania Press, 1999.

Freeman, Hadley. "Under Scrutiny: Self-Penned Revelations by Famous People Rarely Give Us What We Want." *Guardian,* November 24, 2007. http:// www.guardian.co.uk/books/2007/nov/24/bestbooksoftheyear.bestbooks 7?INTCMP=SRCH.

Gagnier, Regenia. *Subjectivities: A History of Self-Representation in Britain, 1832– 1920.* New York: Oxford University Press, 1991.

Gallagher, Catherine. "Gender, Property, and the Rise of the Novel." *Modern Language Quarterly* 53.3 (1992): 263–77.

———. *Nobody's Story: The Vanishing Acts of Women Writers in the Marketplace, 1670–1820.* Berkeley: University of California Press, 1994.

———. "The Rise of Fictionality." In *The Novel,* vol. 1, *History, Geography, and Culture,* ed. Franco Moretti, 336–63. Princeton, NJ: Princeton University Press, 2006.

———. "What Would Napoleon Do? Historical, Fictional, and Counterfactual Characters." *New Literary History* 42.2 (2011): 315–36.

Gelpi, Barbara Charlesworth. "The Innocent 'I': Dickens' Influence on Victorian Autobiography." In *The Worlds of Victorian Fiction*, ed. Jerome H. Buckley, 57–71. Cambridge: Harvard University Press, 1975.

Genette, Gérard. *Narrative Discourse: An Essay in Method*. Trans. Jane E. Lewin. Ithaca, NY: Cornell University Press, 1983.

———. *Paratexts: Thresholds of Interpretation*. Trans. Jane E. Lewin. New York: Cambridge University Press, 1997.

Gibson, Anna. "Charlotte Brontë's First Person." *Narrative* 25.2 (2017): 203–26.

Giddens, Anthony. *Modernity and Self-Identity: Self and Society in the Late Modern Age*. Stanford, CA: Stanford University Press, 1991.

Gilbert, Sandra, and Susan Gubar. *The Madwoman in the Attic: The Woman Writer and the Nineteenth-Century Literary Imagination*. 2nd ed. New Haven, CT: Yale University Press, 2000.

Gilead, Sarah. "Trollope's *Autobiography*: The Strategies of Self-Production." *Modern Language Quarterly* 47.3 (1986): 272–90.

Gill, Stephen. *Wordsworth and the Victorians*. Oxford: Clarendon Press, 1998.

Gillooly, Eileen. "Paterfamilias." In *Contemporary Dickens*, ed. Eileen Gillooly and Deirdre David, 209–30. Columbus: Ohio State University Press, 2009.

Gilmour, Robin. *The Victorian Period: The Intellectual and Cultural Context of English Literature, 1830–1890*. New York: Longman Group, 1993.

Glowínski, Michál. "On the First-Person Novel." Trans. Rochelle Stone. *New Literary History* 9.1 (1977): 103–14.

Goffman, Erving. *The Presentation of Self in Everyday Life*. Garden Court, NY: Doubleday, 1959.

Goldberg, Carl. "The Pursuit of the Fictional Self." *American Journal of Psychotherapy* 58.2 (2004): 209–19.

Green, Laura. "'I Recognized Myself in Her': Identifying with the Reader in George Eliot's *The Mill on the Floss* and Simone de Beauvoir's *Memoirs of a Dutiful Daughter*." *Tulsa Studies in Women's Literature* 24.1 (2005): 57–79.

Greiner, Rae. *Sympathetic Realism in Nineteenth-Century British Fiction*. Baltimore: Johns Hopkins University Press, 2012.

Hadley, Elaine. *Living Liberalism: Practical Citizenship in Mid-Victorian Britain*. Chicago: University of Chicago Press, 2010.

Hardy, Thomas. *Tess of the D'Urbervilles: A Pure Woman*. Ed. James Wood. New York: Modern Library Classics, 2001.

Harrison, Mary-Catherine. "The Paradox of Fiction and the Ethics of Empathy: Reconceiving Dickens' Realism." *Narrative* 16.3 (2008): 256–78.

Hawthorne, Julian. *Confessions and Criticisms*. Boston: Ticknor, 1887.

Heady, Emily. "The Polis's Different Voices: Narrating England's Progress in Dickens's *Bleak House*." *Texas Studies in Literature and Language* 48.4 (2006): 312–39.

Henderson, Heather. *The Victorian Self: Autobiography and Biblical Narrative*. Ithaca, NY: Cornell University Press, 1989.

Hennelly, Mark M., Jr. "*Jane Eyre*'s Reading Lesson." *ELH* 51.4 (1984): 693–717.

Hinnant, Charles Haskell. "*Moll Flanders, Roxana*, and the French Tradition of the Pseudo-Memoir." *The Age of Johnson* 17 (2006): 203–31.

Hobsbawm, Eric. *Industry and Empire: From 1750 to the Present Day*. New York: New Press, 1999.

Hughes, John. "The Affective World of Bronte's *Villette*." *Studies in English Literature* 40.4 (2000): 711–26.

Hume, David. *A Treatise of Human Nature*. 1738. Project Gutenberg, http://www.gutenberg.org/ebooks/4705.

Iser, Wolfgang. *The Act of Reading: A Theory of Aesthetic Response*. Baltimore: Johns Hopkins University Press, 1978.

———. *The Fictive and the Imaginary: Charting Literary Anthropology*. Baltimore: Johns Hopkins University Press, 1993.

———. *The Implied Reader: Patterns of Communication in Prose Fiction from Bunyan to Beckett*. Baltimore: Johns Hopkins University Press, 1978.

———. "The Reading Process: A Phenomenological Approach." *New Literary History* 3.2 (1972): 279–99.

Jaffe, Audrey. *Scenes of Sympathy: Identity and Representation in Victorian Fiction*. Ithaca, NY: Cornell University Press, 2000.

Jameson, Fredric. "Marxism and Historicism." In *The Ideologies of Theory: Essays, 1971–1986*, vol. 2, *The Syntax of History*, 148–77. Minneapolis: University of Minnesota Press, 1988.

———. "On Interpretation: Literature as a Socially Symbolic Act" (excerpted from *The Political Unconscious*). In *The Jameson Reader*, ed. Michael Hardt and Kathi Weeks, 33–60. Oxford: Blackwell, 2000.

Jay, Paul. *Being in the Text: Self-Representation from Wordsworth to Roland Barthes*. Ithaca, NY: Cornell University Press, 1984.

Jeffares, Bo. *The Artist in Nineteenth-Century English Fiction*. Gerrards Cross, UK: Colin Smythe, 1979.

Johnston, Susan. *Women and Domestic Experience in Victorian Political Fiction*. London: Greenwood, 2001.

Jordan, John O. *Supposing "Bleak House."* Charlottesville: University of Virginia Press, 2011.

Joyce, Simon. *The Victorians in the Rearview Mirror*. Athens: Ohio University Press, 2007.

Kaplan, Cora. "Girl Talk: *Jane Eyre* and the Romance of Women's Narration." *Novel* 30.1 (1996): 5–31.

Keen, Suzanne. *Empathy and the Novel*. London: Oxford University Press, 2007.

———. "Introduction: Narrative and the Emotions." *Poetics Today* 32.1 (2011): 1–52.

Kerby, Anthony Paul. *Narrative and the Self*. Bloomington: Indiana University Press, 1991.

Köppe, Tillman, and Julia Langkau. "Fiction, Self-Knowledge and Knowledge of the Self." *Diegesis* 6.1 (2017): 46–57.

Kreilkamp, Ivan. "Unuttered: Withheld Speech and Female Authorship in *Jane Eyre* and *Villette*." *Novel* 32.3 (1999): 331–54.

Kuizenga, Donna. Introduction to *Memoirs of the Life of Henriette-Sylvie de Molière*, by Madame de Villedieu, 1–25. Trans. and ed. Donna Kuizenga. Chicago: University of Chicago Press, 2004.

Lanser, Susan Sniader. *Fictions of Authority: Women Writers and Narrative Voice*. Ithaca, NY: Cornell University Press, 1992.

Lea, Richard. "Very Now: Has Present-Tense Narration Really Taken Over Fiction?" *Guardian*, September 14, 2010. http://www.guardian.co.uk/books/booksblog/2010/sep/14/present-tense-narration.

Lee, Hsiao-Hung. *Possibilities of Hidden Things: Narrative Transgression in Victorian Fictional Autobiographies*. New York: Peter Lang, 1996.

Lee, Julia Sun-Joo. *The American Slave Narrative and the Victorian Novel*. Oxford: Oxford University Press, 2010.

Lejeune, Philippe. *On Autobiography*. Trans. Katherine Leary. Ed. Paul John Eakin. Minneapolis: University of Minnesota Press, 1988.

Levine, George. *The Realistic Imagination: English Fiction from Frankenstein to Lady Chatterley*. Chicago: University of Chicago Press, 1981.

Linton, Eliza Lynn. *The Autobiography of Christopher Kirkland*. London: Richard Bentley, 1885. Victorian Women Writers Project, Indiana University, http://purl.dlib.indiana.edu/iudl/vwwp/VAB7017.

Locke, John. *An Essay concerning Human Understanding*. Reproduced from the 2nd ed. (1690). Project Gutenberg, http://www.gutenberg.net/1/0/6/1/10615/.

Löschnigg, Martin. "English Autobiography and Its Fictional Other: A Diachronic View along Narratological Lines." In *Anglistentag 1999 Mainz: Proceedings*, ed. Bernhard Reitz and Sigrid Rieuwertz, 403–14. Trier, Germany: Wissenschaftlicher, 2000.

Lukács, Georg. *The Theory of the Novel*. Trans. Anna Bostock. Cambridge: MIT Press, 1971.

Lynch, Dierdre. *The Economy of Character: Novels, Market Culture, and the Business of Inner Meaning*. Chicago: University of Chicago Press, 1998.

Machann, Clinton. *The Genre of Autobiography in Victorian Literature*. Ann Arbor: University of Michigan Press, 1997.

Marcus, Steven. "Conceptions of the Self in an Age of Progress." In *Progress and Its Discontents*, ed. Gabriel A. Almond, Marvin Chodorow, and Roy Harvey Pearce, 431–48. Berkeley: University of California Press, 1977.

Marshall, Gregory. *Shaped by Stories: The Ethical Power of Narratives*. Notre Dame, IN: University of Notre Dame Press, 2009.

Mascuch, Michael. *Origins of the Individualist Self: Autobiography and Self-Identity in England, 1591–1791*. Stanford, CA: Stanford University Press, 1996.

May, Leila Silvana. "The Strong-Arming of Desire: A Reconsideration of Nancy Armstrong's *Desire and Domestic Fiction*." *ELH* 68.1 (2001): 267–85.

Mayer, Jed. *Forging a Vocabulary: English Usage and Abusage from Wordsworth's Preface to Pater's Conclusion*. PhD diss., Washington University in St. Louis, 2001.

McKee, Patricia. *Reading Constellations: Urban Modernity in Victorian Fiction*. New York: Oxford University Press, 2014.

McKeon, Michael. *The Origins of the English Novel, 1600–1740*. Baltimore: Johns Hopkins University Press, 2002.

———. *The Secret History of Domesticity: Public, Private, and the Division of Knowledge*. Baltimore: Johns Hopkins University Press, 2005.

McLauchlan, Juliet. "*The Mill on the Floss*: Fiction or Autobiography?" *Cahiers victoriens & édouardiens* 27 (1988): 127–39.

Menke, Richard. *Telegraphic Realism: Victorian Fiction and Other Information Systems*. Stanford: Stanford University Press, 2008.

Mill, John Stuart. *On Liberty*. London: Walter Scott Publishing. Project Gutenberg, http://www.gutenberg.org/files/34901/34901-h/34901-h.htm.

Miller, D. A. *The Novel and the Police*. Berkeley: University of California Press, 1988.

Miller, J. Hillis. "The Function of Rhetorical Study at the Present Time." *ADE Bulletin* 62 (1979): 10–18.

———. *Victorian Subjects*. Durham, NC: Duke University Press, 1991.

Mitchell, Rebecca N. *Victorian Lessons in Empathy and Difference*. Columbus: Ohio State University Press, 2011.

Mitchell, Sally. *Daily Life in Victorian England*. 2nd ed. Westport, CT: Greenwood, 2009.

Moglen, Helene. *Charlotte Bronte: The Self Conceived*. Madison: University of Wisconsin Press, 1984.

Moretti, Franco. *The Way of the World: The* Bildungsroman *in European Culture*. New York: Verso, 1987.

Morgan, Nicola. "Nicola Morgan's Top 10 Present Tense Books." *Guardian*, April 5, 2012. http://www.guardian.co.uk/childrens-books-site/2012/apr/05/top-10-nicola-morgan-present-tense.

Morris, John N. *Versions of the Self*. New York: Basic Books, 1966.

Mugglestone, Lynn. *Lost for Words: The Hidden History of the Oxford English Dictionary*. New Haven, CT: Yale University Press, 2005.

National Endowment for the Arts. "Reading on the Rise: A New Chapter in American Literacy." Washington, DC: National Endowment for the Arts, 2009. https://www.arts.gov/sites/default/files/ReadingonRise.pdf.

———. *To Read or Not to Read: A Question of National Consequence*. Washington, DC: National Endowment for the Arts, 2007. https://www.arts.gov/sites/default/files/ToRead.pdf.

Nayder, Lillian. *Unequal Partners: Charles Dickens, Wilkie Collins, and Victorian Authorship.* Ithaca, NY: Cornell University Press, 2002.

Newsom, Robert. "*Villette* and *Bleak House*: Authorizing Women." *Nineteenth-Century Literature* 46.1 (1991): 54–81.

Nietzsche, Friedrich. *The Will to Power.* Trans. Walter Kaufmann and R. J. Hollingdale. New York: Random House, 1968.

Nunning, Angsar. "Deconstructing and Reconceptualizing the Implied Author: The Implied Author—Still a Subject of Debate." *Anglistik* 8.2 (1997): 95–116.

O'Brien, Joseph. "Riffing on *The Hunger Games*: Class Warfare, First-Person Present-Tense Narration, and the Murderous Game Show Genre." *Popular Fiction*, February 20, 2012. http://popularfiction.wordpress.com /2012/02/20/riffing-on-the-hunger-games-class-warfare-first-person-present-tense-narration-and-the-murderous-game-show-genre/.

Olney, James. *Metaphors of Self: The Meaning of Autobiography.* Princeton, NJ: Princeton University Press, 1972.

Paige, Nicholas. *Before Fiction: The Ancien Régime of the Novel.* Philadelphia: University of Pennsylvania Press, 2011.

———. *Being Interior: Autobiography and the Contradiction of Modernity in Seventeenth-Century France.* Philadelphia: University of Pennsylvania Press, 2001.

Pascal, Roy. *Design and Truth in Autobiography.* Cambridge: Harvard University Press, 1960.

Peel, Katie. "The 'Thoroughly and Radically *Incredible*' Lucy Snowe: Performativity in Bronte's *Villette*." *Victorians Institute Journal* 36 (2008): 231–44.

Peltason, Timothy. "The Esther Problem." In *Approaches to Teaching Dickens' "Bleak House,"* ed. John O. Jordan and Gordon Bigelow, 71–78. New York: Modern Language Association, 2008.

Peterson, Linda. *Becoming a Woman of Letters: Myths of Authorship and Facts of the Victorian Market.* Princeton, NJ: Princeton University Press, 2009.

———. *Traditions of Victorian Women's Autobiographies: The Poetics and Politics of Life Writing.* Charlottesville: University of Virginia Press, 1999.

———. *Victorian Autobiography: The Tradition of Self-Interpretation.* New Haven, CT: Yale University Press, 1986.

Phelan, James. "Dual Focalization, Retrospective Fictional Autobiography, and the Ethics of *Lolita*." In *Narrative and Consciousness: Literature, Psychology, and the Brain*, ed. Gary D. Fireman, Ted E. McVay Jr., and Owen J. Flanagan, 129–46. Oxford: Oxford University Press, 2003.

———. "Estranging Unreliability, Bonding Unreliability, and the Ethics of *Lolita*." *Narrative* 15.2 (2007): 222–38.

———. *Living to Tell about It: A Rhetoric and Ethics of Character Narration.* Ithaca, NY: Cornell University Press, 2005.

———. "My Narratology." *Diegesis* 4.2 (2015). https://www.diegesis.uni-wuppertal.de/index.php/diegesis/article/view/200/273.

———. *Narrative as Rhetoric: Technique, Audience, Ethics, Ideology.* Columbus: Ohio State University Press, 1996.

Picker, John. "The Soundproof Study: Victorian Professionals, Workspace, and Urban Noise." *Victorian Studies* 42.3 (1999): 427–53.

Pinch, Adela. *Thinking about Other People in Nineteenth-Century British Writing.* Cambridge: Cambridge University Press, 2010.

Poovey, Mary. *Uneven Developments: The Ideological Work of Gender in Mid-Victorian England.* Chicago: University of Chicago Press, 1988.

Posnock, Ross. "A Great Memoir! At Last!" *New Republic*, February 19, 2010. http://www.tnr.com/book/review/great-memoir-last.

Qualls, Barry. *The Secular Pilgrims of Victorian Fiction: The Novel as Book of Life.* Cambridge: Cambridge University Press, 1982.

Rabinowitz, Peter J. "Truth in Fiction: A Re-examination of Audiences." *Critical Inquiry* 4.1 (1977): 121–41.

Rich, Adrienne. "Jane Eyre: The Temptations of a Motherless Woman (1973)." In *On Lies, Secrets, and Silence: Selected Prose, 1966–1978*, by Adrienne Rich, 89–106. New York: W. W. Norton, 1995.

Rigby, Elizabeth. "1. *Vanity Fair; A Novel without a Hero*; 2. *Jane Eyre: An Autobiography*; 3. Governesses' Benevolence Institution—Report for 1847." Review of *Vanity Fair*, by William Thackeray, and *Jane Eyre*, by Charlotte Brontë. *Quarterly Review* 84.167 (1848): 497–511.

Rimmon-Kenan, Shlomith. *Narrative Fiction: Contemporary Poetics.* London: Routledge, 2002.

Rousseau, Jean-Jacques. *The Confessions.* Trans. and ed. J. M. Cohen. New York: Penguin Classics, 1953.

Routledge Encyclopedia of Narrative Theory. Ed. David Herman, Manfred Jahn, and Marie-Laure Ryan. London: Routledge, 2005.

Ruth, Jennifer. *Novel Professions: Interested Disinterest and the Making of the Professional in the Victorian Novel.* Columbus: Ohio State University Press, 2006.

Ryan, Marie-Laure. *Possible Worlds, Artificial Intelligence, and Narrative Theory.* Bloomington: Indiana University Press, 1991.

———. "Postmodernism and the Doctrine of Panfictionality." *Narrative* 5.2 (1997): 165–87.

Rylance, Rick. *Victorian Psychology and British Culture, 1850–1880.* London: Oxford University Press, 2000.

Scarry, Elaine. *The Body in Pain: The Making and Unmaking of the World.* New York: Oxford University Press, 1985.

Shaw, Harry. *Narrating Reality: Austen, Scott, Eliot.* Ithaca, NY: Cornell University Press, 1999.

Shockley, Evie. "The Horrors of Homelessness: Gothic Doubling in Kincaid's *Lucy* and Brontë's *Villette*." In *Jamaica Kincaid and Caribbean Double Crossings*, ed. Linda Lang-Peralta, 45–62. Newark: University of Delaware Press, 2006.

Shumaker, Wayne. *English Autobiography: Its Emergence, Materials, and Forms.* Berkeley: University of California Press, 1954.

Shuttleworth, Sally. *Charlotte Brontë and Victorian Psychology.* Cambridge: Cambridge University Press, 1996.

———. *George Eliot and Nineteenth-Century Science: The Make-Believe of a Beginning.* Cambridge: Cambridge University Press, 1984.

Sider, Justin. "'Modern-Antiques,' Ballad Imitation, and the Aesthetics of Anachronism." *Victorian Poetry* 54.4 (2016): 455–75.

Sieminski, Greg. "Suited for Satire: Butler's Retailoring of *Sartor Resartus* in *The Way of All Flesh*." *English Literature in Transition* 31.3 (1988): 29–37.

Simmel, Georg. "The Conflict in Modern Culture." In *The Conflict in Modern Culture and Other Essays*, ed. K. Peter Etzkorn, 11–26. New York: Teachers College Press, Columbia University, 1968.

Simpson, Vicky. "'The Eagerness of a Listener Quickens the Tongue of a Narrator': Storytelling and Autobiography in *Jane Eyre*." *Nineteenth Century Gender Studies* 4.3 (2008). http://www.ncgsjournal.com/issue43/simpson.htm.

Siskin, Clifford. *The Work of Writing: Literature and Social Change in Britain, 1700–1830.* Baltimore: Johns Hopkins University Press, 1998.

Slater, Michael. *Charles Dickens: A Life Defined by Writing.* New Haven, CT: Yale University Press, 2009.

———. "Dickens, Charles John Huffam (1812–1870)." In *Oxford Dictionary of National Biography*, ed. H. C. G. Matthew and Brian Harrison. Oxford University Press, 2004. Online edition ed. Lawrence Goldman. http://www.oxforddnb.com/view/article/7599.

Smith, Adam. *The Theory of Moral Sentiments, to Which Is Added a Dissertation on the Origin of Languages.* New Edition. London: G. Bell, 1911. Hathi Trust, https://babel.hathitrust.org/cgi/pt?id=mdp.49015000787300;view=1up;seq=7.

Smith, Sidonie, and Watson, Julia. *Reading Autobiography: A Guide for Interpreting Life Narratives.* Minneapolis: University of Minnesota Press, 2001.

Smith, Vicky. "Getting a Little Tense." *Young Adult* (blog). *Kirkus Reviews*, July 31, 2012. http://www.kirkusreviews.com/blog/young-adult/getting-little-tense/.

Speer, Nicole K., Jeremy R. Reynolds, Khena M. Swallow, and Jeffrey M. Zacks. "Reading Stories Activates Neural Representations of Visual and Motor Experiences." *Psychological Science* 20.8 (2009): 989–99.

Spence, Donald. *Narrative Truth and Historical Truth: Meaning and Interpretation in Psychoanalysis.* London: W. W. Norton, 1982.

Spiegel, Alix, and Lulu Miller. "The Personality Myth." *Invisibilia*, radio broadcast and podcast, June 24, 2016. National Public Radio. http://www.npr.org/2016/06/24/482837932/read-the-transcript.

Spivak, Gayatri. "Three Women's Texts and a Critique of Imperialism." *Critical Inquiry* 12.1 (1985): 243–61.

Stephen, Leslie. "Autobiography: No. II—Rambles among Books." *Cornhill Magazine* 43 (1881): 410–29.

Sternberg, Meir. "How Narrativity Makes a Difference." *Narrative* 9.2 (2001): 115–22.

———. *The Poetics of Biblical Narrative: Ideological Literature and the Drama of Reading*. Bloomington: Indiana University Press, 1987.

Stewart, Garrett. *Dear Reader: The Conscripted Audience in Nineteenth-Century British Fiction*. Baltimore: Johns Hopkins University Press, 1996.

———. *Dickens and the Trials of Imagination*. Cambridge: Harvard University Press, 1974.

Taylor, Charles. *Sources of the Self: The Making of Modern Identity*. New York: Cambridge University Press, 1989.

Thackeray, William Makepeace. *Barry Lyndon*. In *The Prose Works of William Makepeace Thackeray*, ed. Walter Jerrold. London: J. M. Dent, 1902. Project Gutenberg, http://www.gutenberg.org/files/4558/4558-h/4558-h.htm.

———. *The History of Henry Esmond*. New York: Oxford University Press, 1991.

Thompson, F. M. L. *The Rise of Respectable Society: A Social History of Victorian Britain, 1830–1900*. Cambridge: Harvard University Press, 1988.

Tillotson, Geoffrey, and Donald Hawes, eds. *Thackeray: The Critical Heritage*. Boston: Routledge and Kegan Paul, 1968.

Titolo, Matthew. "The Clerk's Tale: Liberalism, Accountability, and Mimesis in *David Copperfield*." *ELH* 70.1 (2003): 171–95.

Treadwell, James. *Autobiographical Writing and British Literature, 1783–1834*. Oxford: Oxford University Press, 2005.

Tressler, Beth. "Waking Dreams: George Eliot and the Poetics of Double Consciousness." *Victorian Literature and Culture* 39.2 (2011): 483–98.

Trollope, Anthony. *An Autobiography*. Ed. Michael Sadlier. Oxford: Oxford University Press, 2008.

Uzgalis, William. "The Influence of John Locke's Works." Supplement to "John Locke," *Stanford Encyclopedia of Philosophy* (Summer 2017 Edition), ed. Edward N. Zalta. Stanford University. https://plato.stanford.edu/archives/sum2017/entries/locke/.

Vanden Bossche, Chris R. "Cookery, not Rookery: Family and Class in *David Copperfield*." *Dickens Studies Annual: Essays on Victorian Fiction* 15 (1986): 87–109.

Vermeule, Blakey. *Why Do We Care about Literary Characters?* Baltimore: Johns Hopkins University Press, 2010.

Walsh, Richard. *The Rhetoric of Fictionality: Narrative Theory and the Idea of Fiction*. Columbus: Ohio State University Press, 2007.

Warhol, Robyn. "Double Gender, Double Genre in *Jane Eyre* and *Villette*." *Studies in English Literature* 36.4 (1996): 857–75.

———. *Gendered Interventions: Narrative Discourse in the Victorian Novel*. New Brunswick: Rutgers University Press, 1989.

Watt, Ian. *The Rise of the Novel: Studies in Defoe, Richardson and Fielding*. Berkeley: University of California Press, 1957.

Welsh, Alexander. *From Copyright to Copperfield: The Identity of Dickens*. Cambridge: Harvard University Press, 1987.

———. "Writing and Copying in the Age of Steam." In *Victorian Literature and Society*, ed. James R. Kincaid and Albert J. Kuhn, 30–45. Columbus: Ohio State University Press, 1984.

Wilson, Timothy. *Redirect: The Surprising New Science of Psychological Change*. New York: Little, Brown, 2011.

Winchester, Simon. *The Meaning of Everything: The Story of the Oxford English Dictionary*. Oxford: Oxford University Press, 2004.

Winnicott, D. W. *The Maturational Process and the Facilitating Environment: Studies in the Theory of Emotional Development*. London: Hogarth Press and the Institute of Psycho-Analysis, 1965.

———. *Playing and Reality*. New York: Routledge, 1971.

Young, Kay. *Imagining Minds: The Neuro-Aesthetics of Austen, Eliot, and Hardy*. Columbus: Ohio State University Press, 2010.

Zunshine, Lisa. *Why We Read Fiction: Theory of Mind and the Novel*. Columbus: Ohio State University Press, 2006.

Zwerdling, Alex. "Esther Summerson Rehabilitated." *PMLA* 88.3 (1973): 429–39.

Index

Note: page numbers followed by n refer to notes, with note number.

similarities to Eliot's Maggie Tulliver, 28–29; yearning for individual fulfillment and communal engagement in, 89

Eyre, Jane, reader inclusion strategies used by, 30, 31, 33, 88–100; and animation of narrative, 90; direct address as, 96–99, 189–90n58; efforts to improve believability and, 95–96; and gap between author and reader, 89–90; and gap between essential self and socially constructed self, 89–90; and gaps in narrative, 4, 6, 90, 97, 100; simultaneous invitation and resistance of readers' input, 89–90

Eyre, Jane, self-creation by: and anxieties of readerly misprision, 94; as challenge to essentialist conception of identity, 34; and defining of selfhood through orchestration of social influences, 93–94; and delayed initiation of direct address to reader, 96; efforts to control readers' contribution to, 96–99; enhanced emotional impact of text and, 98; Jane's recognition of role of narrative style in, 95–96; and linearly maturing authorial voice, 96; reader participation in, ambivalence about curative power of, 90; Reeds' usurping of, 90, 91–92, 92–94; required reciprocity of, 100; similarity to real-world process, 4–5, 31, 32–33; as struggle, 90–96

facts: accuracy of, in fictional vs. nonfictional autobiography, 20; genres requiring emphasis on, 199n27; modern readers' desire for truth through, 160–61, 161–62

fake news, Internet culture and, 199n31

family, as safe space to work through larger social issues, 103

feeling, as inseparable from interiority, 103

Feinberg, Monica, 110, 191n20

fiction: as buffer against identity construction of readers and authors, 86; capacity to teach feeling and understanding, 55–56; characteristics vs. fictional autobiography, 12–13, 16; consanguinity with fictional and nonfictional autobiography, 40, 44–51; as defined by reader's understanding of author's ontological relation to work, 13; as device for understanding real world, 34; as exercise of capacity for narrative understanding, 55–56; hermeneutic view of, 56, 184n58; history of, 44–45, 48–51, 157, 183n33; importance for understanding ourselves and our affective connections, 174; interpretive ends of, vs. fictional or nonfictional autobiography, 48; Lukács on, 46–47; and modern focus on individual self, 45, 47–48; modern readers' distaste for, 161, 162, 165–66, 167; as quest for lost unity, 47; relevance to readers' real world, as basis of enjoyment, 55; as secure space for suppositional play, 52, 55; self-knowledge gained from, 184n58; validation of self in social world as focus of, 44–45

fiction, as genre, Victorian public's awareness of: as precondition for critique of self-creation, 6; and understanding of truth claims made by fiction, 49; and understanding of truth claims made by fictional autobiography, 40–41

"Fiction, Self-Knowledge and Knowledge of the Self" (Köppe and Langkau), 184n58

fictional autobiography: accuracy of knowing and telling as issue in, 20–21, 23; as autodiegetic first-person narrative, 24; characteristics vs. first-person fiction, 12–13, 16, 24–26; characteristics vs. nonfiction autobiography, 12–13, 15–16, 19–23, 64–66, 95, 186n78; characteristics vs. "omniscient" realist novel, 26–34; characteristics vs. protofictional autobiography, 50; consanguinity with